CW00434188

Women's Movement: women under immigration, nationality and refugee law

10

Women's Movement:
women under immigration, nationality and refugee law

Jacqueline Bhabha and Sue Shutter

Trentham Books

First published in 1994 by Trentham Books Limited

Trentham Books Limited
Westview House
734 London Road
Oakhill
Stoke-on-Trent
Staffordshire
England ST4 5NP

© Jacqueline Bhabha and Sue Shutter 1994

All rights reserved.

Apart from any fair dealing for the purposes of [research or private study, or] criticism or review as permitted under the [terms of the] UK Copyright, Designs and Patents Act, 1988, this publication may not be reproduced, stored or transmitted, in any form or by any means, without the prior permission in writing of the publishers, or in the case of reprographic reproduction only in accordance with the terms of the licences issued by the Copyright Licensing Agency in the UK, or in accordance with the terms of licences issued by the appropriate Reproduction Rights Organisation outside the UK. Enquiries concerning reproduction outside the terms stated here should be sent to the publishers at the address printed on this page.

All rights reserved. No part of this publication may be reproduced in any material form (including photocopying or storing it in any medium by electronic means and whether or not transiently or incidentally to some other use of this publication) without the [prior] written permission of the copyright owner, except in accordance with the provisions of the Copyright, Designs and Patents Act 1988 or under the terms of a licence issued by the Copyright Licensing Agency, 90 Tottenham Court Road, London WIP 9HE. Applications for the copyright owner's written permission to reproduce any part of this publication should be addressed [in the first instance] to the publisher.

British Cataloguing in Publication Data
A catalogue record for this book is available from the British Library.

ISBN: 1 85856 007 1

Cover photograph: Myrna Simpson, mother of Joy Gardner, calling for a public inquiry into her daughter's death, at 10 Downing Street, the office of the British Prime Minister.
The Independent/Glynn Griffiths

Designed and typeset by Trentham Print Design Ltd, Chester
and printed in Great Britain by Bemrose Shafron Ltd, Chester

This book is dedicated to the memory of Joy Gardner,
the first woman killed in the implementation of
British immigration control.

Jacqueline Bhabha is a solicitor at North Islington Law Centre who has worked and written on immigration and refugee issues for many years.

Sue Shutter works at the Joint Council for the Welfare of Immigrants, formerly as an adviser and for the past four years on information and training. She is the main author of the *JCWI immigration and nationality law handbook.*

Contents

Acknowledgements xi

Preface xiii

Introduction 1

Chapter 1
'As a woman I have no country': women and nationality 15

Chapter 2
Travelling third class: women and immigration 29

Chapter 3
Till laws us do part: the ban on husbands 55

Chapter 4
Divide and rule: wives under immigration law 93

Chapter 5
Childless mothers: children kept out 129

Chapter 6
Hard labour: migrant women workers 163

Chapter 7
Sex equality and race division: migration and Fortress Europe 199

Chapter 8
A well-founded fear of exclusion: the legal problems of women refugees 229

Conclusion 259
Glossary 265
Notes 271
Selected bibliography 289
Index 293

Acknowledgements

Seven women wrote *Worlds Apart: women under immigration and nationality law*, which was published in 1985. Apart from the authors of this book they were Hansa Chudasama, Mary Dimech, Francesca Klug, Leena Sevak and Nira Yuval-Davis. Even in those collective and cooperative days, a subgroup of editors was necessary to produce a manuscript for publication, and this consisted of Francesca Klug and the two of us. Most of the historical material in this book is taken from *Worlds Apart.* Chapters one and two have scarcely been altered. Stepping behind the collective veil for a moment, we would like to acknowledge that the research and writing of these chapters was primarily the work of Francesca Klug and to thank her for allowing us to reproduce them here. Chapters three, four, five and six have been extensively revised and updated; only chapters seven and eight are completely new. Our debt to the original *Worlds Apart* collective is therefore substantial and enduring.

During the spring of 1993, a lecture series on 'Immigration law and the family' was organised by the Joint Council for the Welfare of Immigrants and the Group for Ethnic Minority Studies at the School of Oriental and African Studies, University of London. The idea that *Worlds Apart* should be revised and updated was sparked off by the lectures and can be attributed directly to one of the lecturers, also a co-author of *Worlds Apart,* Nira Yuval-Davis. Had it not been for her initiative and support this book would never have been envisaged, let alone written. We are most grateful to her for getting us going.

Most of the case studies are drawn from the experiences of clients at our workplaces, the Joint Council for the Welfare of Immigrants and North Islington Law Centre, though real names have only been used when they have already appeared in published material. We are grateful to our colleagues for delving into their filing cabinets and tolerating our persistent requests and queries.

Several friends and colleagues have contributed ideas and material for this book; we would like to thank Jawaid Luqmani for details of one of his cases, Southall Black Sisters for information about Rabia Janjua, the Aire Centre for assistance with European case law, Janet Llewellyn from the Department of Employment for digging out statistics, Shainul Kassam from the Runnymede Trust for information and encouragement, Steve Cohen for updates on Manchester campaigns, Christine Harvey for information from her unpublished dissertation on children of deportees and Stonewall for information about the immigration position of same-sex couples in Europe.

Nony Ardill, Vicky Guedalla and Elspeth Guild made extensive comments on the manuscript and we greatly appreciate their assistance. We wish to thank our publisher, Gillian Klein, for her unfailing optimism and inspired title suggestion; and *The Independent* for permission to use the cover photograph by Glynn Griffiths.

Francesca Klug and Nira Yuval-Davis have already been mentioned; however we owe them a special debt of gratitude for their invaluable contributions to our discussions on the introduction and conclusion of the book. It has been reassuring to discover how, over the last ten years, our ideas have evolved in the same directions. Though we are responsible for the final product, they will recognise their insights and suggestions throughout those sections. Working together with them made us nostalgic for the special quality of generous, non-competitive collaboration that characterised the production of *Worlds Apart.*

Our nearest and dearest have contributed in a range of ways to the process of writing the book. Clearing the breakfast table to make way for the laptop, scribbling on our notes, sleeping through the clicking of computer keys, entertaining possible sources of disturbance, hearing interminable discussions on the book's progress, providing delicious refreshments for the body and uncomfortable queries for the mind — many thanks to Carol, Michaela, Homi, Anna, Ishan, Satya and Leah.

Jacqueline Bhabha and Sue Shutter, London
October 1993

Preface

The first edition of this book was published as *Worlds Apart* and written in 1983-84, by seven women active in the Women, Immigration and Nationality Group (WING). This group was formed after a national conference, timed to take place just before the 1981 British Nationality Act came into force. The conference was organised by women concerned with the legal and political aspects of British immigration and nationality law, and with the effect on women of the forthcoming nationality changes. It was attended by over 200 women, and was the first time black and white women had jointly addressed the position of women under these laws. As a result of the conference, WING was established and given the task of producing a pamphlet (which grew into a book) on the history of British immigration and nationality legislation and women's position within that history. The book had a dual aim: to provide detailed information for those opposing race and sex discrimination in immigration law, thereby adding fuel to the campaign to change the laws; and to insert a feminist analysis into the immigration debate.

Despite the growing interest in questions of race and gender, and the expanding feminist scholarship on issues relating to citizenship, the voluminous literature on immigration law contained no substantial study on the different ways in which the law operated against women and men. British nationality law had never been written about from this perspective either. Where women were discussed, their position was usually subsumed to that of men. Conversely, much feminist literature on women and citizenship tended to ignore the importance of nationality and immigration legislation in defining the nation, and in excluding women, especially those from specific ethnic groupings, from full rights as citizens. *Worlds Apart* is still the only book written on this subject; yet it has been out of print for some time.

When *Worlds Apart* was written, the main areas of sex discrimination in British nationality law had recently been removed; but sex discrimination in immigration law and practice was increasingly the subject of attack and campaigning. Ten years on, the political agenda has shifted. In addition to explaining the clear discrimination written into British immigration law, the focus is now on uncovering the more subtle processes by which some of the same ends are achieved. The book explores the interplay between race and sex discrimination in the exercise of official discretion.

This new edition, now called *Women's Movement*, appears at a time when the creation of 'Fortress Europe', with stringent harmonised external border controls and discriminatory internal checks, highlights the divisions between those who are European Community nationals, and those, whether settled or refugees, who are not; when a profound economic recession in Europe has eroded the standard of living and other gains made by women and ethnic minority groups over the last three decades and fuelled the growth of chauvinism and the greatest resurgence of racist activity and violence in Europe since the Second World War. Much of the apparatus of restriction and control is now concentrated on refugees; moreover there are important recent developments relating specifically to women refugees, which at the time of writing have scarcely been discussed in Britain.

Though the main targets of immigration controls have been migrants and refugees, black EC nationals have not been exempt — witness the notorious difficulties of black day-trippers to France. Some of these are new issues which raise questions and pose problems not considered in *Worlds Apart*. As this book is being revised, the story of Joy Gardner, the Jamaican woman killed by British police officers enforcing her deportation, unfurls in banner headlines. Questions of race, nationality and immigration are front page news.

Equally significant, if less publicised, are the growing moves to counter these developments by forging links across national boundaries, ethnic divisions and specialist interest groups; to bridge the gaps between migrant workers and refugee groups, between community activists and academic human rights lawyers, between French, German, Spanish, British and other anti-racist organisations. The book describes some of the significant immigration campaigns in detail. It also makes considerable use throughout of real case histories to illustrate the argument without technical legal terminology. Though primarily about British immigration and nationality law, it is within this wider European context that *Women's Movement* seeks to make its contribution. One successful outcome would be to inspire feminists in other European countries to undertake a similar task!

Introduction

Rohini Deb has been married for three years. During that time she has lived in Britain, her husband in Bangladesh. British immigration law has kept them apart. Rohini is a British citizen, born in London. The Home Office, the British government department that deals with immigration matters, claimed that the main reason, the 'primary purpose', for which her husband married her was to come to Britain. It therefore refused him permission to live in Britain. If Rohini wants to live with her husband she must do so in Bangladesh. She could also be reunited with her husband if she uprooted herself and went to work in another European Community country — European family reunion rights do not depend on the scrutiny of underlying motives. Her brother Nazrul also chose a partner from Bangladesh. The immigration officers allowed his wife to join him in Britain; the assumption built into the administration of immigration law is that Bangladeshi wives will follow their husbands. Unlike his sister, Nazrul does not have to choose between his home and his spouse. But the letter of the law which governs their choice of home is the same for women and men; what is different is the practice.

Judith Winfield, a white British citizen, married a Canadian. She too had no difficulty bringing him to live with her. The Home Office did not question his motives for coming to Britain. The effect of immigration law is to exclude black and non-western people.

Immigration law and administration are integral parts of government racism in Britain today. But what these examples illustrate is the complex interaction of racism and sexism in the way immigration laws operate in practice, despite formal sex equality. Eleven years ago, sex discrimination was removed from British nationality law, after long and heated debate. But in immigration law, sex discrimination was rampant and growing. In spite of other gains made by the feminist movement in the twentieth century, in immigration matters developments went against the tide.

The legal position has now changed. In 1984 three women took the British government to the European Court of Human Rights in Strasbourg to challenge the sex discrimination in the immigration rules. Their determination, and the campaign that supported their cases, succeeded where the women's movement had previously failed. In May 1985, the European Court of Human Rights delivered its judgement: the British government had breached the European Convention on Human Rights. The Court held that the sex discrimination in the immigration rules was not justified and that the women affected had no effective remedy for their grievance. The British government therefore was forced to change the immigration rules for spouses. It did so by removing rights from men to put them in the same formal position as women.

Over the next eight years, piecemeal changes in the immigration rules produced greater equality: women workers, for example, were eventually given the same rights as men to be joined by their spouses. However, much official effort has gone into ensuring that formally equal immigration rules are implemented differently on race and sex grounds so that they have a discriminatory effect. Particular groups have been targeted to prevent them from achieving family reunion in Britain. The main category affected are Asian women living, indeed often born, in Britain; the group excluded are their 'foreign' husbands. Successive ministers have portrayed the choice by this group of women, to live with their husbands in the country in which they have long been settled, as an abuse, an illegitimate device to swell black immigrant numbers. The government's main exclusionary tool has been the so-called 'primary purpose rule'. The assumption is that Asian men following their wives to Britain must have had immigration as their primary purpose in marriage. Assumptions about family relationships and the primacy of male work and male decision-making still influence policy and the exercise of discretion.

It was not until 1993, 10 years after the nationality changes, that the government explicitly considered the problem of sex discrimination in immigration law. On 21 July 1993, the Home Office published a consultative document which proposed a complete redrafting of the immigration rules. One of the reasons given was 'in order not to discriminate between family members on grounds of sex'. This in itself is a positive objective. However only one of the specific proposals — to allow female students to bring in their spouses, something male students have always been entitled to do — will, if implemented, benefit women. The other proposals — to remove special provisions for widowed mothers and young women under 21 — take rights away from women.[1]

When *Worlds Apart* was written, in 1983-4, sex discrimination in the law, and government justifications for it, seemed very firmly entrenched. Ten years later, the government's stated intention to reverse this is welcome. However, equality has largely been obtained through a levelling-down process. In 1984, for example, most men living in Britain had an absolute right to be joined by their wives from abroad; at present, nobody has such an unqualified right. What is more, although the law formally applies almost equally to men and women, the practical implementation is still clearly biased. Since the rules require applicants to 'satisfy' officials that they qualify, this means that they can be (and are) operated in discriminatory ways, so that particular groups are disproportionately affected. In the case of the marriage rules, these have been men from the Indian subcontinent and Filipino and Thai women. Although the clear-cut sex discrimination of 10 years ago can no longer be found in immigration law, it is evident that more subtle discriminatory processes are still at work.

Women's Movement chronicles the treatment of women as a distinct social group under immigration and nationality law, a chapter of British social and legal history ignored until the publication of *Worlds Apart.* In recent years, interest has grown in questions of citizenship in general, and women's citizenship in particular. Different parts of the political spectrum, from Charter 88 to the government's Citizen's Charter, have appropriated the concept, not just in the technical sense of the right to hold a specific passport but as a term which sums up the relationship between individual and state, or community (whether local, national or supranational). 'There appears to be a great yearning for [citizenship], even though no one actually knows what it is'.[2] Feminist scholarship on women and citizenship has shown how women were excluded from the basic constitution of the modern nation-state which introduced citizenship as a male fraternity;[3] that men received citizenship not only as individuals but as heads of households, representing the women who remained in the private sphere, the state's relationship with them being through their father or husband.[4] This book describes how women have been defined under nationality law since the Middle Ages and relates this to the ways men have exercised power over women and children.

The purpose of nationality law is to define who does and who does not form part of a nation, while immigration law determines who is allowed to enter or stay in a country. This book covers both areas of law and relates them by showing how immigration laws passed in the second half of this century to prevent black British people from coming here made their citizenship meaningless. It also shows, conversely, how the European harmonisation and single market developments of the 1980s and 1990s have increasingly divided people living within the EC into two sharply contrasting immigration categories. EC nationals (predominantly white) have first class immigration rights, and non-EC nationals, about eight million in number, are excluded from those rights despite being long term residents, unless they happen to be nationals of prosperous 'European' nations like Norway or Austria.

The interaction between nationality and immigration legislation, and the use of the former to serve the purposes of the latter, is a recurring theme of the book. The 1914 and 1948 Nationality Acts, reflecting Britain's imperial domination, had defined all inhabitants of colonies and ex-colonies as British subjects. This was an attempt to legitimise British control over the colonised territories, but was not intended to encourage the colonised people to settle in the 'mother country'. When black British subjects did start to come to Britain after the Second World War, and following a decline in the British economy, a series of immigration acts was passed to stop them. The 1981 Nationality Act was similarly based on the principle of exclusion. Reflecting the end of British imperialist rule, it redefined who 'belonged' to Britain in line with immigration law. Underlying this process was a view that membership of the British nation should be restricted as much as possible to white Anglo-Saxons. This process was carried a stage further in the definition of 'British nationals' for European Community purposes; these were British citizens (which including the white Falkland Islanders after the 1982 war) and citizens from Gibraltar, but not from any other British dependent territory. The overriding importance of race was beyond doubt.

The removal of the right to British nationality simply by birth in the UK further demonstrated this. Immigration status became an equally important criterion. Far from using immigration control to 'improve race relations' as so often claimed,[5] this measure at a stroke excluded a group of children born in Britain from the benefits of citizenship. This is true of other European countries too: second or third generation Turkish children born in Germany, for example, are still Turkish, not German (though there is debate on changing German nationality law); but, because of their 'German blood', hundreds of thousands of 'ethnic Germans', whose families had lived outside Germany for three generations, have been able to take up settlement rights. Given European developments — wide-ranging immigration controls at the external borders of the European Community, increased internal checks to detect 'illegals', the dramatic growth of racism and racist attacks — the protection afforded by citizenship in preventing deportation and securing political representation is ever more crucial. The Campaign against Racism and Fascism states:

> ...[A] pan-European movement to secure citizenship rights is as fundamental today as was the struggle of the labour movement in the nineteenth century to establish the right to organise in trade unions. Where once a strong labour movement was the prerequisite for all other social and political rights — for example, the right to combine against exploitation, the right to withhold labour — a movement for citizenship rights today is fundamental if black people are to fight back against the rising tide of racism and fascism without fear'.[6]

The racially divisive use of nationality law is but one manifestation of the underlying obsession with the numbers of black people in the country that has been evident in Britain from the 1960s onwards. By the end of the 1970s it created a climate where speeches by mainstream politicians about 'swamping' by 'people with a different culture' could be made for electoral gain.[7]

From this perspective the greater the obstacles and restrictions on their entry the better. Though the precise terminology may have changed since Margaret Thatcher's pronouncements, the underlying attitudes are still widely current in prominent circles throughout Europe. In Britain, Winston Churchill MP, grandson of the Second World War leader, stated in 1993: 'We must call a halt to the relentless flow of immigrants to this country, especially from the Indian sub-continent. The population of many of our Northern cities is now well over 50% immigrant'.[8] In fact the 1991 census shows that under 6% of the population as a whole, and 8% of that in West Yorkshire, the Northern region with the largest black population, comes from the ethnic minorities; of these 75% have British nationality and 45% were born in Britain.

Other European politicians have been equally explicit: immediately after his appointment to the government following the 1993 French general elections, the French Interior Minister Charles Pasqua stated: 'The goal we set, given the seriousness of the economic situation, is to tend towards zero immigration...the only way to resolve the integration problem is to get a firm grip on immigration'.[9] Yet one of the package of new anti-immigrant laws introduced by this government strips immigrants' children born in France of the century-old right to automatic French citizenship, a measure which will clearly exacerbate 'the integration problem'. Marriages involving immigrants, and their family reunion rights, have also come under sharp attack. It is as if the loss of nationhood implied by the construction of the European Community is being compensated for by this exclusionary demarcation of fully-fledged citizenship from within. The quest for 'real' citizens can be taken to extraordinary lengths, as demonstrated by the case of Naheed Ejaz and her children,[10] whom the Home Office deprived of their British citizenship of years, and overnight reclassified as illegal entrants because of questions surrounding her husband's status, about which she had no knowledge or control; woman as appendage once again, although Naheed won the first stage of her legal fight against this.

The view of immigrant and black women, as wives and mothers responding to life choices made by men, rather than as initiators of families in their own right, has pervaded official thinking and moulded the relevant immigration rules. Black and immigrant women have had severely curtailed rights to create the family of their choice in their own home country, the assumption being that this is a male prerogative. This has been true for women (particularly those of Asian origin) whose home has always been in Britain but who have chosen husbands from abroad, as well as for women who have taken the initiative of travelling to Britain for work or study and have then wanted to be united here with preexisting families. Indeed there has been persistent official denial of the fact that immigrant women could have this dual role, as workers or students, when they are at the same time wives or mothers. As this book sets out, resident domestic workers recruited from abroad only qualified for the necessary work permits to come if they were unmarried and without children.

In fact, thousands of women have come to Britain as independent workers from Asia, Africa, the Caribbean, Southern Europe and elsewhere, in contradiction to the prevailing view that women have generally immigrated as the dependants of men. Many women were even recruited in their home countries, both by the British government and by the private sector — particularly the hotel and catering industry, the National Health Service and the clothing trade. Some had skilled catering or nursing jobs; others were brought in to take badly-paid, unpopular jobs.

Ideological and economic factors perpetuated the second-class status accorded to women under immigration law. Like male workers, they came here in the 1950s, 1960s and even the early 1970s, when the relatively buoyant economy still required cheap labour. As the economy began to contract, immigration for *settlement* was increasingly restricted and *migrant* workers were recruited for particular industries to match labour requirements. It was more economical to recruit migrants who could be compelled to leave when the work dried up than immigrants who would stay on. The social costs of female migrant workers were even fewer — until 1989 they were prohibited from bringing their families to join them. But by then a severe economic recession had effectively put an end to the need for migrant workers and work permits for the jobs carried out by most migrant women ceased to be available. The only growth area has been the most exploitative of women — domestic workers or 'slaves' as they have accurately been described. This group of workers, long hidden from sight but estimated to number 20,000,[11] has become more visible due to several campaigns and highly publicised court cases. But the government has so far been impervious to demands for effective protection for this particularly vulnerable group.

Women's Movement also describes the modern history of the resistance to racism and sexism in immigration and nationality law. From the suffragettes and feminists at the beginning of this century to the black and immigrant groups of today, women have challenged discrimination in these areas of law. But not all women. While the feminist movement in its early years vigorously opposed sex (though not race) discrimination in nationality law, the same could not be said more recently. Despite some lobbying by equal rights campaigners against sex discrimination (especially when white women were affected), the prevailing ethnocentrism of the 1970s feminist movement meant immigration and nationality issues were mainly ignored.

The 1980s were to prove a crucial decade for the fight against sex discrimination in both nationality and immigration law in Britain. As regards nationality, women had long been mere agents for the transmission of nationality through the male line. Until 1983 British women had not been able to pass on their nationality to their children in their own right; in this sense Britain had been a patrilineal society. This legal structure reflected traditional attitudes to women as occupiers of a private, domestic space rather than a public, political one; the concept of women as fully fledged citizens independent of their husbands, agents in the public sphere, had no place in this scheme of thinking. This is why British women marrying 'foreign men' lost their citizenship until 1948, whereas women from abroad who married British men automatically became British. After prolonged campaigning, British women finally gained the right to pass on their own citizenship when the 1981 British Nationality Act came into force.

Sex discrimination in immigration law was also dramatically reduced by developments that took place in the 1980s. The European Court of Human Rights decision in 1985 was a watershed. But, as the book explains, the government responded to the letter rather than the spirit of the decision, by levelling down: most men living in Britain now had to meet the same obstacles that had formerly only been in place for women.

Collective campaigning, which reached a peak in the 1980s, also had an impact. The book documents several important campaigns — the Resident Domestics Campaign and the Immigration Widows Campaign for example — which were influential in changing immigration law as it affected women. However with the Conservative government in power and effectively unopposed for over a decade, the impact of campaigning has declined. Recent mass campaigns, such as the protest against the removal of rights of appeal for visitors, short-term students and prospective students in the Asylum and Immigration Appeals Act 1993, have had little effect.

Partly as a result of the lack of success of public campaigns and demonstrations, opponents of government immigration policy have resorted to legal challenges, wherever possible, to achieve change. While this has limited the scope for campaigning to areas where a legal point can be found, it has meant that some of the most far-reaching inroads into government policy have resulted from the successful outcome of individual court cases — an effective means of creating precedents for the future. Thus not only British but European courts, both the European Court of Justice and the European Court of Human Rights, have had a profound effect on British immigration law.

In the 1990s immigration issues have once more moved into the headlines, as in periods during the 1960s and 1970s. Now, however, it is not only domestic, national concerns that are voiced, but those relating to the new political, economic and social order, the European Community. Where once politicians only spoke of overcrowded islands or preserving the home-bred stock, now it is the European way of life that is supposedly at stake, threatened by ever-expanding numbers of would-be immigrants. They come from Asia, Africa, Latin America, but also, increasingly, from countries whose peoples were formerly conveniently kept away by the Iron Curtain, Russia, Bulgaria, Romania and the war-torn Balkans. The political collapse of the Soviet bloc and the concomitant opening up of borders and economic disintegration have produced a vast pool of potential immigrants. Until recently the restrictions on free movement imposed by the Soviet bloc were paraded as examples of the oppressive nature of Communism in contrast to the virtues of Western democracy. Now these self-appointed custodians of 'real' human rights are concertedly erecting barriers with which to fence off their privileged life-style.

Another difference exists between the immigration issues of the post-war decades and those of the last eight or ten years. It is not the entry of dependants or of migrant workers that provokes the most heated controversy, particularly as ever more restrictive provisions have all but closed off these sources of immigration. Instead, attention has increasingly focused on refugees. People fleeing for their lives from torture, arbitrary killings, war and the complete devastation of any means of survival have been publicly berated as liars and scroungers, mere 'economic migrants.'

The desperate attempt to survive has, by means of a demonic logic, been re-classified as something akin to a crime. Growing numbers of refugees reaching the European Community have been detained without trial for long periods while their cases are considered. For many it has been a case of out of the frying pan and into the fire.

Women's Movement shows how women refugees have encountered distinctive problems, analogous to those outlined earlier for black and immigrant women in general. As members of male-led refugee families or as dependants within such families they have not encountered particular hostility or difficulty; but women fleeing outside such family contexts have had difficulty qualifying for protection as refugees (though many have been allowed to stay 'exceptionally' in Britain, at the mercy of government discretion). The notion that male activities form the archetype of the 'political', and the assumption that acts by or affecting women are somehow private or purely 'personal' and thus not within the political sphere, operates to this day. Where conventional political protests resulting in imprisonment or torture have attracted the protection of refugee status, refusal to wear the veil or to abide by customary rules concerning marriage have not, even though these are political activities and the resulting and feared persecution may be as severe.

The specific problems encountered by refugee women are not explicitly covered by the main international instrument governing the treatment of refugees, the 1951 Geneva Convention on the Status of Refugees. Gender is not included as a ground of persecution: race, religion, nationality, membership of a particular social group or political opinion are the only categories recognised. This may not present problems for the many women who flee persecution on the same basis as their male counterparts; if Aung San Suu Kyi, the leader of the Burmese National League for Democracy, were to seek protection outside her country, she would doubtless be granted refugee status. It does however create difficulties for those women whose fears of persecution arise out of forms of protest or ill-treatment not considered 'political', for example opposition to the veil, or rape. The book describes these difficulties, but also the trend-setting recent developments in Canada where the specific persecution affecting women has been officially recognised for the first time.

This book is written to document the history of women under British immigration, nationality and refugee law, and the campaigns to give women independent status and equal rights under those laws. It argues that all people living in Britain, women and men, workers, refugees, students, people allowed to stay 'exceptionally', should have the right to bring their families to join them. It also maintains that all the various living arrangements people may choose for themselves should receive equal treatment under immigration law. This applies to members of extended families, lone parents, lesbians and gay men, heterosexual couples living in non-marital relationships and polygamous marriages, as much as to conventionally married couples. It is not for the government to decide what kind of family life people may enjoy, or where.

The focus on the discrimination women have faced under nationality law and the campaigns for equal rights in this field should not be taken to imply support for nationalism or for the idea that British people should be given more rights than others living here. Indeed the imperialist foundations and racist nature of the British nation are recurring themes of the book.[12] Similar points are made in the discussion on Europe and on the evolution of European Community rights. But given the present division of the world and the potentially drastic effects of statelessness, the importance of preserving, indeed extending, people's citizenship rights cannot be overestimated. Similarly, focus on the race and sex discrimination of British immigration control should not be taken to imply an uncritical view of other aspects of the system; rather our stance is to reveal the way the present system particularly operates against black and other ethnic minority women and men.

When *Worlds Apart* was published in 1985 it included the following prophecy: 'The nature of the [immigration] system is such that even if black and Third World women were to gain the rights under immigration law that this book is calling for [women to have the same family reunion rights as men], they would still be up against the racist nature of immigration control in general. Its operation would undoubtedly erode their formal rights, much as it has done for black and Third World men.' Unfortunately, this is exactly what happened. The entire basis of the system needs changing. The family reunion rights which citizens of European Community countries have within the EC, applied generally, could provide a model for a fairer system.

Throughout the text, the limitations of terminology and language are apparent. The word 'black' is used in a political sense to refer to people mainly of African and Asian descent who have suffered from both racism and colonialism; where the experiences of women from the Indian sub-continent are being discussed, the word 'Asian' is used; where women who came to Britain to settle are described, the word 'immigrant' is used, in contrast to the 'migrant' women who came on work permits. Since immigration, nationality and refugee law form our basic subject-matter, in many instances words have a specific legal meaning. Words like 'dependant' or 'alien' are Home Office terms. A glossary has been provided to explain some of the specialist terms used.

Women's Movement does not, of course, look at *all* the ways in which racism is directed against women in Britain. It does not attempt to give an account of the experiences of women in different migrant, immigrant and refugee communities in Britain, except insofar as immigration, nationality and refugee law impinged upon them. The focus, accordingly, is on immigrant women from Africa, the Caribbean and the Indian subcontinent, as those primarily affected. However, the experiences of women from many other minority and refugee communities including Arab, Chinese, Cypriot, Filipino, Jewish, Kurdish, Latin American, and Turkish women are discussed where relevant. While Irish women may also be immigrants and suffer oppression through anti-terrorist legislation, their problems are not specifically addressed here because they have otherwise never been subjected to British immigration control.

The first two chapters of *Women's Movement* are virtually unchanged from the first chapters of *Worlds Apart*, and were researched and written by Francesca Klug. The next four chapters have been substantially revised and updated, mainly by Sue Shutter. The last two chapters, by Jacqueline Bhabha, are new, reflecting the new emphases and concerns which have developed since 1985.

Chapter 1 concentrates on nationality. It traces the history of women's treatment under nationality law from the Middle Ages, when they had no independent rights, to the 1948 British Nationality Act. The main focus of the chapter is on the struggles of the feminist movement in the early part of this century to stop women losing their nationality on marriage.

Chapter 2 turns to the immigration laws. It considers the status of women under each Immigration Act in turn, from the 1905 Aliens Act to the present day. It looks at how racism and sexism have interacted in these Acts and ends with a discussion of the 1981 British Nationality Act.

Chapter 3 looks at those sections of the Immigration Rules that have prevented women living in Britain from bringing their husbands to join them, both in the past and up to the present day. It explains the effects of these Rules on women's lives, analyses the reasons why successive governments maintained this discrimination and describes some of the ways in which women challenged this in order to create the present formally-equal position. It also documents how same-sex and unmarried couples have been kept apart by these laws.

Chapter 4 shifts the focus from women in Britain to women abroad seeking to join their husbands. It shows how men's legal entitlement to bring in their wives has been hedged about by restrictions as a result of racist policies. The chapter concentrates on the particular hurdles women from the Indian subcontinent and the Philippines have to overcome in order to join their husbands in Britain, as well as looking at the implications for women of being treated as dependants under immigration law. Some of the campaigns mounted to change this are described.

Chapter 5 explains how the immigration law assumption that women are dependants has restricted their independent family life choices. It shows the obstacles placed in the way of children and other relatives coming to join women 'heads of households'. It is especially concerned with the systematic attacks on the rights of lone mothers from the Caribbean to be joined by their children and also discusses the immigration difficulties of keeping in contact with extended family members.

Chapter 6 shows how the stereotyped view of immigrant women as dependants of men took no account of the thousands of women who came to Britain as independent workers. It explains how female migrant workers faced particular discrimination when trying to bring their families to join them. Their situation is highlighted by the story of the Home Office's attack on Filipino workers in Britain and their resistance to this. This chapter also discusses the current situation of nurses, domestic 'slaves' and au pairs, and briefly sketches the growing apparatus of internal immigration controls.

Chapter 7 moves from concentrating on Britain to consider the European Community. It shows how EC migration policy and law has developed since the 1950s, with an increasing impact on individual European countries. This body of law has never discriminated on grounds of sex. Rather, the crucial distinction has been that based on nationality, between predominantly white EC nationals and non-Europeans, so-called 'third-country nationals'. The chapter describes the creation of 'Fortress Europe', a process of consolidating the racist immigration restrictions of individual European countries into harmonised Europe-wide controls. It also details the contrast between the relatively generous EC family reunion provisions and the restrictive British rules.

Chapter 8 discusses the increasingly important issue of refugees. There are now an estimated 17.5 million refugees worldwide. Even though only a small proportion are in Europe, Britain witnessed a tenfold increase in the number of people seeking asylum between 1985 and 1991. The chapter describes the ever-escalating measures taken against refugees throughout Europe. It also discusses the 1951 Geneva Convention relating to the status of refugees and its interpretation. It shows that, as the Convention does not include gender as a ground of persecution, women fleeing gender-specific persecution have been excluded from protection as refugees.

The 1993 United Nations World Conference on Human Rights included in its *Declaration and Programme of Action* the proposition that

> The human rights of women and of the girl-child are an inalienable, integral and indivisible part of universal human rights...the eradication of all forms of discrimination on grounds of sex are priority objectives of the international community.[13]

That this seemingly self-evident statement should have required a concerted campaign before being accepted is evidence of the ground that still needs to be covered. But it is also an encouraging signal. This book hopes to contribute to that movement for change.

Chapter 1

'As a woman I have no country': women and nationality

To dig into the annals of British nationality law is to uncover a long history of effective statelessness for married women. Once married, women who were born in Britain were considered, according to law or custom, to have the same nationality as their husband. All women were anyway denied most citizenship rights which stemmed from British nationality and such national rights as they did possess they were unable to pass on to their children. This was the state of affairs until well into the twentieth century. Indeed, it was not until 1983 that British women could transmit their nationality to their children on the same terms as men.

Patriarchy in the Middle Ages

But to begin at the beginning... Traditionally, English nationality law was concerned with the allegiance of subjects to the monarch and was largely governed by common law (that is, law derived from custom) with little interference from Parliament. This aspect of common law remains shrouded in obscurity, but legal researchers have attempted to piece together the history of the status of British subjects by examining documents on individual cases together with early legislation.[1]

Generally speaking, under medieval common law everyone was either an English subject or an alien. All people born on English soil, regardless of parentage, owed allegiance to, and were therefore subjects of, the monarch. With some exceptions, their descendants born abroad were all aliens. However, this was modified by an Act passed in 1351 during the reign of Edward III which ruled that children born abroad whose fathers *and* mothers at the time of their birth

> shall be at the Faith and Ligeance of the King of England, shall have, and shall enjoy, the same benefits and advantages... as other inheritors [provided that] the Mothers of such Children do pass the Sea by the License and Wills of their husbands.[2]

This meant that children born abroad to English parents who were in allegiance to the monarch were, in effect, English subjects.[3]

Whilst this law suggests that the subject status of *both* parents was significant in determining that of their children, women, it seems, could not transmit their English status to their children as free agents. It is not difficult to guess why the law was framed in this way. As the prime purpose of this statute was to develop a clear legal basis to inheritance, the law-makers had to face the ancient problem of how men can identify and control their offspring. Their solution was to control women. Children born abroad to women who had travelled without the consent of their husbands would not be inheritors. Along with children born abroad to unmarried women, they were effectively delegitimised and placed outside the boundaries of the English nation. The patriarchal nature of English nationality law was imprinted from the outset.

Records of individual cases concerning disputed inheritance show that in practice the wife's subject status was not always treated as relevant in determining that of her children. There were numerous instances where children born abroad to an alien mother were able to claim allegiance to the English crown provided they had an English-born father (or British-born, after the annexation of Scotland by the Act of Union in 1707). But the reverse rarely, if ever, applied. For example, in a case of disputed inheritance in the seventeenth century, the judge Lord Hale held that

> it is without question that if an English woman go beyond the Seas and marry an Alien, and have Issue born beyond the Seas, the Issue are Aliens, for the wife was *sub potestate viri* [under the power of the man].[4]

This question was clarified by the British Nationality Act of 1730 which declared that children born abroad would be British provided that their *fathers* were natural-born British subjects (that is, they had been born in Britain). The word 'mother' had now been removed from the statute. In the same way as women had no legal right to custody over their children, they could not pass on their nationality to them.

Victorian values

It was not only as mothers that women were discriminated against under nationality law. Although common law never developed any particular rules on the nationality of married women, legal historians generally agree that in practice they were treated as having the same nationality as their husbands.[5] The 1844 Naturalisation Act clarified the situation so that from then on any foreign woman married to a British subject automatically became British (although she did not necessarily lose her nationality of birth and could therefore have two citizenships).

Following the same principle, the 1870 Naturalisation Act deprived British-born women who had married aliens of their British nationality. The Act simply stated that 'a married woman shall be deemed to be a subject of the state of which her husband is for the time being a subject.' According to the 1923 Select Committee Report, *The Nationality of Married Women,* Parliament's main consideration in 1870 was to make British law conform with international law.[6] The fact that women born and brought up in Britain lost any claim to British nationality on marriage to a non-British man was considered by the male law-makers to be of no consequence. Even Queen Victoria's marriage to a German national was apparently not sufficient to draw Parliament's attention to the implications of this legislation for British women.

Imperialism and British nationality

From the sixteenth century onwards Britain had been acquiring territories in all corners of the world, conferring the status of British subject on their inhabitants whilst taking away their independence and extracting their wealth. After the passing of the 1914 British Nationality and Status of Aliens Act, there was no longer any *legal* distinction between the status of inhabitants of the colonies and of Britain — they were all British subjects (the term citizen was not officially used until 1948). The medieval concept of allegiance to the crown was, by this Act, extended all over the British Empire.

All-party support for Britain's imperial domination meant that the imposition of British subject status on the peoples of vast areas of the world did not create any major conflict in Parliament. Where controversy did arise was over the question of the status of married women. The law-makers could no longer ride roughshod over the rights of women without arousing protest. The growing feminist movement was beginning to make itself felt.

Speaker after speaker in the parliamentary debate on the 1914 Bill alluded to this fact. For example, Aneurin Williams MP stated that

> there is already enough bitterness on the part of women outside with regard to questions affecting their position in the country. This is not the time, surely, to pass a law in this House which is utterly opposed by the great majority of the organised women in this country.[7]

Indeed, feminist ideas were so influential at this period as to persuade one opponent of the Bill (Edward Harvey MP) to argue that

> We must feel that there is something ironical in a Parliament of men, elected by men, settling once and for all the citizenship and civic rights of women who have no voice in the matter directly at all.

But this groundswell of opinion did not lead to any significant improvement in the status of married women under British nationality law. The feminist movement failed in its attempts to persuade the Liberal government to alter the law in their favour during the passage of the 1914 Nationality Bill. Their only achievement was a minor amendment allowing women to retain their own nationality if their husband relinquished British nationality *after* marriage. In addition, the Act allowed British-born widows or divorcées who had lost their British subject status on marriage to reapply for it and permitted the Home Secretary to waive the usual residential qualifications if he accepted their application. But they still had to pay to reacquire their nationality of birth and the process was not automatic. As for women who were not legally divorced, they could not regain the British nationality they had lost on marriage for as long as their husband lived.

The almost total dependence of a woman on her husband, as far as nationality was concerned, continued as before. They were still treated as 'chattels and appendages of their husbands' and placed in the same class as 'lunatics, minors and idiots'.[8] But according to the Secretary of State for the Colonies, Lewis Harcourt, speaking on behalf of the government in the debate on the 1914 Bill, to allow a woman to retain her own nationality 'when she deliberately marries an alien' would be 'departing from the practice of the whole civilised world... with the exception of Venezuela and Spain'.

It is interesting to speculate on the reasons why the government refused to give married women equal nationality rights.

Successive governments disregarded pressure from numerous women's lobbies on this issue until the late 1940s. This was in spite of the fact that the reduction in women's rights brought about by the 1870 Act came at the very dawn of a whole series of other laws which granted women citizenship rights they had previously been denied. In 1882, married women acquired the legal right to hold property in their own names for the first time. The Franchise Act of 1918 gave women over 30 the vote and the 1919 Sex Disqualification (Removal) Act declared that no one should be barred from holding public office on the grounds of sex or marital status. Women householders could for the first time sit on juries and become JPs. Yet even after full equal franchise was obtained by women (in 1928) successive governments refused to grant married women equality in nationality law.

A likely explanation for this lies in the importance attached to nationality by the British state during this and subsequent periods. At the height of 'Great' Britain's imperial power, the question of who was and who was not included in the category of British subject assumed a significance not reached before. The colonised were defined 'in' after 1914, thus emphasising their subjugation to the dominant power — they were all British subjects. (As will be shown, this incorporation was gradually to be removed once Britain's black subjects began to take up their right of residence after the Second World War.)

At the same time, women who married foreigners were defined 'out'. If there had to be coherence in the Empire, all the more so in the family. Thus, the argument went, women had to give up their own nationality to follow that of their husband. In this case subjugation resulted in exclusion. The British lineage was clearly male. The only role for women was as reproducers of the next generation of British children. They could neither retain their nationality of birth if they married 'out' nor pass on their nationality to their children born abroad. On the other hand, until as recently as 1983, men could transmit their British nationality to an unlimited number of generations, regardless of where they were born.

A further clue to understanding the government's policy over the nationality of married women is the fact that those who were most affected by the law as it stood in the early 1900s were poor women living in the East End of London. As the MP for Stepney, W.S. Glyn-Jones, explained in the debate over the 1914 Act, they were 'British-born Jewesses who are married to Jews who have not become naturalised and have lost their British nationality in consequence.' In fact, it was in this period that the first Act to control immigration to Britain was passed — the Aliens Act of 1905, whose aim was to reduce Jewish immigration to Britain from eastern Europe.

Feminism and nationalism

Women's groups in general, and the feminist movement in particular, waged a persistent battle to gain equal nationality rights for women regardless of whom they married. Organised feminist campaigning on this issue, which largely took the form of conventional lobbying, was initiated at a 1905 meeting of the International Council of Women, a body to which 25 national councils were affiliated. Women's groups ranging from the National Union of Women Workers to the Mothers' Union petitioned the British Imperial Conferences of 1918 and 1921 on the matter. The International Woman Suffrage Alliance was particularly active, serving as the focal point for women's lobbying on the question of nationality throughout Europe and America. The patriarchal nature of nationality law was almost universal.

It is worth questioning why women were so active in demanding the right to retain their nationality of birth regardless of whom they married. First, there was the fundamental principle of equality between men and women and the role which inequality in nationality status implied for women — that of appendages to their husbands and the reproducers of the next generation.

Second, there was the possibility of women becoming stateless if they married men from countries which did not allow husbands to pass on their citizenship automatically to their wives. For example, this applied to women who married American men after 1922 (when the United States altered its nationality laws).

Third, the citizenship rights which flow from nationality are a passport to a whole series of other rights (and duties).[9] Women who lost their British nationality on marriage to non-British men were deprived of the opportunity to vote in general elections. (This applied only after women over 30 finally won this right in 1918 following a long and bitter struggle.) As aliens, they had no automatic right to live in Britain at all. If they did live in Britain they and their husbands had to register regularly with the police. Unless they were born on British soil, their children were also aliens and had no claim to live in Britain either.

The story of one couple who suffered under the effects of the discriminatory legislation illustrates the hardship it inflicted on thousands of women over the years. An old man who had lived in Britain for 67 years, having been brought over from Germany by his father, applied for a pension on retirement. He was informed that as his father had never sought to have him naturalised as a British subject he was ineligible. His wife, however, was born in England, where she had lived all her life. Because her husband had been in England since childhood, it did not occur to her when she married him that he was not a British subject. So the woman discovered when she was over 60 years old that she had been an alien since her marriage. As the wife of a German national she was in fact, treated as an enemy alien during the First World War.[10]

Women had practical and political reasons, therefore, for wanting to retain their British nationality on marriage. The struggle feminists waged for equal nationality rights did not necessarily mean that they adhered to the widely accepted nationalism and patriotism of their day. The famous quotation by the feminist writer Virginia Woolf — 'as a woman I have no country, as a woman I want no country, as a woman my country is the whole world' — expressed the internationalist ideology which characterised some sections of the women's movement from its inception.

At the same time, the First World War brought out the extreme nationalism of some of the suffragette leaders and completely split the feminist movement, with the nationalists using the suffragette movement for war work.[11] This rapid change from internationalism to nationalism was illustrated by the development of the militant Women's Social and Political Union (WSPU). Its first journal, *Votes for Women*, founded in 1903, included among its dedications one to 'women all over the world of whatever race or creed'. After the war broke out the WSPU's new journal, *The Suffragette*, edited by Christabel Pankhurst, argued that 'the supreme reason why we have fought for the vote is that we might obtain the power to help in making British civilisation an even finer contribution to the civilisation of the world than it has been in the past'.[12] In October 1914, *The Suffragette* was renamed *The Britannia* and carried a new slogan: 'War Till Victory and Britain for the British'.

Such expressions of patriotic fervour were by no means unusual during the First World War, both inside and outside the suffragette movement. Even in other contexts, however, feminist journals expressed ethnocentric and racist views which were characteristic of imperialist Britain. For example, an article by Laura Aberconway on nationality in *Jus Suffragii*, the journal of the International Woman Suffrage Alliance, cited inter-racial marriages as one of the reasons for supporting married women's right to retain British nationality:

> Throughout our Empire the numbers of British subjects who became the wives of men of coloured races are very large. These women have urgent need for the protection of our laws and should not be cast out from citizenship of our Empire except by their own desires.'[13]

This kind of reasoning was not used again in the numerous articles that appeared in *Jus Suffragii* over the years on the subject of married women's nationality. But neither did those articles pay any attention whatsoever to the imperialist nature of Britain's nationality laws.

Feminists fight on

After the war ended, the feminist movement turned its attention to the nationality question once more. The Home Secretary refused to meet a deputation of women to discuss the issue of women's nationality in 1918; in the same year attempts were made to amend the 1914 Act to remove the inequalities against married women. These failed, except for a small concession which allowed the British-born wife of an 'enemy alien' to resume her British nationality in times of war at the discretion of the Home Secretary.[14] This was more a consequence of the First World War and the anti-German nationalism which it engendered than of any pro-feminist sentiment.

At the same time, the rights of British women were actually reduced under another 1918 amendment which allowed the Home Secretary to deprive women of their British citizenship as a result of the actions of their husbands.[15] This applied in circumstances where a man who had become British through naturalisation had his citizenship revoked because of fraud or 'bad character' or for some similar reason. The Home Secretary then had the discretion to take away the citizenship of his wife and minor children as well. In exceptional circumstances, such strictures could even apply to British-born women. This was probably the first and only time that British-born subjects could be deprived of their citizenship at the will of the Home Secretary.

In 1922, a Bill was drawn up by the Conservative MP for York, John Butcher, to equalise the nationality status of men and women.[16] It was supported by 59 women's organisations including the National Federation of Women's Institutes, the International Woman Suffrage Alliance and the Women's International League for Peace and Freedom. It did not, however proceed beyond the second reading in the House of Commons. Instead, the government referred the issue to the 1923 Select Committee. Consisting of five members from each House of Parliament, it had been specifically appointed to consider the issue of the nationality of married women.[17]

In their evidence to the Committee, spokesmen from the Foreign and Home Offices declared that family unity and matrimonial harmony depended on women maintaining the same national identity as their husbands. In addition, any change to the law would, they argued, cause considerable 'inconvenience', for it would put Britain out of line with other nations on this matter. In making this point they ignored the fact that both the United States and the fledgling Soviet Union had recently passed laws which allowed women to retain their own nationality on marriage and that Argentina, Belgium and Chile already had legislation to this effect.

In the event, the Committee did not reach any agreement about the issue. A report by John Butcher — the proposer of the failed 1922 Bill — which argued that a woman should have the right to choose whether or not to take her husband's nationality on marriage, failed to obtain the support of the five Lords on the Committee. They objected to his argument on the grounds that 'by marriage a woman is merged in the unit of the family and that within the family it is at present the husband who is head.'

The Hague Convention of 1930, which met to consider questions relating to conflicts between different countries' nationality laws also considered the issue of married women's nationality. Whilst proposing some changes to avoid married women becoming literally stateless, the Convention did not demand full equality between the sexes on this issue.

As these proposals fell far short of the demands of the women's lobby, women's organisations campaigned to have the matter raised again at the League of Nations (the predecessor to the United Nations) the following year. On that occasion, Ramsay MacDonald's coalition government finally endorsed the principle that marriage should not necessarily alter a woman's national status.[18] The long hard years of lobbying by the feminist movement and their supporters in Parliament had at last begun to have an effect.

Nevertheless, a Bill introduced in 1932 to establish this change in married women's status once again failed. The following year the government sponsored the 1933 British Nationality and Status of Aliens Bill specifically to alter the position of married women to fall in line with the recommendations of the Hague Convention. Henceforth, a woman no longer became stateless on marriage to an alien if the laws of his country did not allow her to take his nationality. Under those conditions alone, she would be allowed to retain her citizenship of birth. This change was spurred on by the difficulties that had developed over marriages between British women and American men. As the Act was retrospective the result, in effect, was to restore British nationality to many stateless women. The Home Secretary also issued a new Order in 1933 which exempted British women married to aliens from having to register with the police. This followed the stand taken by Winifred James, who refused to register as an alien after she married an American. A summons was taken out against her and she made it clear that she was prepared to go to prison over the issue.[19]

But the relatively minor changes of 1933 were of no help to the thousands of women who still suffered under the discriminatory effects of British nationality law. One MP stated that he had a box filled with letters at home amounting to 400 cases of women experiencing hardship under the nationality legislation. Many of these were the wives of non-British seamen who had deserted them: ‘They live at some port in this country and are condemned for the rest of their lives to be aliens in their own country.’[20]

Whilst women’s organisations decried the narrowness of the changes brought about in 1933, the coalition government continued to declare its newly formed commitment to equal nationality rights between men and women. This, the government argued, would be translated into law once the dominions, Britain’s self-governing territories within the Empire, accepted the principle. No less than the unity of the Empire was at stake! On these same grounds, a further attempt to equalise the nationality status of women failed in 1938 when yet another Bill on the issue was unable to gain government support.

Winds of change

In the event, women had to wait another ten years, until 1948, to obtain the right to retain their own nationality on marriage. By this time the Second World War was over and women who had married non-British soldiers discovered they had lost their citizenship of birth (provided they did not become stateless in the process). One such woman, Esther Weinberg, who was serving in the ATS (the army’s women’s corps), had married a Jewish refugee from Czechoslovakia who was fighting with the Czech brigade. After he was killed in action she discovered that she had lost her British citizenship on marriage and had to reapply for it. As a Czechoslovakian Jew, her husband’s citizenship had in fact been worthless so, in spite of the 1933 Act, Esther had been made effectively stateless — at the very time when she was serving in Britain’s wartime army.

Throughout this period, the women’s lobby kept up the pressure on British and other Commonwealth governments. Once Canada unilaterally changed its own nationality laws in 1946, the question of unity of the Commonwealth and Empire could no longer be used by successive governments as a justification for delaying the 17-year-old commitment to provide equality for married women on the issue of nationality. Finally, the 1948 British Nationality Act, which remained in force until 1983, was introduced by the post-war Labour government, partly to settle the issue of the nationality of married women once and for all. Among other far-reaching changes, this Act produced the all-embracing citizenship of the UK and Colonies. This was acquired by all citizens of countries which were still part of the British Empire. When colonies later became independent their inhabitants lost their UK citizenship and became citizens of the newly independent countries; as Commonwealth citizens, they were still British subjects (the terms were interchangeable). Along with Irish citizens, British subjects had the right to live in Britain where, unlike aliens, they could vote, serve on juries, take employment without first obtaining work permits, work in public services and stand for public office. As British subjects they even had the right to fight and die for 'King and Country' — which many of them did in both world wars.

Under the 1948 Act marriage no longer had any automatic effect on nationality. British women would not lose their British nationality on marriage to an alien unless they declared that they wished to. As for women who had already lost their British nationality when they married, they became UK citizens once more.

Under the original draft of the Bill, an alien woman would no longer have an automatic entitlement to British nationality on marriage to a British man. It was proposed that a woman would not have the opportunity to take on her husband's nationality without first securing the Home Secretary's agreement. The reason for this was the spectre of the 'bogus marriage' — a phantom that has haunted immigration debates ever since (although in recent years it has more often been men than women who have posed the alleged threat). Licences for brothels had recently been withdrawn in France and it was claimed by some MPs from both major parties that there was

> a certain number of alien women who come here either for scandalous and immoral purposes or as spies and who pay British subjects to marry them merely in order that they may qualify as British subjects.
>
> All of us on both sides of the House, and almost everybody in this country, are extremely jealous of the good reputation of British citizenship. We do not want people in this country who can do a great deal of harm by being British citizens and who have no loyalty at all to Britain or to the things in which we believe.[21]

Against this argument, the traditionalist lobby which supported automatic citizenship for the wives of British men again argued that the unity of the family could depend on the unity of passport. Viscount Maugham stated in the House of Lords that 'marriage is a very singular thing: a woman is supposed to lose some of her identity.' In addition, it was feared that all women married to British men who were refused registration by the Home Secretary would henceforth be branded as 'harlots'! Finally, MPs asserted that to give the Home Secretary discretion as to whether or not he would bestow British citizenship on a woman married to a British man was tantamount to 'giving the Home Secretary an entirely new power over Englishmen'. Is it not wrong, it was asked, 'to give the Home Secretary complete discretion to exclude the wife of a British subject living in this country?'

In the end, the Labour government accepted an amendment to the effect that alien women were *entitled* to register as UK citizens (a much cheaper and speedier process than naturalisation) on marriage to British men, provided they swore an oath of allegiance to the British crown. It was this element of choice which the feminist movement had been calling for all along. It applied to any woman who had been married to a UK citizen at any time, even if she had since been divorced or widowed.

But the reverse did not apply to men. They had no right to register as UK citizens on marriage to British women but had to go through the longer and more expensive process of applying for naturalisation, along with all other aliens. In fact, there was no mention of the possibility of husbands being treated in the same way as wives in any of the debates on the Act. This reflected the assumption that wives should take the nationality of their husbands, but not vice versa. Thus the indignation of MPs over the proposal that this almost sacrosanct principle should be relegated to the discretion of the Home Secretary. Justifying the continuing inequality between men and women under nationality law, Labour Home Secretary John Chuter Ede asserted that

> I do not myself subscribe to the doctrine that everything that happens to a man must of necessity happen to a woman. We are getting dangerously near the position when we shall be told that if a married couple have twins the man must be expected to suckle one of them.[22]

Nearly ten years later, in August 1957, Britain ratified the United Nations Convention on the Nationality of Married Women,[23] which provided that neither marriage, nor divorce, nor the change of nationality by a husband during marriage, should have any automatic effect on the nationality of his wife. The 1948 Nationality Act had already incorporated these proposals, so the Convention did not in fact require any change to Britain's nationality law.

So what had been achieved in the half-century of campaigning for equal rights for women in nationality law? For the first time in 100 years, British law did not interfere with a woman's right to retain her nationality regardless of whom she married. Possibly for the first time in British history, it was recognised in *practice* that a woman did not take on the national identity of a man simply because she married him.

But there was still no question of a woman being able to pass on her citizenship to her own children. Nationality through descent could be traced only through the father. Under section 7 of the 1948 Act the Home Secretary could, at his discretion, register as British any minor child (then under 21); in practice, he would never do so without the father's permission. Generally, the policy was, until as late as 1979, to refuse applications to register the children of British mothers if they were likely to live outside Britain or, if they lived in Britain, if their father had not applied to become a UK citizen.[24] In all the debates over changing the nationality status of married women, the fact that citizenship was transmitted through the male line only was either ignored or referred to as an immutable state of affairs which could not, and should not, be altered in the name of equality for women. This, of course, was the very principle which had been opposed by the International Woman Suffrage Alliance since the First World War.

More than three decades were to pass before women obtained the right to pass on their nationality to their children. In the intervening years, a series of Immigration Acts rendered UK citizenship worthless for thousands of black holders of that status. Before reviewing the current nationality status of women, it is necessary to look at those Immigration Acts whose provisions were eventually translated into nationality law under the 1981 British Nationality Act.

Chapter 2

Travelling third class: women and immigration

A form of immigration control has existed in England since medieval times when monarchs claimed a prerogative power to expel aliens from the country. One of the earliest known examples of this was when all Jews were expelled from England in 1290. The last English monarch to use the royal prerogative to expel foreigners from the realm was Elizabeth I. In 1596 she sent an open letter to the Mayor of London telling him that

> Her majesty understanding that several blackamoors have lately been brought into this realm, of which kind of people there are already too many here... her majesty's pleasure therefore is that those kind of people should be expelled from the land.[1]

A series of Acts in the eighteenth and nineteenth centuries culminating in the Removal of Aliens Act 1848, empowered the Home Secretary to expel aliens for the 'preservation of peace and tranquillity of the realm'.[2] However, it was not until Jews started to immigrate to Britain in large numbers at the end of the nineteenth century, to escape persecution in eastern Europe, that the modern system of immigration control on entry was set up.

Following a build-up of public and parliamentary agitation against Jewish immigration, the 1905 Aliens Act was passed to exclude 'undesirables'. The spectre of a menacing influx of 'alien people' whose entry had to be controlled for the sake of the British nation had found legislative expression. The makers of British immigration law have been obsessed by this fear ever since.

The Aliens Acts

The 1905 Act set up a system of immigration control which has many analogies to that which exists today. Immigration officers and medical inspectors were appointed to enforce control and Immigration Boards were established to hear appeals from would-be immigrants. Although a special clause in the Act allowed entry for refugees from political and religious persecution, in practice it was those very people — Jews and socialists fleeing from Russia and Eastern Europe — whom the Act sought to exclude. In particular, the Act restricted the entry of 'undesirable aliens' who, it was feared, would be a burden on the state unless their 'sponsors' in England could demonstrate that they would be able to support them. Single women alleged to be prostitutes were among those deported as 'undesirables'.

Then as now, families were split up as a result of the workings of the Act. Immigrants settled in Britain had no right to send for their relatives abroad. 'Dependants' had no greater entitlement to come to Britain than anyone else. The crux of the matter was whether they could be supported.

The *Jewish Chronicle* newspaper related numerous examples of this. In one case, a girl who came to England from Russia in June 1907 to join her fiancé was turned back even though her sister had been admitted the previous day. In another case, Sara Ntzwiech was refused permission to stay in Britain even though her sister and cousin appeared before the Immigration Board vouching to maintain her for two years.

As was to happen decades later, working-class support for immigration control developed as an easy (and false) answer to economic misery. This was encouraged and exploited by a powerful pro-nationalist lobby which brought the proto-fascist British Brothers League together with an assortment of writers, MPs and other establishment figures. One of these, W.H. Wilkins, specifically evoked the British woman's lot in his call for the restriction of Jewish immigration. In his book *The Alien Invasion*, published in 1892, he devoted an entire chapter to the miserable conditions of 'the weaker sex' who, he alleged, were suffering intolerable competition in the clothing trade from the 'influx of foreigners'. Aliens were to blame, he concluded, for leaving 'these poor creatures with no time for the pure tender delights of motherhood'.

The 1914 British Nationality and Status of Aliens Act conferred British subject status on all the inhabitants of the British Empire, setting the seal on the enforced incorporation of the colonised. (It was not until 1962 that they became subject to immigration control.) At the same time, aliens became subject to ever-increasing restrictions. Once the 1905 Act was passed, legitimising the belief that alien immigration was a threat to Britain, the anti-aliens lobby never ceased to agitate for tighter controls. The 1914 Aliens Restriction Act was passed on the first day of the First World War, going through all its parliamentary stages in one afternoon. This Act and the 1919 Aliens Restriction (Amendment) Act, passed after the defeat of Germany in the war, were introduced amidst a welter of anti-German nationalism. Both provided the Home Secretary with wide powers to deport anyone whose departure was considered to be 'conducive to the public good'. Thereafter, the 1919 Act was renewed every year by Aliens Orders. The 1953 Order remained in force for 20 years until the 1971 Immigration Act was implemented in 1973. Under this series of Orders, entry to Britain was still allowed only if an alien could 'support himself and his dependants in the United Kingdom'. To obtain employment, a work permit had to be acquired.

Instructions to immigration officers laying out how these Orders were to be implemented were not published until 1970 (although, according to the Home Office, the instruction governing the entry of dependants varied little during the entire period in which the Aliens Orders were in force). These instructions stipulated that work permit holders could bring in their dependants provided that they limited 'their stay to the date on which the husband's/father's conditions expire' and that they were supported and accommodated 'without recourse to public funds'. This meant that male migrant workers could bring their families to join them but women who were not settled in Britain had no right to bring in their husbands at all. As for a woman who was settled (that is, a woman with no time limit on her right to remain), the question of allowing in her husband depended on 'whether hardship would be likely to result if she and her husband were obliged to live abroad' — a question that was left to the immigration officer's discretion. The presumption clearly was that wives should live where their husbands dictated.

Even the foreign husband of a British subject could settle in Britain only if his wife had been born in the UK and had lived there all her life or had 'substantial connections with the country and is well established here'. Such men were allowed in for 12 months in the first instance and could remain thereafter only if the marriage was still lasting. By contrast, the foreign wives of British men were, as already explained, automatically entitled to UK citizenship on marriage and were consequently allowed to come to Britain free of all conditions.[3]

During the interwar years the number of aliens settling in Britain dropped sharply and most work permits issued were for domestic servants. In spite of this, the agitation of the anti-aliens lobby did not cease. Whilst the government encouraged British emigration to the Empire, alien immigration to Britain was discouraged. As Paul Foot has pointed out, 'the immigration process was fine provided that British people were immigrating to another country.'[4]

As the 1930s progressed and Jews sought refuge in Britain from Nazism in Germany and elsewhere, the anti-aliens lobby returned to its anti-semitic rhetoric of earlier years. Some Labour MPs complained over and over again that immigration officers were sending Jews back to Germany and that the first question asked of aliens seeking entry to Britain was whether they were Jewish. They were allowed entry only if they had a 'sponsor' in the UK. But in spite of pressure from certain sections of the Labour Party, the Home Secretary refused to amend the aliens laws and allow Jews unrestricted asylum in Britain. As the doors were shut on Jewish people throughout the world, they were left to be slaughtered by Europe's Nazis.[5]

Labour shortages and immigration

After the Second World War, when women who had been keeping industry going were shunted back into the home, there was a need for an alternative source of cheap labour to help rebuild the shattered British economy. As a result, the Labour government introduced the European Voluntary Workers Scheme (EVWS), by which thousands of workers, mainly from eastern Europe, were recruited for employment in Britain. This scheme was introduced *outside* the Aliens Act which remained in force as a sop to the anti-aliens lobby, whilst foreign labour was freely enlisted to fill vital labour needs.

For the first six months after EVWS was introduced, dependants were allowed to join the workers in Britain: sometimes families would be split up, with husbands working in one part of the country and wives in another. After January 1948, however, only single people could be recruited. They had to sign a declaration that they were 'single, unattached and had no dependent relatives'. Later still, under the Distressed Relatives Scheme, dependants could be brought over provided that work and accommodation could be guaranteed, but not many relatives came over under this procedure.

Despite EVWS, labour shortages continued. As both the newly created National Health Service and London Transport were grossly understaffed, the government took steps to recruit workers from Britain's Caribbean colonies. A 1968 study showed that migration from the Caribbean rose and fell according to the demand for labour from year to year between 1957 and 1961, when rumours about impending immigration control disturbed this pattern.[6]

From the 1950s onwards, Commonwealth citizens from Africa, Asia, the Far East and Cyprus, as well as the Caribbean, came to Britain in greater numbers than ever before. Many of them were in fact UK citizens and, as British subjects, they were entitled to live and work in the 'motherland'. Any restrictions on doing so came, quite illegally, from the colonial governments in the country of origin, rather than the law in Britain. In Cyprus as far back as the 1930s, for example, regulations stated that before people would be issued with passports to come to Britain, they had to show they could speak English and had a job to come to, as well as providing an affidavit from someone in Britain confirming support. If these regulations were not satisfied, the passport could be endorsed 'not valid for the UK'. Alternatively, Cypriots might be issued with certificates of identity, rather than passports, which did not specify their place of birth. This meant they might be refused entry to Britain as they had no evidence they were British subjects. British government attitudes to Cypriot migration were equally unwelcoming:

> 'the intention of the whole system was, and is, to prevent jobless and unassimilable Cypriots flocking to the UK and increasing the popu-

> lation of spivs in the Tottenham Court Road area or having their babies on the National Health Service without contributing toward it'[7]

Thus even when there was no immigration control of Commonwealth citizens, there was emigration control in the colonies! The system was clearly thought worth copying by other colonial governments in the 1950s:

> 'recent regulations, modelled to a certain extent on [those of Cyprus], have been introduced for Jamaicans and West Indians because of the concern caused to the Ministry of Labour, the Public Assistance and other authorities here by the unrestricted arrival of 700 to 800 per boat, many landing entirely without resources'[8]

Thus the government acted to recruit the workers it required for the British economy but to restrict other potential migrants.

A new wave of chauvinism and racism swelled in Britain, both inside and outside Parliament. Black colonised people who were fighting the British for freedom in their homelands faced overt hostility when they came to Britain. The racist ideology that had cemented British imperialism was now used against the black subjects of the declining Empire when they came to find work in Britain. Not only did they face systematic discrimination and segregation in housing, jobs and other services; they also had to confront the growing violence that culminated in the 1958 riots in Nottingham and Notting Hill. Working-class opposition to immigration was encouraged and exploited by politicians, commentators and neo-fascist groups. The government's reaction to the hostility of its white subjects to its black subjects was to take away the automatic right of the latter to enter Britain. From now on, they would be allowed to come to the UK only if the labour market explicitly required them.

Women under the 1962 Commonwealth Immigrants Act

It was in this context that the Tory government introduced the first Immigration Act to control the entry of British subjects to Britain — the 1962 Commonwealth Immigrants Act. In this way the proposition that the 'problem' lay with immigrants rather than with the racist elements within British society once again found expression in the law. Instead of challenging that chauvinism, this legislation and those Acts which followed it were to fuel the insatiable demands of racist ideology.

The 1962 Act began the process, completed in 1971, of transforming the status of Commonwealth citizens into that of migrant workers. Within a decade their right to live in Britain was severely eroded. Along with other foreign workers, their only passport to Britain would soon be the possession of the specific skills that the British economy required at any given time.[9]

The Act introduced immigration control for all British subjects except those born in the UK or Ireland or those who were holders of UK passports which had been issued by the *British* government (or a government representative overseas, such as a High Commissioner in a former colony). This meant that citizens of the UK and Colonies who obtained their passports from the government of a *colony* were subject to British immigration control for the first time, as were citizens of independent Commonwealth countries, even though they were still British subjects. To enter Britain they had to obtain an employment voucher, issued by the Ministry of Labour. The debates surrounding the Act showed that it was primarily designed to restrict black Commonwealth immigration. It did, however, also affect many white people, such as Australians and Canadians.

In its original form, the Bill did not give immigrants any automatic right to bring their spouses with them to the UK. After much debate on this issue, the Home Secretary, R.A. Butler, moved an amendment to allow Commonwealth husbands to bring over their wives and children aged under 16. 'Common law wives', however, were not given automatic entry under the Act. The Home Secretary argued that it was impossible to put their right of entry into statutory form, but immigration officers were given the discretion to let in 'a woman who has been living in permanent association with a man' where 'the association is really firm and permanent'.[10] Immigration officers were also instructed to 'bear in mind any local customs or traditions tending to establish the permanence of the association'.[11] (Labour MP John Chuter Ede felt obliged to point out that such customs were not 'British in any way: there is no suggestion that they have anything to do with the Christian religion.')

An amendment proposed by Labour MP Eirene White to alter the word 'wife' to 'spouse' so that women would also be entitled to bring in their husbands was not even selected for debate. Her colleague Judith Hart remarked that she 'was surprised that the Home Secretary did not mention his reason for applying sex discrimination as well as racial discrimination to the Bill.'

The 1962 Act also contained inequalities in its deportation provisions. Whilst the wife of a man exempt from deportation was herself exempt, this did not apply to a husband. Also exempt from deportation were people with a British-born father (but not mother). Defending this inequality — described by Labour MP John Diamond as evidence that 'it is a patriarchy ... that we are subscribing to' — Home Office minister David Renton argued that children, or more specifically sons, retain a connection with the country of birth of their father and not of their mother. Supporting an amendment in opposition to this, Labour MP Edwin Wainwright argued: 'I think it is the African countries, the coloured countries, which are behind the objection to this amendment. Had only the white races been involved, I do not think we should have had objections from the government on this issue.'

Clearly, the deportation exemption clause excluded most black Commonwealth citizens anyway, as few had British-born fathers or mothers at this time. But in making this point, Wainwright hit upon what was, in fact, to become a pattern in future immigration legislation. Sexism and a general contempt for the rights of women were to be used whenever possible to restrict further the immigration of black people to Britain. When it was feared that such proposals would also adversely affect white men they were generally not implemented until the late 1980s, when men's rights were progressively reduced.

However, under the Instructions to immigration officers, which explained how the Act was to be implemented, Commonwealth husbands of settled women were allowed to enter as 'the normal rule'. Those who wished to work did not need to obtain employment vouchers, but they would be refused admission if there was 'no reasonable prospect of maintenance for the man himself or his family without recourse to public funds' (a qualification which did not yet apply to Commonwealth wives). The instructions stated that 'in a doubtful case the immigration officer should take into account the strength of the wife's connections with the United Kingdom, including her length of residence here.'[12] In other words, it would be easier for white women who had lived all their lives in Britain to bring in their husbands than for black women who had recently immigrated.

Working wives

To justify sex discrimination in immigration law and in particular why it has always been made more difficult for husbands to come here than wives, successive governments resorted to two related arguments. First, they insisted that immigration policy only reflected the common practice that men determine where the family should live. Explaining why women were not given the same right as men to bring over their spouses under the 1962 Act, Renton argued that 'in the Bill, as in our nationality law, we have assumed that the husband is the head of the family and that the wife acquires his domicile.' He did however add that 'in the interesting case of the career wife who is here, normally her husband will be let in.' When husbands were allowed to join their wives, this is described as a 'concession' and not a right.

Second, and even more commonly, governments have argued that immigrant men posed more of a threat to the labour force than immigrant women. By 1962 the British economy was already beginning to enter a prolonged period of contraction. As MP Judith Hart suggested in the debate over the 1962 Bill, some MPs thought that 'husbands who come in with wives are more likely to constitute a danger to the employment situation than wives entering with husbands.' In fact, black Commonwealth men did usually come to Britain as workers and they generally emigrated before their wives, although the timing of migration varied from community to community. This is reflected in the fact that whereas by the late 1960s there were almost as many African-Caribbean immigrant women as immigrant men in Britain, among Asians (especially Bangladeshis and Pakistanis) the ratio of men to women was still much higher. As will be explained in the discussion on the position of wives, in spite of their legal right to be joined by their dependants, many Asian men faced huge difficulties in bringing their wives and children over: they were blocked by the arbitrary and unjust way in which immigration control is administered.

However, the pattern of migration where men came to Britain as breadwinners and women followed as wives did not always hold. In spite of stereotypes to the contrary, thousands of women have come to Britain as independent workers rather than as dependent wives. Between 1963 and 1972 nearly 20 per cent of all Commonwealth workers and almost half of all non-Commonwealth workers who came to Britain on employment vouchers or work permits were women. In the next decade, nearly a third of workers from all countries who were issued permits to work in Britain were women recruited for the sectors of the economy seen as appropriate for female labour (see tables in Chapter 6).

In spite of these facts, immigration policy has been predicated on the notion that women come over as dependants and men as breadwinners. The latter alone are perceived as an asset or threat to the British economy (depending on its condition at the time). However, this not only ignores the hundreds of thousands of women who have come over as workers to take jobs that people living in Britain would not do, but also the many women who, although not entering on work permits, take employment once in Britain — often for the sake of a family's economic survival.

According to the 1966 census, nearly 74,000 women in Britain who were born in the Caribbean were in paid employment. For Asian women the figure was nearly 40,000. By the time of the 1971 census, almost 171,000 women from New Commonwealth countries had a paid job, amounting to over 50 per cent of all New Commonwealth women in Britain (which included women from such countries as Cyprus, Hong Kong and Malaysia, as well as Africa, the Caribbean and the Indian subcontinent).

Surveys have shown that black women tend to be more likely to be in or seeking work than white women. The 1974 Political and Economic Planning survey found that 74 per cent of African-Caribbean women and 45 per cent of non-Muslim Asian women were in paid employment, compared with 43 per cent of women from 'the general population'. Among Muslim women, as many as 39 per cent also had a paid job provided they spoke fairly good English. By 1981, the proportion of non-Muslim Asian women who were in or seeking work had risen to 57 per cent. Ten years later, 53 per cent of women in Britain were in paid employment; this included 71 per cent of Caribbean women and 55 per cent of Indian women.[13]

These figures belie successive governments' assertions that immigrant women do not seek to enter the labour market. They also conceal the fact that the only kind of work that most black women were able to find was in industries where low pay and bad conditions prevailed. These included the textile industry — both the large mills in the North West of England and the small, family-based sweated businesses in the East End of London

— and hospitals and other service industries where, more often than not, they worked as cleaners or orderlies. It is beyond the scope of this book to elaborate further on the process by which race and sex discrimination, entrenched in all levels of British society, prevented black women from gaining access to other, less exploitative, types of work.

No entry for East African Asians

When in opposition, the Labour Party had voted and campaigned vigorously against the 1962 Act. Once returned to power in 1964, however, the Labour government decreased the number of vouchers which could be issued to Commonwealth citizens, tying the employment voucher scheme even more closely to the needs of the British economy. Such reversals of policy were to become the pattern of Labour's approach to immigration legislation.

Meanwhile more and more colonies had gained independence from Britain and usually their inhabitants automatically became citizens of the newly independent countries. Under the 1962 Act they had lost their right of entry to Britain. However, under the law of some East African countries — Malawi, Kenya and Uganda, for instance — this process was not automatic for everybody. Asian settlers, who had been brought over by the British to help build up the colonies, were discriminated against by the independence laws. Often they did not automatically become citizens of the new independent countries. They were then given the option to renounce their UK citizenship in order to become citizens of the countries in which they lived.

Faced with this choice, many East African Asians chose to retain their citizenship of the UK and Colonies for the sake of security. As there was no longer any *colonial* government in these countries, those who maintained their UK citizenship were issued with passports by the British government itself (via its East African representatives) and were therefore exempt from immigration control under the 1962 Act.

The 'Africanisation' policy of some East African countries led many British Asians to exercise their right as UK passport holders to come to Britain.[14] Tory MPs Enoch Powell and Duncan Sandys led a campaign to deprive these UK citizens of their right of entry. The Labour government responded by introducing the Commonwealth Immigrants Bill in 1968 which passed through all its parliamentary stages in three days. Richard

Crossman, who was a member of that government, explained the Cabinet's motives in pushing through this legislation in a report to *The Times* in September 1972:

> It was widely felt that our improved majority in 1966 was due to our new tough line on immigration control. That is why as a government we were panicked in the autumn of 1967 by top secret reports predicting a mass expulsion of Asians from East Africa and began to make contingency plans for legislation which we realised would have been declared unconstitutional in any country with a written constitution.

The Commonwealth Immigrants Act 1968 denied the right to settle in Britain to all United Kingdom passport holders who were not born in Britain, or who had no parents or grandparents who were UK citizens. The purpose of this carefully worded Act was to deprive British Asians of their right of entry to the only country of which they were citizens. Distinctions in 1962 between the different rights of UK citizens were based on where their passports had been issued. By 1968, ancestry had become the decisive factor in determining the right of entry to Britain. The Labour government was responsible for the most explicitly racist legislation to date.

Women under the 1968 Commonwealth Immigrants Act

In the original formulation of the Bill, the right to enter Britain was to be traced through the male line only. As Lena Jeger MP argued, 'We are proposing to give special rights to people who happen to have a white grandfather but not a white grandmother.'[15] In the event, the Labour government accepted an amendment from its own party allowing ancestry for the purpose of immigration to Britain to be traced through the male *and* female lines. Of course, this did nothing for the East African Asians against whom the Act was aimed, but was a theoretical gain for white women. In practice, however, as women were still not able to pass on their citizenship to their children born abroad (except at the discretion of the Home Secretary) UK citizens born outside Britain mainly obtained their citizenship through their father and were therefore entitled to live in Britain anyway.

As a concession, the government issued a discretionary allowance of special vouchers to UK passport holders whose entry to Britain was barred by the 1968 Act, to control the number who would be allowed entry each year. This system continues to operate to this day. Vouchers are issued to 'heads of households', for them and their families. Translated, this means they are issued only to men unless a woman is widowed, divorced or single, preventing British women married to non-British men from ever settling in Britain. When attempts were made to alter this during the passage of the Bill, Home Office minister David Ennals simply stated that 'there is no element of sex discrimination at all in the Bill.' Summing up the contents of the Bill, Lena Jeger MP declared: 'So many things in this Bill, which is sodden with racialism, are sodden with anti-feminism. Discrimination is indivisible: discrimination in one direction leads to discrimination in another '

In addition, the Instructions to immigration officers that explained how the 1968 Act was to be administered introduced the 'sole responsibility' rule which is also still in operation. This means that where only one parent lives in this country, dependent children under 18 can join that parent only on demonstration that he or she has had 'sole responsibility for the child's upbringing'.[16] In discussing this clause, MPs noted the fact that many women from the Caribbean came to Britain as independent workers and later sent for their children who were being cared for by relatives at home. The legislators were therefore fully aware that this new Rule represented a severe attack on the rights of Caribbean women who clearly did not have *sole* responsibility for the children they were supporting in those circumstances. As will be shown in Chapter 5, many such women have remained separated from their children indefinitely as a result of this policy.

Women under the 1971 Immigration Act

The next Conservative government, not to be outdone by the last Labour administration, committed itself to tightening immigration control still further. The 1971 Immigration Act which came into force on 1 January 1973 replaced virtually all previous immigration legislation and has formed the basis of immigration control ever since. This Act introduced the explicitly racist concept of patriality. Whereas the previous legislation had divided people into 'subjects' and 'aliens', the new Act divided the world into 'patrials' and 'non-patrials' — those who had the 'right of abode' in the UK and those who did not.

Generally speaking, patrials were citizens of the UK and Colonies born, adopted, registered or naturalised in Britain or UK citizens born abroad with a parent or grandparent (of either sex) who had obtained UK citizenship by one of those means; UK citizens born abroad who had been settled in Britain for five years or more; and Commonwealth citizens born to or adopted by UK citizens born in the UK. Under the previous Commonwealth Immigrants Acts, Commonwealth citizens without UK passports — whether they were from Australia, Cyprus, India or any other former British colony — had been prevented from coming to settle in Britain. However, under the 1971 Act these restrictions were actually lifted from Commonwealth citizens with British-born grandparents — mainly Australians and Canadians.

This meant that patrials were generally white, whereas non-patrial UK citizens were likely to be black (although there were of course black patrials who were born in Britain). Patrials were free from immigration control, restrictions on employment and deportation. They thus had rights normally associated with citizenship and nationality. Yet many patrials, such as Canadian citizens whose mothers were born in Britain, did not have UK citizenship. At the same time, many UK citizens did not have British ancestry and so were non-patrials with no right to settle in Britain. The majority of these were UK passport holders living in East Africa or Malaysia. This was the result of an immigration policy primarily based on the intention of keeping black people out of Britain.

One of the effects of patriality was to enable female patrials to confer immigration rights on their children born abroad for the first time. Although women still could not pass on their citizenship to their children, a far larger group than in 1968 could now transmit one of the most important rights associated with British citizenship — an entitlement to live in that country. However, as most black women, except those born in Britain, were not patrial this once again benefited mainly white women.

In addition, all female Commonwealth citizens married to patrial men (including those who had at any time been married to a patrial UK citizen, even if they were widowed or divorced) were given patrial status by the Act. As patriality, rather than UK citizenship, was now the passport to living in Britain, this was in effect an extension of the right of British men to pass on their citizenship to their wives. Of course, there was no equivalent provision for women to pass on their patriality to their husbands.

Female appendages under the Immigration Rules

The way the Immigration Act is administered is not contained in the Act itself but is set out in the Immigration Rules which can be changed by a single vote in Parliament without having to go through the lengthy procedures involved in legislation (there have been eight major changes to the Rules since 1973). The Rules regulate the entry and stay of visitors, students, workers and dependants, none of whom are covered by the Act itself. They also detail the 'general considerations' which should be borne in mind by immigration officers in their work, including that they 'will carry out their duties without regard to the race, colour or religion of people seeking to enter the UK.' They demonstrate the degree of discretion left in the hands of immigration officials in that 'the fact that the applicant satisfies the formal requirements of these rules' does not mean that 'he' will be allowed to stay in Britain if, for example, it is felt that 'in the light of his character, conduct or associations it is undesirable to permit him to remain.'[17]

As well as the published Immigration Rules, there are also secret, unpublished Instructions to immigration officers, three fat loose-leaf folders, for use by immigration officers abroad, by officers at ports and airports in Britain and by Home Office staff. These go into much greater detail about the criteria and reasons immigration officers must use in secretly making decisions, and are constantly being updated by the Home Office.

The combined effect of the Act and the Rules has been to prevent all further immigration by people without the right of abode except as dependants of immigrants already settled or as work permit holders recruited to take jobs which cannot be filled by anyone living in Britain. In this way, the extra rights which Commonwealth citizens had compared to non-Commonwealth citizens were progressively eroded. This coincided with the shift in the economic interests of Britain's rulers from the Commonwealth to the Common Market. On the same date that the 1971 Immigration Act came into force, 1 January 1973, Britain joined the EC and thus gave millions of European workers the automatic right to enter Britain to seek work — rights which Commonwealth workers had lost.

The statutory right which men previously had to bring in their wives and children ended with the passing of the 1971 Act. However, the wives and children of Commonwealth men (including UK citizens) who had settled in Britain before the Act came into force were guaranteed the right to live there with their husbands and fathers. The Act stated that

> The rules shall be so framed that Commonwealth citizens settled in the United Kingdom at the coming into force of this Act and their *wives and children* are not, by virtue of anything in the rules, any less free to come into and go from the United Kingdom than if this Act had not been passed. [Our emphasis]

As for the wives and children of men who settled in Britain after 1973, they were not given such legislative protection but their right to enter was governed by the Immigration Rules which, as already explained, can be altered much more easily than Acts of Parliament.

This point did not escape Parliament during the debate on the 1971 Act. In summing up the debate, Enoch Powell MP prophesied that 'already in the first few months of this new legislation,' the Home Secretary 'is contemplating quite fundamental alterations in those rules to which in future the right of admission of dependants will be consigned.' As he explained, by consigning the right of entry of dependants to the Immigration Rules, rather than to the Act itself — a decision he wholeheartedly supported — the government had 'the means, whenever we decide, to change this policy by administrative action.'[18]

When David Steel MP introduced an amendment to provide for a statutory right of entry for the *husband,* as well as the wife or child, of everyone settled in the UK, the government opposed this with the frank admission that such rights were maintained in the Immigration Rules so that, where necessary, Parliament can 'have the right to make alterations in rules at short notice.' But this completely ignored the fact that husbands were *not* allowed to join their wives at all under these Rules (except under exceptional conditions which are outlined in the next chapter). Home Office minister Richard Sharples simply asserted that 'it was the policy of the government to allow people lawfully entering the country to be accompanied or to be joined by their wives and young children.' The presumption that family unity meant the right of men to bring over their wives and children was so strong that the granting of the equivalent right to women was just skipped over in the debate.

Generally speaking, women were largely invisible in the Immigration Rules, and in immigration legislation as a whole; where their existence was recognised, it was almost entirely in relation to men. The notion of women's supposed dependence on men was reflected in all aspects of the Rules. It was not only men settled in Britain who could bring in their families; 'the wife and children under 18' of 'persons' here to study or for employment were allowed to accompany the 'head of household'. The equivalent right was not afforded to female students or work permit holders. Wives and children under 18 of men who were deported could also be deported, but this draconian regulation did not apply to the husbands of female deportees. Men had to show that they could 'maintain and accommodate' their wives and children (unless they were UK citizens or Commonwealth men who settled in Britain before 1973), but husbands did not have to be supported by their wives.

'Illegitimacy' and rape

During the debate over the 1971 Immigration Act, Conservative MP Jill Knight expressed anxiety about 'opening the floodgates' to 'illegitimate' children by allowing patriality to be traced by children born outside marriage. According to Knight, in the West Indies 'marriage is often thought to be quite unnecessary' so that 'there may well be large numbers of illegitimate children of British residents.' However, Home Office minister Richard Sharples assured her that she had no cause to worry: 'The rights of patriality... are confined to those whose descent is legitimate. That is the government's clear intention.'

Eventually, as a concession to the demands of the Labour opposition, the government accepted that so-called 'illegitimate' children could claim patriality (and therefore the automatic right to live in Britain) through their mother, but not their father. This was in sharp contrast to nationality law under which citizenship was traceable through the male line only. 'Illegitimate' children born abroad to British parents could be born stateless — they had no automatic entitlement to British nationality unless their parents subsequently married. The reason for permitting patriality to be traced through the female but not the male line was not only to follow other recent legislation which gave rights to the children of unmarried mothers and not of unmarried fathers; it was also to limit the status of patriality to those whom it was intended to benefit — white Commonwealth citizens.

Throughout the Empire, British men had raped women or taken them as their mistresses as a matter of course. So there were far more children born outside marriage to patrial men than to patrial women in those countries. A government spokesman in the parliamentary debate on the Bill underlined this point. The most common example of 'illegitimate' children born to patrial fathers, he said, would be the Anglo-Indian child brought up by an Indian mother 'in Indian surroundings, perhaps without even the English language... so that he [the child] would not be the sort of person for whom patriality was really designed.' A similar situation would occur in the West Indies, the minister explained, but this would be less common. However, on occasions where the *mother* was patrial, she would have 'passed on to the child who is with her the contacts and ideas of this country.'

The reverse argument — that women were *less* likely to pass on their 'British heritage' to their children than men — had been used on previous occasions to justify denying women the possibility of passing on their nationality or other rights to their children born abroad.'[19] Once again, the overriding consideration of limiting black immigration to Britain was such that *any* argument would be used in support of this — even if it contradicted a previous one devised for the same purpose.

The question of the rights of 'illegitimate' children under immigration and nationality law also provides an illuminating insight into the indispensability of marriage in maintaining a patriarchal society. If, as Frederick Bennett, Conservative MP, remarked during the debate on the 1971 Act, 'paternity must always be an assumption: the only thing that is absolutely certain is descent by maternity,' then the institution of marriage has traditionally functioned to decrease the 'uncertainty' of paternity. If children were nevertheless born out of wedlock, they were simply defined as 'illegitimate' and discounted for the purposes of tracing benefits through the male line.

The Middle Ages revisited

The debate about equal nationality rights for women, and in particular whether British nationality should be traced through the female line, was revived in the 1970s. In 1977 the Labour government published a Green Paper[20] which discussed various alternative schemes for a new British Nationality Act. The importance of sex equality was unquestioningly accepted in the document. This might have been expected, given that the same government had been responsible for introducing the Sex Discrimination Act only the year before. However, that Act exempted all legislation passed before it came into force, so that the Equal Opportunities Commission, which was set up by the Act, was powerless to intervene in cases where women could not pass on their citizenship on equal terms with men. All the EOC felt it could do was to let the government know its disagreement with the discrimination against women in nationality legislation. Most of its recommendations were then translated into the policies outlined in the Green Paper.

The Labour government failed to act on these proposals despite pressure to do so. Articles periodically appeared in newspapers such as the *The Guardian* about the effects of the discrimination; letters of protest from aggrieved women were sent to the Home Secretary. Then in early 1979 Jill Knight MP introduced her British Nationality (Amendment) Bill to force the Home Secretary to register minor children born abroad to women born in the UK provided *both* parents wished this to occur. In response, the Labour Home Secretary Merlyn Rees announced on 7 February that a woman born in the United Kingdom would normally be able to have her child registered as British if there was no well-founded objection by the father. The situation was now back to where it was in the fourteenth century, when children born abroad to English women were themselves considered to be English provided that their mothers left the country 'by the License and Wills of their husbands'.

For some mothers this change came too late. Children who were over 18 when it was introduced were too old to benefit from it. Leila Saadawi had to wait nine years to obtain UK citizenship from the time she first applied for it. Her mother was a UK citizen born in Britain who had married an Egyptian man. Leila was born in Egypt in 1959 but had lived in the UK for nearly five years when she was an infant. Her mother later left her father and came back to Britain, where Leila joined her when she was 14. Mrs Saadawi applied for her daughter to be registered as a UK citizen straightaway, but the Home Office shelved the case because Leila went back to Egypt. When she tried to return to Britain in April 1978 she was given only six months to stay in the country. She was eventually allowed to remain permanently — but only after intervention from her mother's MP.

By this time, Rees had announced that he was prepared to register the minor children of British women born abroad. Leila, however, was informed that as she was now over 18 she was too old and would have to apply for naturalisation like any other 'alien' adult. Her mother had first applied for her to become a UK citizen when she was only 14, but the new regulation was not retrospective. Leila was told she would have to pay the then full fee of £150 to obtain UK citizenship after meeting the statutory. residence requirements. Her mother was very angry. She wrote in a letter to her lawyers that

> We believe that the Home Office is making a profit out of this nationality business and that Leila is just being made to pay because they cannot be bothered to deal fairly and justly with individual claims. It is more profitable to pressurise applicants into paying.

Mrs Saadawi's son, Abdul, was able to be registered as a British citizen because he was still under 18 when the new regulation was introduced in February 1979. However, even this was granted only after his father's written consent had been obtained.

The 1981 British Nationality Act

Two months after Rees gave women some choice over their children's nationality, Margaret Thatcher's Conservative government was swept to victory on a manifesto committed to further immigration control and a new Nationality Act. This was necessary, the new Home Secretary William Whitelaw explained in a speech at a Conservative Party meeting in April 1978, to 'remove some of the possible sources of future immigration'. And this was just what the new Act did — it was a translation of immigration legislation into nationality law.

There were large discrepancies between Britain's nationality and immigration laws at that time. Citizens of the UK and Colonies did not necessarily have the right to live in Britain, at the same time, this right was held by many people of British ancestry who were not UK citizens. The Nationality Act was introduced to eradicate these anomalies. Rather than increase the rights of British subjects, however, it in fact brought nationality law in line with immigration law and hence introduced further restrictions. While the new Act ended the discrimination against women that had been a feature of all previous British nationality legislation, it consolidated the discrimination against black Commonwealth citizens. Reflecting the demise of the British Empire, it abolished most of the remaining categories under which the colonised or ex-colonised were included as part of the British nation.

The 1981 Nationality Act, which came into force on 1 January 1983, created three new statuses out of the old citizenship of the UK and Colonies — British citizenship, British Dependent Territories citizenship and British Overseas citizenship. Those who belong to the first group are largely white; the members of the other two groups are almost exclusively black, and have fewer or no rights attached to their citizenship.

Technically speaking, British citizenship is an entirely new status. British citizens are those who used to be called patrial UK and Colonies citizens (terms phased out by the 1981 Act). They have the right of entry and settlement either because they were born in the UK; or because they have a parent or grandparent who was born there; or because they became British by registration or naturalisation there; or because they had settled and lived there for five years or more before 1983. The rights connected to their citizenship are defined mainly in immigration terms, since the other civic rights that they possess (such as voting or standing for public office) are shared by all Commonwealth and Irish citizens in the UK. British citizens are not subject to immigration control but, as will be explained below, for many years their sex made a difference to the conditions on which others might join them in Britain. (Irish citizens are not subject to immigration control either, both because of the 'common travel area' between Britain and Ireland and because they are EC citizens. Nevertheless Irish citizens can be deported under the Prevention of Terrorism Act.)

British Dependent Territories citizens (BDTCs) are people who were born in, or had a parent born in, a place still designated a British colony, or who became British by naturalisation or registration in a British colony such as Hong Kong or St Helena. The inhabitants of Gibraltar, however, are given British citizenship if they ask for it, without having to fulfil any other conditions. After the 1982 conflict between Argentina and Britain, a special exception was made for the Falkland Islanders who automatically became British citizens (although they had previously been accorded BDTC status). While the few remaining British colonies are very different places, all their inhabitants thus share the same citizenship, provided they meet the above requirements — a citizenship which does not give them any rights anywhere except in the particular colony with which they are connected.

British Overseas citizens (BOCs) are people who were able to retain their UK citizenship when the colony in which they were living became independent. As explained above, this applied mainly to Asians in East African countries who lost the right to live in Britain under the 1968 Commonwealth Immigrants Act. The 1981 Nationality Act rounded off this outrageous story by depriving the East African Asians (and others, mainly Malaysians) of the status of UK citizenship altogether. To come to Britain they still have to queue for special vouchers (a queue which peaked at seven years in 1983 in India) and after living in Britain for five years they can register as British citizens and so regain the rights which the 1968 Labour government took away from them in the first place.

Women under the 1981 British Nationality Act

The 1981 Nationality Act affected women in three main ways. First, it took away the automatic right of women who had at any time been married to British men to register as British citizens, although there was a five-year transitional period which ended in 1988 during which time women who were *still* married to British men could register as British. Women who married after 1 January 1983 also lost their automatic right to patriality (that is, the right of abode in Britain), for the Act replaced 'patriality' with 'British citizenship' so that no one could *become* patrial after it came into force.

This reduction in women's rights was done in the name of equality. The government boasted that for the first time men and women were in the same position as far as acquiring British nationality on marriage was concerned. Prior to the enforcement of the 1981 Act, the foreign husbands of UK women citizens had no advantages over other non-citizens in naturalising as British: both had to be resident in Britain for five years before applying. This contrasted with the wives of British men who automatically had the right to register as British citizens. Under the new Act, all husbands and wives married to British citizens are required to live in Britain for three years (compared to five years for most other categories of would-be citizens) before applying for citizenship. There is no guarantee that their applications will be accepted for although there is no language test for the spouses of British citizens, proof of 'good character' is required — which involves police and immigration service checks on criminal records, political activities and security matters. Before citizenship is finally granted, spouses have to pay £135 to the Home Office (compared to £170 for most other applicants). Thus the equality under the new Act involved a levelling-down for women. Furthermore, as the husbands of many British women could not come to Britain in the first place at the time the Act was passed (see below), the advantages it conferred on such men were illusory.

The British government clearly had a duty to publicise the loss of rights and choices for women under the new Act. Numerous voluntary organisations and women's groups attempted to do this in the period leading up to the 1 January 1983 deadline, through leafleting, campaigns and public meetings. The government, however, consistently failed to do likewise, despite earlier assurances on this point that it would. In fact, far from publicising the changes and helping those affected by them to come to informed decisions about how best to protect their status and that of their families, it seems that in certain quarters the government positively hindered people.

This entitlement to register as British was of particular significance to Asian women in East Africa, who were married to men who had formerly been UK citizens in that, provided they registered before the new Act came into force, they became full British citizens rather than British Overseas citizens. On a fact-finding trip to Kenya, the Joint Council for the Welfare of Immigrants found that there was no sign that the British High Commission had made any effort to alert such women to their imminent loss of entitlement to register. In fact, the High Commission refused to accept some women's applications for such registration until after 31 December 1982, by which time it was too late.[21]

Second, the new Nationality Act took away the automatic right of all children born in Britain to British citizenship — a right which had existed since the Middle Ages. Children born in Britain are now British only if one of their parents is British or settled here at the time of their birth. So, for example, a baby born in Britain to a Turkish au pair or to an Egyptian woman on a work permit will not obtain British citizenship unless she or her husband later becomes settled in the country. Not all countries allow women to pass on their citizenship to their children born abroad; hence, if a woman from such a country is unmarried or married to a refugee or other non-settled man and gives birth in Britain while subject to immigration restrictions, her child will be born stateless.

Third, the 1981 Nationality Act allowed women to pass on their citizenship to their children born abroad for the first time. This includes children adopted in Britain, who had previously been British only if that was the nationality of their adoptive father. As such, the government claimed to be heralding a new dawn of sex equality. The Nationality Act did indeed provide women with equal citizenship rights for the first time in British history. In making this change, however, Britain was hardly ahead of the times — other governments which had already granted women this right included Australia, Canada, Denmark, France, New Zealand, the United States and West Germany. Nevertheless, the struggle which British women began at the beginning of the century was finally won.

The new sex equality was not introduced without some rearguard action by two parliamentary patriarchs. Enoch Powell, supported by fellow-rightwinger Ivor Stanbrook, put forward an amendment to prevent women from passing on their citizenship to their children on the grounds that, in the words of Powell, 'Nationality, in the last resort, is tested by fighting. A man's nation is the nation for which he will fight'; women, on the other hand, are involved in 'the preservation and the care of life'. By a fantastic twist of logic, this means that women are less fit to bequeath their nationality to their children than are men.[22]

But in spite of the absence of a comparable feminist lobby to that which had petitioned Parliament on this issue at the beginning of the century, the general acceptance of 'equal rights for women' had percolated into nationality law and the Powell-Stanbrook amendment failed. 'The relationship between men and women has altered,' Home Office minister Timothy Raison announced when explaining the changes. According to the Home Secretary William Whitelaw, the Bill represented 'an important and significant new advance towards sex equality'.

In fact, as will be explained in greater detail in the next chapter, some women were more equal than others. For the year before, the Tory government had passed new Immigration Rules which made it even more difficult than previously for some British women, particularly black women, to bring their husbands over to Britain. Thus, although British women could now pass on their citizenship to their children born abroad (unless they were British Overseas citizens, who could not transmit their citizenship at all) women who were born outside Britain and who had no British ancestry could be forced to leave the country if they wished to live with their foreign-born husband. This applied even if they had registered or naturalised as British citizens! The new provisions for sex equality in the Nationality Act, therefore, must be judged in this context. Equal rights for men and women under nationality law cannot be fully achieved as long as there is inequality in immigration law, for the one is inextricably tied up with the other.

As far as the children of women who were not married were concerned, they could for the first time automatically receive citizenship through the mother, regardless of where they were born. An attempt by Labour MP Jo Richardson to amend the new Act to allow both men and women to pass on their citizenship to children born outside wedlock again failed on the grounds that where a child was 'illegitimate', paternity was impossible to prove.

Conclusion

Clearly, it was the demands of white British-born women which the government was aiming to meet by allowing women to transmit their nationality to their children born abroad. While not in any way minimising the importance of this gain for all women, it was white women married to American or European men who presented the most forceful lobby on the government over this issue and who persuaded all major political parties of the injustice of the situation in an era of sex equality.

But at the very moment that the government was persuaded to provide equal rights for men and women in nationality law, it actually increased the discrimination against women in immigration law. This was for one reason only: to prevent further immigration of black males to Britain.

Chapter 3

Till laws us do part: the ban on husbands

From the late 1960s onwards one major issue came to dominate official policy on immigration: the entry of foreign husbands and fiancés. As more and more stringent controls prevented Commonwealth workers from coming to Britain altogether, the attention of the anti-immigration lobby focused on the only group of people who still had an absolute claim to settle in the UK — the dependants of people already living here. Among general scaremongering about an alleged threat from hordes of illegal immigrants, allegations grew that wives and children seeking to enter Britain were not related to their families here as they claimed. As Commonwealth citizens from the Indian subcontinent generally came to Britain later than African-Caribbeans, it was the former who bore the brunt of this particular agitation. As will be explained in more detail in the next chapter one result of this was the introduction of entry clearance, which meant that Commonwealth citizens intending to settle in Britain had to obtain written permission from British officials in their home countries before coming here.

While it became increasingly difficult for women and children to satisfy entry clearance officers that they were who they said they were, Labour Home Office ministers continued to emphasise that

> there is a fundamental principle — not a privilege, but a right — that it would not be proper to take away: that of a mother and her children to join the father who is already settled in this country.[1]

When asked about the same issue a few months later, Home Secretary James Callaghan replied that

> to prevent a man's wife and children from joining him here leads to social problems in the community. The only way to prevent those problems is to allow families to be reunited.[2]

Whilst the nature of these 'social problems' was not spelt out (on this occasion at least), it is possible to guess that part of the concern was involved with white British men's fears that 'their women' might become sexually associated with these 'wifeless' black men.

In any event, the government had an obvious sop to these cries for further immigration restrictions which would neither contribute to such 'social problems' nor detract from the right of white British men to select their wives from whatever part of the world they wished. The answer was to prevent *women* from bringing in husbands from abroad, even though far fewer husbands than wives came to Britain each year.

1969: 'Concession' to women removed

In response to a parliamentary question in January 1969, Callaghan stated that

> the government has decided that the concession under which male Commonwealth citizens are allowed to settle here in right of their wife must be withdrawn.[3]

This attack on women's rights was ushered in without any debate at all. It was to be the first of ten ways (seven of which were actually implemented) in which successive governments attempted to alter the right of women to bring in foreign-born husbands in a period of nineteen years. Twenty-five years on, some women are still struggling to regain this right that was taken away from them so lightly. Although all women living in Britain, regardless of their citizenship, were affected by this change in the law, its intention was to stop the immigration of Asian men. Justifying the new policy Callaghan claimed that

> It seems that marriage is being used by many young men of working age as a means of entering, working and settling in this country. This abuse of the concession is inconsistent with the general scheme of Commonwealth immigration control.[4]

It is difficult to know what 'concession' the Home Secretary had in mind. During the passage of the 1962 Act when arguments raged about women not being given the same right to bring in their spouses as men, the government assured the opposition that although there would be inequality in the Act itself, under the Instructions to immigration officers, Commonwealth husbands would 'normally' be let in provided their wives were settled in the country.[5] This was indeed the case and was maintained by the 1968 Act.

The only possible interpretation that can be put on this use of the term 'concession' was that the Instructions governing the entry of Commonwealth husbands under the 1962 Act were an improvement on those concerning the entry of alien husbands. As already explained, under the Instructions to immigration officers for aliens, Commonwealth women could bring in their husbands only if the women were born in the UK or had 'substantial connections' with the country. Alien women who were settled in the UK had to prove 'hardship' before their husbands could join them.[6]

Under the new regulation, Commonwealth women, including UK citizens, were placed in the same situation as alien women. The Instructions to immigration officers allowed Commonwealth husbands or fiancés to enter Britain provided they had an entry certificate.[7] This would be granted only if the Home Secretary was satisfied that there were 'special considerations, whether of a family nature or otherwise, which render exclusion [of the man] undesirable.' The example given of such 'special considerations' was 'hardship which, in the particular circumstances of the case, would be caused if the wife had to live outside the United Kingdom in order to be with her husband.'

In practice, this meant that the only women who had any chance of bringing in foreign-born husbands were white women who would have to live in a country without a large European population in order to be with their husbands. Racist and sexist assumptions were such that Asian women who were born and brought up in Britain were unable to persuade the Immigration Appeal Tribunal, which reviewed such cases, of the 'hardship' that would be inflicted on them by having to live in an Asian husband's country. Likewise, white British women were hard-put to persuade the tribunal of the 'hardship' they would suffer by joining a husband in a European state. Unless they could prove 'hardship', such women — including those born in Britain — were forced to leave the country to be with their husbands.

For example, the tribunal turned down an appeal by Mrs Dumont, a British woman married to a Canadian, on the grounds that she was unable to prove sufficient 'hardship' at having to live with her husband in his native land. Similarly, Miss Kaur — who was born and brought up in Birmingham — could not persuade the tribunal to allow her to bring her Indian fiancé to live with her in Britain, even though she had never in her life been to India. In summing up this rejection of her appeal, the adjudicator said that Miss Kaur wanted the best of both worlds — to keep to the marriage customs of her community and enjoy the more free and affluent life of England. 'The normal course for both British and Sikh women is to make their married home where their husband is,' he said. Mrs Roy, on the other hand, won her appeal against having to live with her Punjabi husband in India by putting forward the argument that she would be 'the only Englishwoman living in 50 square miles of the Indian Punjab.'[8]

The Asian community in Britain campaigned to change the law. Two thousand people marched in Birmingham to protest against the ban on husbands and fiancés and a petition signed by 5,000 people was presented to the Home Office. Referring to Enoch Powell's 'rivers of blood' speech, when the MP prophesied that civil unrest would be the outcome of black immigration to Britain, one official of the Southall Indian Workers' Association said: 'This restriction has caused more resentment among Indians and Pakistanis than all the Acts and racialist speeches put together.' Another protester, a Pakistani community leader in Bradford, described the new Rule as 'the first stage of the repatriation of the blacks'.[9]

But this opposition fell on deaf ears. Under the 1973 Immigration Rules introduced to administer the 1971 Immigration Act, husbands and fiancés were still admitted only when it could be shown that the wife would suffer a 'degree of hardship' by having to live outside the UK.[10] This applied to both Commonwealth and non-Commonwealth men alike. For black and migrant women, there was therefore no question of them being able to remain in this country with a husband from the land of their own or their parents' birth. In the case of non-Commonwealth husbands, the restrictions were even more severe. On the rare occasions when they were given permission to live in Britain with a British wife, they were allowed to stay for just 12 months in the first instance, at the end of which period the time limit could be removed if the couple were still living together as husband and wife.[11] As already explained, this was the same condition which had applied to non-Commonwealth men under the 1970 Instructions to immigration officers for aliens.[12]

1974: The Rules are liberalised

As cases of British women separated from their husbands under these Rules mounted, there was increasing pressure on the new Labour administration to change the regulations once again. In March 1974, Fenner Brockway tabled a question in the House of Lords requesting equality of treatment for men and women in the marriage rules. In response, Tory peer Viscount Colville exclaimed:

> This is a small island. Goodness knows there are enough problems as it is in finding housing for those who already live here... to open the floodgates is not likely to be very successful in promoting racial harmony.

'Floodgates', 'swamping'—these terms have been invoked over and over again to refer to *any* number of black people living in Britain. Yet in 1968, the last year that Commonwealth men had been able to join their wives settled in Britain, only 1,676 men were admitted as husbands or fiancés, a figure actually quoted by Viscount Colville himself.[13]

Then, in June 1974, Lena Jeger MP introduced a Bill in Parliament to achieve equality for women in this matter.[14] The Bill received unanimous support from the Labour Party Women's Conference, and, in the words of its sponsor, was designed to

> bring us a little nearer to the end of the traditionally patriarchal society in which a woman is automatically expected to live in the land of her husband as part of his baggage.[15]

When introducing the Bill, Jeger explained that British women had written to her from all over the world saying that they had been unaware that they could not live in the country of their birth with their foreign husbands until the time had come for them to return to Britain. But, she assured fellow MPs, her enormous mail bag had contained just a few cases from Asian countries, while there were large numbers of British women married to Australian, Swiss and Swedish men who could not bring their husbands home to their country of birth. Although she stressed that she was not mentioning this fact in order to gain support for the Bill, it is likely that this point was not lost on the Home Office. A week later, Home Secretary Roy Jenkins announced that he would alter the Rules to allow husbands to enter the country on the same terms as wives. Having reviewed the situation, he was 'persuaded that there are no sufficiently compelling reasons for denying the parties to a marriage the freedom of choice I believe they should have'.[16] The new Rules were introduced in August 1974[17] and Jeger withdrew her Bill. All husbands, regardless of their nationality, could once again join their wives in Britain provided the women had settled status. Fiancés were admitted for three months in the first instance, and allowed to settle once the marriage had taken place. The year's waiting period before settlement would be granted to non-Commonwealth men was removed.

Public opinion, activated by the press and MPs from all parties, was sufficiently outraged over the fact that (white) women born in Britain could not live here with their foreign-born husbands that the Tories did not even force a vote against the change to the Rules. Although there was probably less lobbying by the women's movement over this issue than there had been by feminists at the beginning of the century on the rights of married women under nationality law, the resurgent feminist movement of the late 1960s had brought in its wake a measure of consensus on the issue of equal rights for men and women. The opposition and fear that the growing women's movement in Britain aroused was matched by an increasing recognition of the importance of equality before the law, if only as a sop to the more militant feminist groups. International Women's Year was celebrated in 1974. The following year, the Labour government introduced the Sex Discrimination Act which the Tory Party did not vote against. There was a mood in the country that 'something had to be done' for women.

It is in the context of this rising tide of formal equality for men and women that Jenkins's liberalisation of the Rules must be understood.

However, full equality between men and women under immigration law was not then achieved. In addition to the continuing inequality concerning the transmission of patriality described in the last chapter, male work permit holders and students could, under the Immigration Rules, be accompanied by their wives. Women had no such right. And since 1973, it has been possible to deport women along with their husbands — but not vice versa.

1977: The screws are tightened again

Almost as soon as the Rules were liberalised, the opposition put pressure on the Home Secretary to abandon his 'concessions' to women. Conservative MP David Lane, later to be appointed Chairman of the Commission for Racial Equality, asked Jenkins in December 1974: 'What safeguards are now operating to prevent abuse of the Immigration Rules governing entry of men or women to join spouses settled in the United Kingdom?' He also questioned why the Home Secretary no longer considered that the level of male immigration which would follow from relaxing the marriage rules was likely to be 'substantial'.[18]

The explicitly racist nature of the anxiety many Conservative and some Labour MPs felt about immigration to Britain was revealed in a debate moved by Tory MP Jonathan Aitken in May 1976. Participants noted 'with concern the changing demographic character of Great Britain, particularly the outflow of young people emigrating overseas and the continuing inflow of immigrants from the New Commonwealth.' The right of entry of male and female fiancé(e)s was, in their view, likely to maintain such an 'inflow' *ad infinitum*. For, as William Whitelaw, then opposition spokesman on Home Affairs, pointed out, this meant that 'girls and boys born in this country can seek a fiancé of their own ethnic group from the country from where their parents originally came... a process which could go on for ever'.[19]

It was in the same debate that Enoch Powell disclosed the existence of *The Hawley Report*, a confidential Foreign Office document on the entry clearance system in the Indian subcontinent. Among other issues, the report expressed concern about the so-called 'multiplier' effect of allowing entry to husbands and fiancés as 'it entitles parents, grandparents and allegedly distressed relatives of the fiancé to apply.' The next day the newspapers were filled with Powell's warning that the continuing entry of relatives from the Indian subcontinent would lead to inner-city violence on such a scale that 'compared to those areas, Belfast today will seem an enviable place.'[20]

The foreign husbands issue was raised again in yet another debate on immigration called by the opposition that year. Whitelaw argued:

> In these days of sex equality such discrimination becomes more difficult but... I fear that if it were proved that concessions for fiancés were becoming widely exploited loopholes they would have to be revoked.[21]

Speaking in stronger language still, Ivor Stanbrook MP argued that the relaxation to the Rules,

> in deference to the women's lobby in International Women's Year... was a grave mistake, because it has unnecessarily inflated the numbers of immigrants and it is contrary to the way of life of the people concerned.

Explaining this last comment, he continued:

> It is part of the British way of life for the father to provide a home for the family and it is the same in India. The husband is expected to provide the home for the wife. There is no rational argument in favour of saying that a wife in another country should be in a position to provide a home for her husband and children. It is contrary to all common sense, human nature, and the way of life of both Britain and the subcontinent.[22]

For Home Secretary Roy Jenkins it was 'the arguments of treating men and women on the basis of equality' that had persuaded him to change the Rules in the first place.[23] However, he surrendered this principle to the expediency of pandering to the anti-immigration lobby and, in particular, its scaremongering about 'bogus' marriages.

In March 1977 the government introduced new Rules 'aimed at preventing men from gaining settlement in this country by marriages of convenience'. Three changes were made. A husband or fiancé could be refused entry when there was reason to believe that the marriage was one of 'convenience' where the couple had no intention of living together as 'man and wife'; if granted entry, husbands were allowed to remain for just 12 months at the outset, with checks made at the end of the period to find out if the marriage had lasted. Only then could the husband be granted permanent settlement; where the marriage had ended before the year was out or where there was 'reason to believe' that the marriage took place for immigration purposes, the husband would 'normally' be refused permission to remain in Britain.[24]

These changes, the government assured MPs, were designed to prevent 'bogus marriages', not 'to affect the many genuine and lasting marriages which are arranged in accordance with Asian culture.'[25] Criticising the new Rules on the grounds that they would lead immigration officers to ask highly personal questions to discover whether a marriage was genuine or not, Alex Lyon MP revealed the nub of the matter:

> In 1974 the real pressure came not from Asians or blacks or the New Commonwealth. It came from white university professors at Oxford who were married to white university professors at Harvard and were writing to the Guardian and claiming that it was despicable that they were treated in such a way... who is it among us who thinks that we shall turn up a case of offensive questioning of a white couple in the future, as distinct from a black couple?[26]

There were, predictably, many cases of black couples being subjected to intimate and intrusive questioning before they were allowed to remain together in Britain. Mr Khan, for example, was asked why he had not married before the age of 29, why he and his wife were not going to mark their wedding with a religious ceremony, and how long they had been living together before they were married. Another Asian couple were questioned about the nature of their marriage, whether it was arranged or a love match, whether they had enjoyed their honeymoon and whether they normally slept together.[27]

Thatcher administration attacks black women's rights

As in the past, these new controls only led to demands for more. An all-party Select Committee was set up by the 1978 Labour government to examine the whole question of immigration. Not surprisingly, it was the relatives of those already settled here who provided the main focus of the inquiry. The entry of husbands and male and female fiancé(e)s 'troubled' the Select Committee members the most. Their conclusions were based on the assumption that wives were by definition dependent on their husbands. On this basis, they argued that 'as male fiancés are prospective heads of families... they enter the UK not so much to join a family as to form a new family.' Although the Committee made no specific recommendations concerning husbands and fiancés, its conclusions boded ill for the future:

> While, in a multi-racial society, the cultural patterns of ethnic minorities should be acknowledged, we believe that the members of those minorities should themselves pay greater regard to the mores of their country of adoption and also to their own traditional pattern of the bride joining the husband's family.[28]

The future awaiting 'ethnic minorities' was outlined by William Whitelaw MP, opposition Home Affairs spokesman, in a speech to the Central Council of the Conservative Party in April 1978. Emphasising that 'all countries are entitled as a mark of their national sovereignty to have their own nationality and immigration laws,' he expressed the intention of a future Conservative government to bring in a whole range of measures, including more restrictions on the right of entry of husbands and fiancés. Arguing that 'through the practice of arranged marriages there is abuse' (a correlation that Labour ministers had up until this time been at pains to deny — in their speeches, at least) Whitelaw stated:

> It surely cannot be unreasonable to argue that, in accordance with the customs of Europe and the Indian subcontinent, the abode of the husband in a marriage should normally be viewed as the natural place of residence of the family.[29]

In line with her vote-catching statements about the danger of Britain being 'swamped' by immigrants, Margaret Thatcher was elected to office in April 1979 on a manifesto which pledged to tighten immigration control even further. Husbands and fiancés were to be stopped from coming in altogether, regardless of the nationality of the wife. The irony of the first female prime minister advocating a policy which discriminated so blatantly against women was not lost on her opponents. David Steel, leader of the Liberal Party, observed that

> the right honourable Lady, having gained her unique position as our first woman Prime Minister through the sacrifices of those women who were oppressed in previous generations, appears to be using her first year in office to bring in rules that are oppressive to women.[30]

Feminism and race

The protest which ensued mirrored that of the early 1970s. However, the political climate had changed since the Labour government inflicted the same attack on women in 1969. It was now more difficult for the government openly to discriminate against women — or at least against white women. In the months following the government's election and before the introduction of the new Immigration Rules, organisations like the Women's Institute, the Equal Opportunities Commission (EOC) and the National Council for Civil Liberties, as well as numerous black groups, lobbied against the proposals.

The women's movement as a whole — both the equal rights lobby and the more radical feminist groups — had gained in strength and influence. But their concerns were still largely those of the white, middle-class women who dominated them. A rather crude example of this was found in an EOC briefing document, prepared for a conference on the proposed new Rules, which cited the plight of four white couples who would be separated if the new policy came into operation. Although the document mentioned the effect of the new policy on 'British families of Asian origin [who] still wish to make arranged marriages for their daughters,' it stated that the 'groups of women most likely to be affected are British sportswomen, businesswomen, students studying abroad, women doing voluntary service overseas, actresses and women in marketing and international sales.'[31]

On the whole, feminist groups did not pay much attention to this issue (with some notable exceptions — for example Women Against Racism and Fascism which was active in the late 1970s). This reflected fundamental differences in theory and analysis which went beyond giving priority to the particular problems of white, middle-class women. By denouncing the family as the main source of women's oppression, the feminist movement did not generally address itself to the issue of women being separated from their husbands by the government and the government's attack on the right of black families to be together if they chose. At the root of this was a general failure, which began to be addressed in the 1980s, to recognise the differences between women — particularly those based on class, race, culture or country of origin — as well as the oppression they share in common. As Hazel Carby argued:

> We would not wish to deny that the family can be a source of oppression for us but we also wish to examine how the black family has been a site of political and cultural resistance to racism... The media's 'horror stories' about Asian girls and arranged marriages bear little relation to their experience. The 'feminist' version of the ideology presents Asian women as being in need of liberation, not in terms of their own herstory and needs, but into the 'progressive' social mores and customs of the metropolitan West.[32]

Consequently, from the mid-1970s onwards, black feminists increasingly formed their own groups to organise around issues which were of concern to all women and also those which specifically affected black women. Under the umbrella of the Organisation of Women of African and Asian Descent and its newspaper *FOWAAD*, black women's groups and centres sprang up. But they did not have the same political clout with the government as civil rights groups or the more mainstream elements of the feminist movement. The changes the government made to its proposals for banning the entry of husbands and fiancés reflected that fact.

When the new Rules were eventually set out in a White Paper in November 1979, the original plan of refusing entry to the foreign husbands or fiancés of all women living in Britain was amended. Only women who were not born in Britain were banned from bringing in their husbands — a proposal which was obviously aimed at reducing black male immigration, while providing greater protection to white British women than the original policy.

However, a new wave of protest followed. Stories about the catastrophic effect that the new Rules would have on the lives of British women whose parents happened to have been working abroad at the time of their birth were publicised by the press and became the subject of radio phone-in programmes. Even commercial companies got involved. The Crown Agents, responsible for recruiting British workers to foreign employers, argued that they would find it difficult to place families in which the woman was likely to give birth while working abroad if the proposals were not amended.[33]

Opposition to the White Paper was such that although a majority of 42 voted in favour of it in the parliamentary debate in December 1979, 19 Conservative MPs abstained, causing the first major revolt within the Tories' own ranks since the Thatcher government had come to power. One junior minister, Cyril Townsend, resigned his post as parliamentary private secretary. He argued that after the advances made in achieving greater rights for women during the 1970s, 1979 was a singularly inappropriate year in which to seek to lower their status again.[34]

There was no doubt about the nature of most of this concern for women's rights. White British women were still being penalised under a policy intended to catch immigrant women. As a result, when the new Rules were drawn up in their final form in February 1980, they were amended to take account of 'the needs of British girls who have been born overseas fortuitously'.[35] They allowed UK women citizens with one parent born in Britain, as well as women who were themselves born there, to bring in their husbands and fiancés from abroad.[36] Women who had become British through naturalisation and who were not of British descent could not do so. A two-tier citizenship was explicitly enforced. The Rules were even more discriminatory than in their original form, as it was clear that it was only women of non-British ancestry whose rights were being curtailed. After this, the government was able to swell the majority in its favour to 52 — a ten-vote increase — and the new Rules came into force in March 1980.

Asian marriage system attacked

By 1979 the stated object of official policy on foreign husbands and fiancés had shifted. The 1977 restrictions had been justified by the alleged need to deal with 'bogus marriages' — marriages which were enacted for the sole purpose of allowing a man to stay in Britain and where the couple had no intention of living together as husband and wife. By 1979 it no longer mattered whether the marriage was 'genuine' or not — what was at stake were the 'arranged marriages' practised by some members of the Asian community. Under this system, whole families decide on the suitable marriage partner for their children, rather than just the partners themselves. Sometimes this means that the couple do not meet each other before their wedding day. Although government ministers denied that they actually sought to destroy this tradition, the 1980 Rules contained two new clauses which strongly impeded the arranged marriage system. They are still in force.

First, in order for a husband or fiancé to come to live in Britain the couple have to have met. This applies whether the woman was born here or not. Justifying this new policy, Home Secretary William Whitelaw stated in the 1979 debate on the White Paper that he could not 'see anything wrong in the way in which our country has worked over generations — that people who wish to get married should actually have met before they decide to do so.' In making such a statement Whitelaw ignored the fact that a form of arranged marriage has been common among the British aristocracy for generations. But this pronouncement made it clear that the new policy was intended to make it more difficult for Asian families to continue their arranged marriage system. To do so, they would have to incur the extra expense of ensuring that the couple had met. This clause was clearly designed to reduce Asian immigration, not to prevent 'bogus marriages'.

Second, the new Rules stated that a man would not be able to enter Britain for the purpose of marriage, either as a fiancé or a husband, if the immigration officer had reason to believe that 'the marriage was one entered into primarily to obtain admission to the United Kingdom.'[37] This was based on the allegation that the arranged marriage system was being 'abused' by men who, although they intended to live with their wives for the rest of their lives, and were therefore contemplating perfectly 'genuine' marriages, really married only because they wanted to come and live in the UK. As will be explained below, although this clause was used relatively sparingly at first, it has increasingly operated to keep out Asian husbands and fiancés. Home Office minister Lord Belstead justified this new policy on the grounds that

> The abuse of the arranged marriage system is in itself sexually discriminatory... it uses girls in such a way as to enable men to enter illegally, in effect... we are certain that many of these marriages are arranged to the detriment of girls living in this country.[38]

This cynical evocation of the rights of Asian girls in defence of a policy which was introduced for the sole purpose of reducing the black population of Britain, has been exposed and attacked by Asian women:

> Whether some of us decide to marry at all, let alone have an arranged marriage, is an issue we define and act upon autonomously of the state. We do not require the racist state to intervene on our behalf. To ally and collude with the racist state in a pseudo-feminist struggle would be crass and misguided... Today's arranged marriage system is

Table 1 Husbands and wives[a] accepted for settlement on arrival in the UK or after marriage, 1973-1992

Year	Men	Women
1973[b]	6,280	17,840
1974[c]	5,630	19,770[d]
1975	11,190	19,440
1976	11,060	20,690
1977[e]	5,610	19,890
1978	9,330	18,950
1979	9,900	19,780
1980[f]	9,160	17,430
1981	6,690	16,760
1982	6,090	15,490
1983[g]	5,210	16,800
1984	5,550	16,680
1985[h]	6,680	17,980
1986	6,810	14,110
1987	7,210	14,840
1988[j]	7,950	15,120
1989	9,140	10,900
1990	10,760	16,650
1991	11,610	19,010
1992	10,880	18,540
Totals[k]	**162,740**	**343,870**

Source: Home Office, Control of Immigration: Statistics, London: HMSO

Notes:

- a Commonwealth and non-Commonwealth citizens excluding EC citizens.
- b Includes 'other men' accepted for settlement during 1973.
- c Immigration Rules liberalised in June 1974 allowing entry to husbands of all women settled in UK.
- d Includes 'other women' accepted for settlement during 1973 and 1974.
- e Immigration Rules tightened in March 1977 — husbands not accepted for settlement until after a probationary year.
- f Immigration Rules tightened further in February 1980; banned entry of husbands of women not born in UK or without a parent born there.
- g Immigration Rules slightly liberalised in February 1983; banned entry of husbands of non-British women only, but tightened-up 'primary purpose' clause.
- h Immigration Rules changed to place settled women in the same position as British citizen women.
- j Immigration Rules changed to place the same restrictions on settled and British men and women.
- k The difference in the total number of husbands and wives granted settlement reflects a difference in the number of applications by husbands and wives, as well as government policy restricting entry of husbands.

> qualitatively different from that of yester-year and given that the choices open to Asian women are limited, some actually do support the practice. The system of marriage has operated over a long period of time and cannot be wiped away by legislation.[39]

There was another factor involved in the government policy to ban or restrict the entry of husbands and fiancés — Asian men in Britain also conduct arranged marriages with women from the Indian subcontinent, but the obstacles described above were not originally applied to them. In fact, as Table 1 shows, even in the years when the Rules were liberalised, the number of wives coming over to the UK or being allowed to settle on marriage far exceeded that of husbands. (This of course, reflects the fact that many men, especially from the Indian subcontinent, immigrated to Britain without their wives, while the number of women who migrated on their own was much smaller.) The reason for the sex discrimination as explained by Whitelaw in the debate on the White Paper, was 'the exploitation [by men] of marriage as an instrument of primary immigration'. The use of the word 'primary' is significant. This was a term which was to be frequently employed over the following years. The implication was that male immigration was somehow 'primary' and female immigration 'secondary'.

Elaborating on this theme further, Timothy Raison, Home Office minister with responsibility for immigration, asserted that 'the young man seeking to come to the United Kingdom for the purpose of marriage is economically motivated. The reason why women come here is not primarily economic but so they can build a family.' As explained in the previous chapter, this statement not only ignored the thousands of women who had migrated to Britain as independent workers, but also the fact that wives frequently took employment when they are here. In fact, overall, black women are more likely to be in the labour market than white women. The 1981 Labour Force Survey found that the 'economic activity rate' of all 'non-white' women in Britain was just under 50 per cent compared to just over 47 per cent of white women (68 per cent of African-Caribbean and Guyanese women and 40 per cent of women from the Indian subcontinent were in paid employment). In 1990-91, this rate for both white and 'all ethnic minority' women was 53 per cent; 71 per cent of Caribbean women and 39 per cent of women from the subcontinent being in work.[40] Yet the government persisted with the argument that immigrant women were, by definition, dependants and that immigrant men were a threat to the labour force. On that two-pronged basis, women were denied the right to bring over their spouses, while it was still afforded until 1988 to immigrant men in the name of family unity (although it became increasingly difficult for black men to exercise this right, as will be shown in the next chapter).

However, some sections of the Tory Party remained opposed even to black wives being allowed to come here, justifying their view by extending the logic of the government's argument that black men provide an employment threat to Britain. Conservative MP Keith Hampson complained in the debate on the 1979 White Paper that 'three times as many females from the Indian subcontinent arrive in this country as males. Those women go to the highly populated and industrialised centres and produce children, many of whom are males, who enter the labour force.'

Once a spurious argument is cynically employed to justify a policy which is racially and sexually discriminatory it begets other arguments which go further along the same line. Clearly, if family unity is a fundamental human right, it should apply to all people living in a country regardless of race and sex. Arguments employed to justify any other policy are bound to be illogical and untenable.

Resistance and change: the 1983 Rules

Black and immigrant women who were discriminated against under the complicated but cunning provisions of the 1980 Rules could not, and did not, let the matter rest there. Many individual immigration and anti-deportation campaigns were set up at this time to resist the effects of immigration policy in general. As will be discussed in greater detail later, some specifically concerned women. Examples are Anwar Ditta's campaign to have her children brought over; Najat Chaffee's struggle to remain here after separating from her violent husband; and the Filipino resident domestics' long and determined fight to resist the threat of mass removal.

The first all-women conference on the issue of racism and sexism in immigration law took place in County Hall, London, in October 1982, organised by an *ad hoc* group of black and white feminists. About 200 women of various nationalities came to discuss their experiences of oppression under Britain's immigration policy. They learnt from each other and from legal workers how the racist and sexist nature of the laws combined to affect the lives of black and immigrant women living and working in Britain. The Women, Immigration and Nationality Group was born out of the 1982 conference. It aimed through publicity and lobbying to continue the campaign against current immigration policy and its specific effects on women. Alongside these initiatives, the Joint Council for the Welfare of Immigrants and the National Council for Civil Liberties mounted a new campaign to persuade the government to change the 1980 Rules.

However, the combined forces of these campaigns were not in themselves sufficient to outweigh the pressure from the Tory right against any liberalisation of the Rules. Whereas the women's and civil rights lobbies had influenced the final form of the 1980 Rules and the Nationality Act, passed the following year, it took the European Commission of Human Rights to induce the government to amend the Rules again.

The European Convention on Human Rights, an international human rights instrument which Britain has signed, has been in force since 1953. It was negotiated by the countries of the Council of Europe after the Second World War and is designed to protect individuals against infringements of civil liberties by the state. The European Commission and Court of Human Rights were set up to enforce the Convention. Individuals who feel aggrieved by the actions of their own government can complain to the Commission, which decides whether there is a case for the government in question to answer. If there is, and if the parties cannot arrive at a friendly settlement, the case is referred to the final arbiter, the European Court of Human Rights.

Many women who were separated from their husbands by the 1980 Rules lodged their cases with the Commission. Three test cases were chosen by the Commission for consideration. In all three cases the husbands had been refused permission to live with their wives in Britain because neither the women, nor their parents, had been born in the UK. One woman, Nargis Abdulaziz, was the daughter of UK citizens who were born in Malawi and came to live in Britain in the late 1970s. Another, Sohair Balkandali, was a UK citizen born in Egypt who had been living in Britain since 1973. The third applicant, Arcely Cabales, was a Filipino citizen who had worked as a nurse in British hospitals since 1967.

In December 1980 the Commission decided to hold a hearing to determine whether the cases, which became known as the ABC cases, were 'admissible' — that is, whether the British government had a case to answer. The hearing did not take place for another 17 months. The three women complained that the British government was in breach of Articles 3, 8, 13, and 14 of the European Convention on Human Rights by discriminating on the grounds of race and sex and interfering with family life.

In response to the charge of sex discrimination, the government acknowledged that the Rules did discriminate between men and women. As a justification, the government once again resorted to the assertion that women do not work. It argued that debarring husbands and fiancés was 'justified to protect the labour market of the indigenous and settled population', but that wives do not present the same problem because

> women are not necessarily bound to compete for employment and are unlikely to be breadwinners. Women as breadwinners are unusual, for society still expects the man to go out to work and the woman to stay at home. This is a fact of life, a common pattern. The majority of women do not threaten the labour market, particularly women from the Indian sub-continent.[41]

After the Commission had ruled that there was a case for the British government to answer, in May 1982, the latter felt under sufficient pressure to liberalise the Immigration Rules. It had recently passed the 1981 Nationality Act, with the stated aim of creating classes of citizenship with clear and consistent rights. Yet under the 1980 Rules British women without British ancestry were deprived of the right to live with their foreign-born husbands in Britain while other British women did have this right (albeit one hedged about with numerous restrictions which did not apply to British men). It must have been clear to the government ministers that this two-tier citizenship would make it even more likely that the European Court would rule against them.

From the moment the government stated its intention to liberalise the Rules to allow all British women to bring in their husbands or fiancés, a large group of Conservative backbenchers, aided and abetted by a generally sympathetic press, led a vociferous campaign against the proposed change. In a parliamentary debate in October 1982, more than 50 Tory

MPs abstained in a vote on the White Paper which set out the new proposals. The newspaper coverage which anti-deportation campaigns and groups like WING had such difficulty in obtaining was made freely available to this lobby. Sympathetic leaders appeared in the *Sun, Daily Mail* and *Daily Telegraph*; scare stories about 'arranged marriage agencies' competed for space with items about Asian girls coerced into marriage against their wishes to men from the Indian subcontinent. Better, the perverse logic went, to prevent such girls from having the right to marry men from Asia altogether, whether they wanted to or not. The issue that was behind this mask of pretended concern for Asian girls was, of course, the number of Asian men who would be allowed to come to Britain if the Rules were liberalised once more. However, according to the government, which was equally obsessed with numbers, this would have involved only another 2,500 to 3,000 men a year. But for the Tory right, this was still too many. As Harvey Proctor MP put it: 'If the new Rules increased the inflow by one I should feel obliged to vote against them.[42]

In the end, to appease the right wing of its party, the government introduced 'safeguards' with the new Rules which incorporated new restrictions on and after entry. Nevertheless, this did not prevent Margaret Thatcher experiencing one of the few defeats of her government. Twenty-three Conservative MPs ignored a three-line whip and joined the major opposition parties (who were opposed to the liberalisation for not going far enough) to defeat the government by a majority of 18 on the vote over the new Rules in December 1982. A further 28 Tories abstained, revealing the extent to which a large number of Conservative MPs were prepared to go to prevent any more black people having the right to settle in Britain. The Home Secretary then had 40 days to draw up new Rules, and persuade the 'rebels' to change their minds. Tactics used, according to Proctor, included 'a whisky here, a trip to the Far East there, the friendly chat, the unfriendly chat, appeals to party loyalty... threats of weaker rules still to be carried with Opposition acquiescence.'[43] The main concrete offer held out to the Tory rebels was a statement that the new policy would be subject to a 'continuous re-examination in the light of changing circumstances'.

Those efforts reaped their rewards. Second time round, the government managed to rally a majority of 37 in favour of the Rules; only 15 Tories abstained or voted against. These new Rules came into force in February 1983. They allowed all women with British citizenship, regardless of their ancestry, to bring in foreign-born husbands and fiancés. However, the Rules still denied this right to women settled here but not naturalised as British, as well as to those who worked or studied in Britain under immigration restrictions. In addition, they provided one new 'safeguard' (two others contained in the December Rules were dropped). The Rules transferred the onus of proof on to the *applicant*. For a husband or fiancé of a British woman to be granted entry for an initial period of 12 months, the immigration officer had to be 'satisfied' that the 'primary purpose' of the marriage was not to enable the husband to immigrate and that the couple had met and intended to live together permanently. Under the previous Rules, entry could be refused only if the immigration officer had 'reason to believe' that these requirements were not met. It then became up to the couple to prove that their marriage was 'genuine'. Likewise, a husband would be allowed to stay permanently at the end of the trial period of 12 months only if the Home Secretary was 'satisfied' that all the above conditions had been met, that the marriage has not broken up and that the husband was not in breach of the Immigration Rules or subject to a deportation order before he married his British wife. None of these restrictions applied to British men bringing over their wives. Neither did they apply to women who came over as workers from another EC country. There is no sex discrimination under EC immigration law, which allows all people from EC member states who migrate in search of work to bring their families with them. This means that, in this respect, EC women living in the UK are in a better position than British women.

Continuing separation for non-British women

As far as women without British citizenship were concerned, they had no legal entitlement to bring their foreign husbands over in any circumstances. This applied whether or not they had been settled here for many years. Malika Chabani, for example, came to live in Britain from Morocco with her family when she was 15 years old. She was told that she must return to Morocco with her 2-year-old British son, Sayd, if she wanted to live with Abdesselam, her husband. The rest of her family lived here. Yet, according to the secret Instructions to immigration officers mentioned above, 'discretion would not normally be exercised in favour of applicants in this position because refusal... would not lead to the break-up of a family unit since no such unit has existed.' Women like Malika could not seek protection from the Sex Discrimination Act because it does not cover laws which were passed before it came into force (the Immigration Rules come under the 1971 Immigration Act). The only solution for such women, then, was to become British citizens. Those who were Commonwealth citizens and settled here before 1973 were entitled to register as British. But other women had to be settled in Britain and to have lived here for five years before they could apply; the Home Secretary had the discretion to refuse their applications without giving any reasons (over 6,000 applications for citizenship were refused or withdrawn in 1981 alone). It was also a lengthy and expensive procedure, taking 21 months on average to process applications in 1983 and costing £160 per person.

Moreover, until 1982, married people who wished to naturalise but whose spouse was not resident in Britain were placed in a 'catch-22' situation. In order to become British, all applicants have to intend to live in the UK in the future. As the husbands of non-British women were not allowed to live in Britain at all, the intentions of their wives were felt to be in doubt. They were therefore refused British nationality on this ground and deprived of the only means of bringing their husbands over. After pressure from immigration advice organisations, the Home Office relented and in 1982 dropped the practice of refusing naturalisation to married people whose spouse was not resident in the UK. There were also good reasons for some people to be anxious about naturalising. Many women settled in Britain without British nationality came from countries which did not allow dual citizenship — for instance, India, Malaysia, Ghana or the Philippines. By obtaining British nationality, they not only lost the citizenship of their birth, but, in some cases, important rights. India, for example, allows only Indian citizens to buy property and Malaysia treats its former citizens in exactly the same way as foreign nationals.

The end of sex discrimination?

The 1983 immigration rule changes were not enough to meet the British government's obligations under the European Convention on Human Rights. On 28 May 1985 the European Court of Human Rights gave its decision in the cases of Abdulaziz, Cabales and Balkandali,[44] the ABC cases. The British government was found guilty of a violation of Article 8 of the Convention, which states:

> Everyone has the right to respect for his private and family life, his home and his correspondence. There shall be no interference by a public authority with the exercise of this right except such as is in accordance with the law and is necessary in a democratic society in the interests of national security, public safety or the economic well-being of the country, for the prevention of disorder or crime, for the protection of health or morals, or for the protection of the rights and freedoms of others.

Because of the sex discrimination in the rules about family unity, the government was also held to have violated Article 13, which provides for an effective remedy. The Court decided:

> the advancement of the equality of the sexes is today a major goal in the member states of the Council of Europe. This means that very weighty reasons would have to be advanced before a difference of treatment on the ground of sex could be regarded as compatible with the Convention.... The discrimination...was the result of norms that were in this respect incompatible with the Convention. In this regard, since the UK has not incorporated the Convention into its domestic law, there could be no 'effective remedy'.[45]

The Court rejected the government's arguments that the sex discrimination in the rules was necessary to protect the UK labour market. However the court also came to the strange conclusion that the rules did not discriminate on grounds of race, and did not breach that part of the Convention. Perhaps the wording and operation of the rule, discussed above, was too subtle for the Court.

Soon after the court's judgement, however, the government made it clear that it did not intend to give women the right to be joined by partners from abroad. David (now Lord) Waddington, then Minister at the Home Office, stated:

> It would be absurd if, having tightened up the work permit system to prevent young men coming here and going on to the labour market, we were to allow these same young men to come here by using marriage as a device.... The country would be immensely surprised if, having willed a firm and fair immigration control, we now took the view that anybody who enters into a marriage, irrespective of whether

> that marriage is entered into for immigration purposes, should be able to come here.[46]

He had clearly, like the Bourbons, learned nothing and forgotten nothing, as he was still using the arguments about employment discredited by the Court and expressing racist views on Asian marriages allegedly widely held in the rest of the country. This helps to explain why the 1985 Immigration Rule changes moved towards sex equality mainly by removing rights from men, and subjecting women applying to join their husbands to the same restrictions as men. Waddington's views also foreshadow the main plank of government policy on immigration control of marriages for the next 10 years — the investigation of motives for marriage and the refusal of people who could not prove that their marriage was not entered into primarily for immigration reasons.

'Primary purpose'

The primary purpose rule has continued to prevent large numbers of women from living in Britain with their foreign husbands, especially if the men came from the Indian subcontinent. The 'primary purpose' clause of the Rules has been operated much more stringently than in former years since the onus was placed on the couple to prove their intentions on marriage. As discussed on page 75, it is not just a question of satisfying the immigration officer that they intend their marriage to last for ever after. Even where it is quite clear that the marriage is genuine, that it is not a marriage of convenience, husbands are refused entry if it is suspected that their main motive for getting married is to live in the UK. This stringency matches the assurances which MPs Marcus Fox, Nick Budgen, David Mudd and others said they received from the Home Secretary before they agreed to support the new Rules in their final version.[47] While it is impossible to know exactly what was said to this lobby it is not difficult to guess that there were guarantees that the new 'safeguard' would act severely to limit the number of Asian men allowed to join their British wives and fiancées, in spite of the fact that all British women were theoretically able to bring their husbands over. Budgen delivered a warning to Whitelaw on this point: 'If the predictions of the Home Secretary that the change in the burden of proof will restrict the number of applicants

Table 2 Applications for entry clearance to enter the United Kingdom by husbands and fiancés in the Indian subcontinent 1977-1992

Year	**Husbands and fiancés**				
	Newly received	Granted [a]	Refused	Refusal rate %	Outstanding at end of period
1977[b]	3,330	3,500	140	4	3,400
1978	3,800	2,140	120	6	4,600
1979	3,660	1,990	170	8	5,800
1980	820	1,840	180	9	4,400
1981	900	1,920	210	10	2,700
1982	1,230	800	700	47	2,500
1983	3,300	1,080	970	47	3,300
1984	2,780	1,340	1,120	45	3,300
1985	3,060	1,190	1,160	49	3,800
1986	3,410	1,190	1,470	55	4,100
1987	3,790	1,090	1,570	59	5,000
1988	3,320	1,090	1,850	63	5,000
1989	3,560	1,520	3,040	67	3,600
1990	3,890	1,360	3,010	69	2,400
1991	4,230	1,590	2,590	62	2,800
1992[c]	5,510	3,140	2,500	44	3,600

Source: Home Office, *Control of Immigration: Statistics*, London: HMSO
Notes:

a. Applications granted and refused do not necessarily relate to those received in a given year because of the length of the queue.
b. Figures not available before 1977.
c. This reflected the Home Office announcement that primary purpose would not be used as a reason for refusal in certain cases, discussed on pages 86-7.

is incorrect, honourable members... will remind the Home Secretary of the promise made today.'[48]

As Table 2 shows, the number of Asian husbands and fiancés allowed to join their wives in the UK in 1983 was only 280 more than in 1982, despite the liberalisation to the Rules in February of that year (partly due to the length of the queue for entry clearance in the Indian subcontinent). The overall refusal rate of applications from husbands and fiancés in the Indian subcontinent was 47 per cent in both 1982 and 1983. But Home Office figures reveal a dramatic increase in the proportion of applications turned down partly or wholly on the grounds that the 'primary purpose' of the marriage was immigration to Britain — from 18 per cent in 1982 to 73 per cent in 1983. This proportion remained consistently high; it was 86 per cent in 1991 and 84 per cent in 1992.

Home Office minister David Waddington has explained this spectacular rise in refusals on the grounds of 'primary purpose' in terms of a 'backlog of applications associated with a change in practice under which more applications are decided locally.'[49] But according to the Joint Council for the Welfare of Immigrants, this 'change of practice' refers to the fact that whereas under the previous Rules doubtful cases concerning the intentions of the applicants were referred to the Home Office for further consideration, these are now considered by the immigration officers on the spot.

Secret Instructions issued to immigration officers after the 1983 Rules came into force revealed the kind of interrogation men might face to prove the motive for their marriage. Among other questions, a man may be asked about the nature of his relationship with his fiancée or wife, his reasons for getting married and the circumstances under which he made this decision. Couples have complained that intimate questions about their sex lives have been asked. In one case reported in the press, immigration officers read the couple's love letters and refused the man entry on the ground that the letters were not affectionate enough for the proposed marriage to be genuine.[50]

The Instructions show that applicants may be asked, 'If your fiancée did not live in the United Kingdom, would you still go to her home to live?' If they answer 'no', they are liable to be refused entry to the UK, especially if their 'general circumstances or background together indicate that the marriage is primarily for immigration reasons.' This suggests that a man's very willingness to live in the UK makes him suspect. It is almost as if the best chance a fiancé or husband has for being accorded entry to Britain nowadays is actually to argue that he does not want to live there! The Instructions go on to say that even if an applicant gives a satisfactory answer, the immigration officer must 'assess the applicant's credibility and integrity' before allowing him entry to the UK. This reliance on discretion opens the door to stereotypes and prejudices. As the purpose of the present system of British immigration control is to keep black people out of the country this inevitably influences the attitudes and judgements of individual immigration officers.

At the end of the interrogation, the secret Instructions conclude, the applicant 'should *not* be given the benefit of the doubt' (our emphasis) if the evidence is evenly balanced, for in that case he has not been able to *prove* that the marriage was not primarily for immigration purposes. But what the Instructions do not explain is how to *prove* what is primarily a psychological state of mind — the main *motive* for getting married. And what of cases where the man and the woman have different reasons for getting married? Why is it assumed that the 'primary purpose' of a marriage is that of the man? Under the current application of the Rules, it is *his* intention, as the person abroad, which dictates whether the couple has the right to live together in this country.

The assumption that marriage should be the product of a freely made decision by two individuals romantically attached to each other is, in any case, an idealised Eurocentric notion. How many people, wherever they are from, do not in fact take into account factors like the place of residence of their future spouse or their employment prospects when considering whom to marry? Perhaps David Waddington had seen too many Hollywood films!

Many couples challenged these refusal decisions through the immigration appeals system. In some cases the Immigration Appeal Tribunal interpreted the primary purpose rule more liberally than the Home Office had intended.[51] The Home Office decided to arrange a special tribunal made up of three lawyers in order to obtain 'guidance' on the interpretation of the rule, in line with its views. The tribunal took place on 31 August 1984. It concerned Vijay Kumari who had lived in the UK since 1970. Her fiancé, Vinod Bhatia, had been refused permission to come to Britain to marry her in 1983 on the grounds that the primary purpose of the proposed marriage was immigration. Two out of three of the tribunal members agreed with the Home Office that although 'Vijay's primary purpose and that of her parents is to arrange a suitable match without providing a large dowry, on a balance of probabilities the primary purpose of the appellant is to obtain admission to this country.' The third member, however, dissented on the grounds that 'the evidence comes nowhere near displacing the intention to live together permanently as the primary purpose of this intended marriage.'[52]

The majority decision, which was confirmed by the Divisional Court in April 1985, meant that the Home Office could continue to refuse almost any man applying to come here to join his wife. Hundreds of British women, including those born in Britain, have been affected by the application of the 'primary purpose' rule.

Baljit Kaur, for example, was born and brought up in Birmingham. The Home Office refused her Indian husband entry on the grounds that the main reason he married her was to come to live in the UK. This was in spite of the fact that they had a baby and there could be no question that they intended their marriage to last. When challenged about this couple on the television programme *Eastern Eye* in January 1984, Waddington said it was Baljit 'who was the one who separated the couple' by refusing to live in India.

The development of the primary purpose rule

Primary purpose has remained the government's favoured tool. Throughout the 1980s and early 1990s its use grew. For example, in the Indian subcontinent in 1992, 87 per cent of the men initially refused permission to join their partners in Britain were refused for this reason; 23 per cent of women were refused, 72 per cent for this reason. In 1992, 2360 men and 8250 women and their children were allowed to come to the UK from the subcontinent for marriage (this includes people whose appeals against refusal were successful) but 2500 men and 2160 women and children were refused — a very high proportion. The total number of men allowed in for marriage that year was 5980 and women, 12,700.[53] Most of the applications from other parts of the world were successful on first attempt; this can be inferred from the numbers of appeals against refusal of entry clearance heard. In 1992, 2266 appeals from men refused permission to join their partners in the UK were decided; only 192 of these concerned men not from the Indian subcontinent.[54] In spite of frequent requests for the information, the government has maintained that separate figures for primary purpose refusals are not kept at any post outside the Indian subcontinent except Hong Kong, where the numbers of such refusals are very small. When a matter as important as being able to live together with one's chosen partner is at stake, it can be assumed that most people will appeal against refusals. The figures therefore suggest that the primary purpose rule was not used to any great extent in most other countries, more kept in reserve as a flexible tool for race and sex discrimination when required.

Because of the complexity of showing a negative purpose, and the difficulty of establishing what the primary motivation for two people marrying is, let alone what it is not, many couples unjustly and forcibly separated by the primary purpose rule have challenged the immigration authorities' decisions in the courts, thereby creating legal precedents. The case of Arun Kumar and Santosh Kumari, for example, was decided in July 1986. Arun had first applied to come to the UK as a fiancé in March 1982 and had been refused; the couple married in India in December and he applied again as a husband and was again refused. Santosh stayed with him in India for 13 months but returned to the UK when she was pregnant and ill; she later miscarried. She went back to India in January 1985 and stayed for several weeks and the couple had a child in October 1985. When Arun's appeal was at last heard, it was allowed, the court deciding that events since the marriage could be taken into account and that the 'intervening devotion' between Arun and Santosh had shown that the marriage was not primarily for immigration purposes. The judges clearly found the implications of the immigration rules difficult to justify:

> under the rules a marriage primarily entered into in order to obtain admission to the United Kingdom would still retain its non-qualifying character whatever happened afterwards and even if the husband applied for entry on their golden wedding day.[55]

Two years later, when deciding the cases of Amirul Hoque and Matwinder Singh,[56] who had been refused permission to join their wives in the UK, the Court of Appeal provided a list of ten 'propositions' to be considered in deciding primary purpose cases. These included that it was for the applicant (i.e. the husband) to satisfy the entry clearance officer of his intentions and that it is his, not his wife's, intention which is the central consideration. Furthermore, the court stated:

> where arranged marriages are the norm, the fact that a marriage is an arranged marriage albeit a circumstance to be taken into account, does not show that its purpose is or was to obtain admission to the United Kingdom.

The court also observed:

> It is fatally easy, but wrong, to treat an admission on [the husband's] part that he seeks to obtain admission to the United Kingdom as evidence that this was the primary purpose of the marriage.

This common-sense view was frequently ignored by entry clearance officers in the Indian subcontinent.

Judgements in other cases have commented on the 'breach with tradition' for a man from Pakistan or India coming to his wife's home on marriage, but have decided that where a good reason can be shown for this break with tradition, it should not justify a refusal, particularly when the marriage arrangements have been of long standing. Some judges have also shown more understanding of the arranged marriage system and of the complex reasons for many marriages. Iram Iqbal applied for a judicial review of the refusal to allow her husband Tanveer to come from Pakistan to join her. He had applied to come in 1986 and was refused in 1988; he lost his immigration appeals in 1990 but Iram continued her fight to the courts. In allowing the case, the judge commented that this six-year wait was 'indicative of the couple's constancy and the slowness of our immigration and court procedures' and that:

> in the context of arranged marriages in Muslim society, the absence of such a passionate relationship or indeed of being 'in love' was not of itself indicative of [immigration] being the primary purpose of a marriage...To draw an analogy with English society at the turn of the century, the fact that an American heiress was so keen to be a duchess that she was prepared to marry an Englishman whom she did not love would not lead one to suppose that the primary purpose of the marriage was for her to obtain admission to the UK. She may have been after his title and he after her money.[57]

Economic incentives also should not be overrated, as there will be an economic reason for people from many countries wanting to come to the UK, so officials should consider whether this is the primary reason for the marriage, rather than one of several reasons.[58]

The immigration authorities and the courts have therefore spent a great deal of time trying to interpret the complex motives couples may have for getting married. They have made detailed inquiries into people's intentions on marriage and focused on tiny slips made in the course of an interview which may contain over 100 questions. This history shows the lengths to which the British government is prepared to go to exclude Asian men and to disregard the views and the rights of women of Asian origin living in the UK. The long-standing custom of arranged marriages, with a wide spectrum of relatives concerned and consulted, has often been wilfully misinterpreted to indicate that an economic motive must be paramount. The racism of this approach has combined to exclude men and deny rights to women.

The Rules have also been operated strictly against men who were told they could not remain in the UK before they married (usually because they had overstayed their time limit). As explained, this is one of the conditions which men who marry British women must satisfy before being allowed to settle in Britain. The implication of this policy was that if a woman married a man who had at any time been in breach of the Rules, she might never be able to live with him in this country.

For example, Selim Ajir was unknowingly subject to a deportation order in 1981 because he had stayed longer than the time permitted him. The following year he met his future wife Irma, who was born and brought up in Britain. They lived together for two years and got married as soon as Irma's divorce from her first husband came through. The Ajirs then applied for Selim to stay permanently, but the Home Office refused to lift the deportation order, arguing that the marriage was for immigration purposes only. They were called up to the Home Office and interrogated separately. After a while, an immigration officer informed Irma that her husband had been arrested and was being deported back to Turkey. Although she managed to have him released, his application to remain was refused.

Europe steps in

As with the previous immigration rule changes, it was a decision in Europe which forced the Home Office in June 1992 to make some 'concession' on the operation of the primary purpose rule. However, on this occasion it was not a judgement of the European Court of Human Rights but of the European Court of Justice, which decides conclusively whether actions of individual governments are in harmony with EC law.

As discussed in Chapter 7, EC law allows an EC citizen migrating to another member state for a purpose covered by the EC treaty to be joined there by his or her spouse. This is a right and there is no question of examining the purpose of the marriage, or the couple's intentions for the future. Surinder Singh, an Indian man working in Germany, married Rashpal Purewal, a British citizen, in 1982. The couple lived together in Germany and Ms Purewal also took part-time work there. In 1985 they returned to Britain to set up a shop. When Mr Singh entered the UK, he was admitted for one year initially as a husband. When he applied for settlement at the end of that year, this was refused because the marriage had by then broken down. The Home Office later decided to deport him. He argued that the Home Office had been wrong to admit him only for a year, under British immigration rules; because his wife was an EC national covered by the EC Treaty she was entitled to have her husband living with her. So, it was argued, he had settlement rights arising out of his wife's EC free movement rights. The Immigration Appeal Tribunal agreed but because its decision was based on EC law, it referred the case to the ECJ. This court also agreed[59] that EC nationals exercising free movement rights and then returning to their own country acquired EC rights, including that of family reunion, and that the Home Office had wrongly applied British law.

Another important European case concerning family unity, this time from the European Court of Human Rights, is that of *Berrehab*.[60] It decided that the rights of a Dutch child to respect for her private and family life (guaranteed by Article 8 of the ECHR) were breached when the Dutch government deported her Moroccan father who had been living in the Netherlands. The parents were divorced but the father had continued to see his daughter frequently.

These two cases forced the UK government to alter its practice where children or free movement rights are concerned. Expecting to lose the *Surinder Singh* case, the Home Office announced on 30 June 1992 that it would not use primary purpose as a reason for refusal of a marriage case if the marriage had subsisted for more than five years, or if there was a child or children of the marriage with the right of abode in the UK.

This 'concession' was a very welcome change for many hundreds of couples who had lived apart for long periods and who never expected to have the chance of an ordinary family life. Its effects were shown in statistics, as the numbers of husbands allowed to come in the third quarter of 1992 rose substantially. But it has done nothing to help couples considering marriage, if they do not want to live apart for the first five years of their marriage, or do not want or are unable to have children. The terms of the 'concession' are also revealing about the Home Office's thinking — a grudging concession after the supreme court's ruling on EC rights, which nevertheless ensures that those it wants to keep out can be delayed for a substantial period. It helps to underline that immigration policies are about keeping certain people out, or at least delaying their ability to travel, thereby deterring people in the UK from marrying people abroad.

In January 1993, the Home Office issued secret internal guidance to staff dealing with applications for settlement based on marriage where the person had remained illegally in the UK before the wedding. These suggested that where there were children involved, or where the relationship had subsisted for more than two years, normally deportation should not be carried through. The guidelines demonstrate the impact of ECHR decisions on immigration policy development in Britain. However, as they have not been publicly disclosed, and contradict the published immigration rules, many couples who do not know about them are therefore unable to make decisions about the future based on the guidelines nor can it be ensured that Home Office officials are implementing them.

Immigration Widows Campaign

While the issue of the ban on foreign husbands had been taken up by immigrant and civil rights groups since the late 1960s, it was only around 1983 that campaigns focused on the fact that such exclusion represented a fundamental attack on women's rights.

The first meeting of the North London Foreign Husbands Group took place in September 1983. The group comprised women affected by the Immigration Rules (and those husbands who had not yet been made to leave the country), their legal advisers, and other supporters. It had a two-fold aim: to offer support to women on their own and couples threatened with separation; and to fight to change all the Rules which had put them in that situation.

By early 1984, the group was growing fast. As awareness of the issues involved grew, the group changed its name to the Immigration Widows Campaign, the phrase first coined by WING in its information pack on the issue.[61] A publicity leaflet about the campaign was produced and launched at a press conference at the House of Commons in May 1984. Several Labour MPs pledged support and some Conservative MPs also expressed concern. A delegation of 12 women from the campaign travelled to Strasbourg in September for the hearing of the ABC cases at the European Court of Human Rights, and also met Members of the European Parliament in Brussels who offered their support.

Throughout 1984 and 1985, the group lobbied and campaigned for women to have the same rights as men to be joined by partners from abroad. It argued this in a pamphlet, *Trial by separation.* But the government response to the ABC cases, which was to remove rights from men in order to produce an 'equality of misery' was deeply disappointing. The campaign in London was complemented by the Manchester Immigration Wives and Fiancées Campaign, and groups of women who met in other cities such as Rochdale and Bristol. The most effective public campaigning was in the first half of the decade, when the sex discrimination in the law was most glaring. After the 1985 and 1988 concessions towards equality, which enabled many couples to be together, these campaigns lost some of their momentum. As women of Asian origin once again became the main victims of government racism in this respect, and were isolated from the wider community, the campaign groups attracted less support. During the late 1980s, the Immigration Widows Campaign functioned successfully as a support group, mainly for Asian women separated from their husbands, but had little campaigning success.

As the sex discrimination in the operation of immigration control became less pervasive (while race discrimination continued unabated) the Immigration Widows Campaign decided in 1989 to merge with the long-established Divided Families Campaign group in London, working on all family-related immigration issues. In this form, the group has continued. In December 1990 it produced another pamphlet, *Give us a happy ending: how families are kept apart by British immigration law.* But without the narrow focus of earlier campaigns and in a less favourable political climate, the group has remained small and its effects are limited.

Changes in immigration laws and rules

The rule change of 1985 did not provide sex equality, because the government did not remove the absolute entitlement that Commonwealth citizen men settled before 1973 had to be joined by their wives. However the rules provided that settled women and men outside this group would be subject to the same rules. Thus a partial sex equality was created by subjecting most men to the same legal restrictions as all women. Both women and men applying to join partners had to show that the primary purpose of their marriage was not immigration, that they had met each other, that they intended to stay together permanently as husband and wife and that there was adequate support and accommodation, without recourse to public funds, for them in the UK. Women also were admitted for a probationary year before qualifying for settlement. No change was made in the position of spouses of people living in the UK for temporary purposes, such as work permit holders and businessmen, so that sex discrimination continued.

The final levelling-down of the marriage rules for settled people took place three years later in 1988, in the Immigration Act of that year, when the government did remove the absolute right of British and other Commonwealth citizens settled in the UK before 1973 to be joined by their wives and children under 18. The restrictions on the entry of partners from abroad to which women had long been subjected now applied to all men — including white, British-born men. The 1948 legislators' views on marriage to British men conferring citizenship rights, quoted on page 27, had evaporated. As the rules began to affect them, many British men expressed indignation about this government interference with their rights as husbands.

Beyond marriage

In spite of their inadequacies, the immigration rules do give women settled in the UK a chance to bring in their husbands from abroad. But same-sex couples have no such rights. Irrespective of the length, stability or exclusivity of their relationship, and regardless of its centrality to the life of the individuals concerned, a lesbian or gay partner of someone who is settled here — British citizen or not — has no such right to stay by virtue of that relationship. Indeed, it is as if homosexual relationships do not exist at all, for no mention is made of them in the Immigration Rules. For example, Angela Smith lived with her British lover, Jane Burnett, in the Caribbean for over six years. After Jane could no longer find work as a teacher there and her permit was not renewed, the couple planned to come and live in the UK together. But Angela was refused permission to stay here by the Home Office on the grounds that she did not qualify under any aspect of the Rules. The couple were forced to live apart and only meet on holidays.

Because of this omission from the rules, it is unusual for a lesbian or gay couple to apply to the Home Office for leave to remain on the basis of the relationship. The only case litigated before the British courts, *Wirdestedt*,[62] concerned a Swedish gay man and his British lover. It was lost, but the Home Office followed the court's expressed hope that it would look at the case again and later allowed Lars Wirdestedt to remain exceptionally.

In an unreported Immigration Appeal Tribunal decision on this issue, an Australian overstayer, John, won his appeal against deportation; the Tribunal held that the 'compassionate circumstances' of his nearly seven years' relationship with a British man, Nicholas, as well as other matters, such as his help to Nicholas' widowed mother, who had cancer, and his responsible job, outweighed the 'public interest' in deporting him.[63] But the Home Office had fought the case all the way and did not give in until forced to do so by the Tribunal; no appeal cases fought on the basis of lesbian relationships are known. The Home Office has said that it is less likely to exercise discretion about a homosexual relationship than a heterosexual common-law relationship.[64] There is very little public knowledge of current Home Office practice in dealing with same-sex applications but certainly they are not treated on the same basis as heterosexual relationships. Chapter 7 discusses the possibility of same-sex couples living together in Denmark or the Netherlands, where the law is different, and then returning to Britain.

Heterosexual couples who are not married also lack the rights of married couples in the Rules. As already explained, there was a limited provision for a man to bring in a woman living in 'permanent association' with him, although there was never any corresponding provision permitting an unmarried woman (even if she were British) to bring in her male partner. The rule was rarely used and only if any previous marriage had broken down and if the man had not already brought in a wife or another woman on this basis. Perhaps not surprisingly, it was mainly white couples who benefited from this rule. Women allowed to stay on this basis were, however, normally given permission to remain in the UK for only a year at a time (wives were given settlement immediately). If their relationship broke up, they were in a very vulnerable position. Lilli Luczak, for example, a Canadian national, was allowed to stay in the UK in 1976 because of her relationship with a British man with whom she had a child. The man was violent to her and eventually the relationship broke down. When Lilli tried to return to the UK after attending her grandmother's funeral in Germany she was refused entry.

In the name of sex equality, the immigration rule changes of 1985 removed this provision for granting a woman leave to remain on the basis of a common-law relationship; the Home Office did not want to open this possibility to men. Such applications (for both sexes) are now decided entirely at the discretion of the Home Office, and the guidelines used are contained in the secret Instructions to immigration officials, rather than any published rules. The Home Office may treat such applications similarly to those from married couples but normally requires a higher standard of proof that the partners have had a long-standing relationship. There is no guarantee that the applications will succeed and people are forced to live in extreme uncertainty. Yet there are many reasons why couples may be unable to marry: a previous partner may be unwilling to agree to divorce, or may live in a country which prohibits divorce; there may be no evidence to satisfy a marriage registrar of a divorce or death abroad, or the couple may have principled views against the legal institution of marriage. If one of the partners comes from abroad, these circumstances may result in enforced separation.

Conclusion

The 1980 Immigration Rules which the first Thatcher government introduced soon after coming to power were primarily designed to stop black women from bringing their husbands here. To achieve this, the Rules discriminated on the basis of ancestry. But when it became clear that this discrimination between British citizens violated the European Convention on Human Rights, and that it contradicted the stated intention of the 1981 Nationality Act, the government amended the Rules once more to reduce the extent of discrimination between different kinds of British citizens. At the same time, to soften the Tory outcry which followed, it introduced a new 'safeguard' which shifted the onus of proof on to the applicant. The 'primary purpose' rule proved so successful in keeping people out that later rule changes permitting the husbands of settled women, and then women with work permits and businesswomen, to come to Britain were not strenuously opposed. It is a flexible tool which can be used by governments entirely as they wish. However, its operation has not been unchallenged and decisions in European courts have forced the British government to limit its scope. Legal discussions of the rule have exposed its injustice and the difficulties in operating it.[65] Yet, as indicated in Chapter 7, the British government has found it so useful that it has introduced other EC governments to the concept and it has been incorporated into 1993 EC resolutions on family reunion.

Chapter 4

Divide and rule: wives under immigration law

Women's struggles in Britain for independence and equal treatment since the turn of the century scarcely impinged upon their position under immigration law. Until the 1980s they were still considered to be primarily wives, dependants of men. The preceding chapter has shown how the right of women in Britain to marry and live with whom they choose has been severely restricted. The justification for the restriction has been that women should follow their husbands. In this chapter, the focus is shifted to women attempting to do just this — from women living here seeking to bring in their husbands, to women abroad seeking to join or stay with husbands here.

If the belief that women should follow their husbands were the sole basis for the legislation, then women seeking entry to Britain for that purpose should encounter no difficulty. And indeed there is provision in the Immigration Rules for all men settled here to be joined by their wives. This right remained constant until 1985, in sharp contrast to the vicissitudes of the corresponding rule for women considered earlier. This is a result of consistent government fostering of nuclear family unity.

The belief in the inherent superiority of the nuclear family has characterised all British governments; it has been particularly central to Conservative philosophy.[1] The 'party of the family' has repeatedly made great electoral play of its determination to defend and protect the family against hostile forces (such as socialism or feminism). Women should withdraw from the public sphere and accept their traditional roles as wives and mothers. But the Conservative Party's formal respect for family life maintains the privileged position of white men and the unity of white nuclear families. Black women abroad attempting to join husbands in this country have faced numerous hurdles, part of the process of keeping black immigration to a minimum. Because their exclusion would have run counter to the widely accepted ideology of family unity around a male head of household, an enormously complex system evolved. This system ensured that although lip-service was paid to the right of wives abroad to join their husbands, many black wives were prevented from doing so. It is called the entry clearance system. As the largest number of women seeking entry as wives has been Asian women, they have been the main target of this system. In their case, family unity is encouraged, if at all, when it takes place outside Britain.

The entry clearance system

The methods used to enforce immigration laws have grown in complexity over time.[2] When immigration control was first imposed on Commonwealth citizens in 1962, it all took place at the port or airport of arrival, as the control of aliens usually had, and it was up to the immigration officers there to decide whether a person qualified for entry. At first this decision was taken on the spot and, if refused entry, the person was sent straight back. As the rate of refusal began to increase, organisations and individuals intervened with the immigration officers to try to influence their decisions, sometimes successfully. The criteria which officers used to make their decisions were unknown because their Instructions from the Home Office were not made public. There was no forum in which the evidence for or against a decision to refuse a person could be considered and no system of appeal. In this vacuum, once the immigration officer had refused entry, the only way in which the Home Secretary or the Minister of State with responsibility for immigration could be made to reconsider a case was through pressure from a Member of Parliament acting on behalf of a constituent.

'Entry certificates' were first introduced in 1965; at that stage they were optional. Aliens from some countries already had to obtain visas before travelling here, so the concept of ensuring rights of entry in advance was not new. The idea of putting restrictions on the entry rights of Commonwealth citizens, however, was. Entry certificates were described by the government as a 'facility' for Commonwealth citizens enabling them to find out in advance if they were eligible for admission to Britain. The system quickly became used for other purposes — airlines began to request, or demand, that passengers to Britain, particularly from the Caribbean, had entry clearance because when they were refused entry, it was the airline that had to pay for their return fare.

As the system grew in complexity, with increasing delays and more refusals of entry, demands for improvement grew. In 1967 a committee set up to look into the possibility of appeals against refusal had recommended their introduction in the UK, where evidence could be presented for both sides, the Home Office and the family. The Committee's report[3] and other pressures induced the Home Office to draft the Immigration Appeals Act in 1969 and an unofficial system of appeals began in that year. During the third reading of the Bill, on 1 May 1969, the Home Office announced that entry certificates were to be made compulsory for dependants seeking to join other family members in the UK, this to take effect from 16 May 1969. Thus at a stroke a great hurdle was placed in the way of those seeking to come here. The system of immigration appeals was completely altered and made ineffective as a way of obtaining justice. Instead of the whole family being together at the airport, the person refused was abroad. But since the appeal against refusal took place in Britain, the central witness — the wife herself — was not allowed to take part.

The Home Office denied that the system was intended to create delays and difficulties. James Callaghan, Home Secretary, claimed that the introduction of compulsory entry certificates was in the best interests of 'genuine' immigrants because it reduced the lengthy interrogations at Heathrow Airport.[4] However, the figures for family members travelling from Pakistan alone contradict this. Although 187 people travelled to Britain in March 1969 and 230 in April, only 24 did in June and 40 in

July,[5] after the new policy came into force. At this time, only short delays were experienced by people waiting for entry clearance, but by December 1973 women and children in Bangladesh were waiting for 30 months before they could be interviewed by a British High Commission official; by June 1974 this had reached 38 months. The government used the entry clearance system as a delaying mechanism: the political benefits of keeping annual immigration figures within a politically acceptable quota far outweighed the disadvantages of keeping black families divided.

The introduction of an appeal system was not the only 'improvement' suggested. In 1969, the government set up a working party to look into the feasibility of providing advisory services to people refused entry overseas. But it concluded that these should not be necessary because the man in Britain (at that stage it was assumed always to be a man) should advise his wife: 'he himself initiates the move and he should be able to give his wife and family all the advice they need including help in avoiding any pitfalls.'[6]

Yet Quintin Hogg (now Lord Hailsham, a former Lord Chancellor) had stated back in 1966: 'The thing which appals me the more I think about [immigration] law is its complexity and the difficulty anyone has in finding his [*sic*] way about it. Since I was called to the Bar 34 years ago, the complexity has increased in nearly every aspect. It is a jungle.'[7] A jungle through which women with no experience of the British legal system were expected to find their way unassisted.

Many did not find their way. The Commission for Racial Equality (CRE) noted in its 1985 report, *Immigration control procedures*,[8] discussed further on pages 98-9 and 112-3,

> Between 1977 and 1981, one in five women applying in the Indian subcontinent for clearance to join men claimed to be their husbands for settlement in the United Kingdom were refused entry certificates; more than one in three of the children applying to join men claimed to be their fathers were refused.

Despite the very considerable hurdles, others succeeded. But this was usually only after huge delays. A Labour minister, visiting the Indian subcontinent in January 1975 found that in Bangladesh, for example, 'the waiting time for an interview was approaching four years.'[9] Following this visit, some attempts were made by the then Labour government to speed up the processing of queues of applicants in the Indian subcontinent and to deal with the cases less stringently. These measures were unpopular with British staff in the Embassies and High Commissions abroad. The Foreign Office responded to this discontent by sending a senior Foreign Office official, Donald Hawley, to visit the same posts. His report. referred to in Chapter 3 and leaked to the press by Enoch Powell, argued that it would be wrong to 'lower' the standard of detailed interviewing any further. Things had already gone too far in this direction and any further 'lowering' would make entry clearance officers mere 'rubber stamps' with a consequent 'effect on morale and pride in the job.'[10] Their job was seen as keeping people out; the effect on families attempting to join each other was not mentioned. Hawley also recommended the introduction of a register of dependants, with a cut-off date and an annual quota for dependants admitted.

Assumptions underlying the system

Central to the workings of the entry clearance system are the assumptions made by entry clearance officers. Despite the criteria of the Rules, the final decision about whether a woman qualifies for entry as a wife depends on the subjective assessment by the officer of her veracity, of the reliability and value of her evidence and of whether the whole picture she presents matches the officer's expectations of a genuine application.

The manner in which people operate within any organisation is informed by the institutional ideology of the system of which it is a part. In the case of the immigration control system, that ideology has been remarkably constant and coherent over the past 30 years, since control over Commonwealth immigration was introduced: black people are to be excluded from entry as far as possible, particularly when they are poor. Where legislation alone does not suffice to achieve this, the administration of the system ensures that apparent rights of entry are challenged.

The Home Office stated in its 1978 White Paper about entry clearance procedures in the Indian subcontinent:

> The prevention and detection of attempted evasion and abuse of the control, where it is shown to exist, is one of the main features of the Government's immigration policy... It is a regrettable though inevit-

> able consequence of the need to prevent abuse that some genuine applicants suffer inconvenience...[11]

That people suffered much more than inconvenience is shown throughout this chapter. It was underlined by the CRE investigation:

> the emphasis on the ineligible has gone too far. It has resulted not only in inconvenience — serious and costly as that may be — for genuine applicants, but in an unacceptably high level of risk that applicants who are in fact genuine can fail to satisfy the officer... refusal of the genuine is an unacceptable outcome of the procedure, and the dominant, overriding priority should be to ensure that genuine applicants are enabled to exercise their rights with the minimum of difficulty.[12]

The continued operation of the entry clearance system shows that these exhortations have not been heeded and immigration procedures continue to exclude family applicants.

Whether or not an individual entry clearance officer subscribes to explicitly racist views, therefore, matters not. For, like any other member of a cohesive institution, he or she will internalise its prevailing ideology. Stereotypes fill out the general picture, so that Asians are viewed differently from Afro-Caribbeans, Sylheti Muslims differently from Sikhs. An overall picture is evolved of how 'they' behave within a particular context, and individual officers are taught to spot deviations from a presumed norm, which can then be taken as indicators justifying suspicion. The CRE noted internal documents used by officers at Heathrow Airport, which contained racist assumptions but no details of any 'evidence' on which they were based. One document stated: 'Moroccans from the 'immigrant areas' seem, like Mirpuris, to be both simple and cunning. The only way to discover if their applications are genuine is by thorough and sceptical examination'. Another asserted that 'many [Ghanaians] are like lost and confused children, ill prepared for their proposed travels with no particular reason for undertaking them' and 'like Ghanaians, Nigerians tend to have ambitions and plans out of all proportion to their capabilities and circumstances'.[13]

Racist stereotypes affect every level of decision-making, from the sorts of procedures which are established to process applications, to the attitudes towards particular pieces of evidence. In the case of the Indian subcontinent, for example, the assumption of Asian dishonesty and deceitfulness informs the entire immigration control system. A clear example of this is a document called 'The Sylhet Tax Pattern' which was produced by the British High Commission in Bangladesh. It attempted to explain how '90 per cent of all sponsors seeking entry for dependants attempt to take in bogus children'[14] and how these cases could be identified. General and vague ideas of the average age at which a man or woman from Sylhet married were elevated into immutable facts. Since some men had claimed income-tax relief for non-existent dependants (often while supporting other dependants ineligible for relief under the British tax system), all wives applying for entry who had older children not seeking entry to Britain were suspected. The older children were assumed to be non-existent, invented for tax purposes, and so the wife's application was refused for this reason. The High Commission document advised entry clearance officers to suspect, among other things, 'a wife who does not look her stated age, an applicant [who is] a second wife, a blank or sparse family tree.'[15]

The Immigration Rules for wives

Sexist assumptions and stereotypes are superimposed on and intermeshed in this racist foundation. The 1971 Immigration Act presupposed the existence of a conventional nuclear family as the basic social unit in society, with the man as the head of the household supporting his dependants. Marriage is given primary significance, so that whether or not a couple are married can make all the difference to their immigration status, as indeed to that of their children.

The Immigration Rules until 1985 granted any man *settled* in the UK — that is, living here without any immigration restrictions on his stay — the right to bring his wife here to live. The man did not have to be a British citizen. If he was a Commonwealth citizen settled here since before 1 January 1973 (the date the 1971 Immigration Act came into force) then the right to bring in his wife was absolute. All other men had to prove that they could support and accommodate their wives without recourse to public funds. By contrast, as explained in Chapter 3, the Immigration Rules have always placed restrictions on a woman bringing in her husband and there are numerous qualifications which can prove impossible to fulfil.

It was not only men settled here who had the right to bring in their wives. Male students or work permit holders have always had this right. They can enter with or be joined by their wives for the duration of their stay in this country. The wife's right to be here is completely dependent on the husband's — once his leave runs out, so does hers: in these circumstances she has no independent immigration status. Women workers were allowed to bring in partners from 1989. Women students still have no such rights although a change is under discussion. As explained above, anyone intending to come here to live permanently has to obtain prior entry clearance. This applied to husbands, wives and male fiancés only, until 1985 when it was also imposed on female fiancées. Previously they were allowed in simply on the strength of an undertaking that they would marry within three months.

The absolute right for the wives of Commonwealth men settled here before 1973 to come to join their husbands could continue even after the husband had left. This is illustrated by the case of Sarah Kusah. She had first travelled to Britain from Sierra Leone as a 9-year-old child. In 1961, she married a Ghanaian man and they had two children in Britain within three years. Because of her husband's violence towards her, Sarah returned to Sierra Leone with the children in 1964, and lived there until 1973, when her husband sent tickets to Britain for her and the children. She was re-admitted as a visitor, rather than for settlement, in March 1974, because she had been led to believe that this would be quicker. Her hopes for a reconciliation of her marriage were frustrated, so divorce proceedings had been started by the time she applied for permission to settle again on 3 June 1974. Mr Kusah left the UK on 23 June 1974 and has lived in Ghana ever since. Sarah's application to remain and her appeal were both refused because she could not produce any evidence that her husband had been settled here on 1 January 1973 and at the time of her return. Her own childhood and marriage here, the birth of her children here, her life and work here from 1974 to 1979 did not give her any legal right to remain. Yet when the publicity surrounding her case reached Ghana, her ex-husband eventually provided evidence proving his settled status here (on condition that Sarah accepted divorce on his terms). Sarah was then allowed to remain, but only on the basis of her relationship with a man with whom she had not had close links for five years.

The entry of wives

Regardless of formal rights, throughout the 1970s and 1980s entry clearance and immigration officers subjected some applications from wives seeking entry to join husbands here to intense scrutiny. This was done by calling into question that which gives rise to the right of entry, the marriage itself. As well as denying entry to women, this technique also denied entry to their children, if they were alleged not to be the children of a 'real' marriage. With the advent of DNA testing, discussed in detail on pages 135 et seq, the relationship of parents to children can be scientifically proved, and with this proof a marriage is assumed, so detailed questioning on this score has become superfluous.

Sometimes the marriage was treated as suspect simply because of the character of one or both of the spouses — an example is the concern about the marriages of alleged prostitutes from France to British men, voiced during the parliamentary debates on the 1948 British Nationality Act. Today, however, it is more commonly immigrant men who are suspected of contracting 'primary purpose marriages', marriages whose sole or main purpose is thought to be the immigration advantage they confer.

In practical terms, this suspicion meant that before a woman could gain entry as a wife she had to prove that she really was married to her husband. This was particularly hard in the Indian subcontinent where a vast edifice of questioning was erected, allegedly to detect fraud and deceit. The way women applicants for entry clearance were questioned and the sort of evidence they were expected to produce violated many accepted notions of legality or natural justice.

Applicants had to 'satisfy' the immigration officer that they qualified under the rules. *In theory*, the balance of probabilities was the standard of proof required; *in practice*, a far higher standard of proof was expected. The interview where applicants were assessed consisted of a series of questions. Foreshadowing the techniques used in primary purpose interviews, discussed on pages 80-81, leading questions which misled applicants into thinking a particular answer was required were not excluded from the process as they would be in other areas of legal investigation. The questions were primarily to ascertain whether or not the applicant was 'telling the truth'. Many of the questions had nothing to do with the actual process of qualifying. Rather, they were designed to test out the answers of different applicants against each other, to reveal 'discrepancies' which were then taken as evidence of dishonesty and used to refuse entry. Questions ranged from taking down a comprehensive 'family tree' to details about what happened on the wedding night to descriptions of farm animals ('How many spots does your smallest goat have?') to enquiries about village architecture ('How many windows does your cousin's house have?'). This is an excerpt from an entry clearance interview in Pakistan:

> I asked the applicant to name the occupants of her house. She said that she, the other applicants and her mother-in-law lived there. I asked her to describe to me in detail the construction and situation of the house. She said that it was a single-storey brick building comprising 5 rooms: a kitchen/dining room, a bedroom, a guest room, a store room and an animal room. She said that two other houses were attached to her own, one belonging to Samina Bi, the other to Mirza Khan. I asked her if her home was served by electricity and she said that it was not. I asked her what means of illumination were employed during the hours of darkness and she replied that there were two oil lamps in the house. I asked her from whence the household obtained its water supply and she said that it was drawn from a well situated in a lane next to the house. I asked her if she possessed a sewing machine. She said that she did not. I asked her if there was a radio in the house. She said that there was and that it had been brought by the sponsor on his return to Pakistan. I asked her if there were any bicycles in the house and she replied that Jaweed had a bicycle which he had owned for the past five or six years.
>
> I asked Inamai Bi if any animals were kept by her family. She said that they had none but that 4 years prior to the interview they had sold 2 oxen and 3 cows. I asked her from where she purchased milk and she replied that this was obtained from a neighbour, Mirza Khan. I asked her if her family possessed any land...[16]

Behind this questioning lay assumptions about the way families and relationships were constructed which were plainly inapplicable to the communities from which most Asian immigrants to Britain came. A Western Christian model of marriage was assumed where the couple choose each other as exclusive companions because of their mutual love. Other practices were at best ignored but more often treated with racist contempt. Immigration officers and adjudicators regularly delivered themselves of unashamedly unjudicial pronouncements. For example, in an appeal against deportation by a young woman and her child, both victims of her ex-husband's violence, the adjudicator had this to say:

> her knowledge of English is limited and her association with this country is largely concerned with the better standard of living she enjoys here... the overriding reason of all her actions since coming here has been a desire to obtain a residential qualification by marriage to almost anyone of acceptable age... or in any other way open to her.[17]

The story of Nasreen Akhtar, a Pakistani widow who came to Britain with her two daughters, after marrying Abdul Majid over the telephone, also illustrates official attitudes.

Nasreen's marriage was considered valid under Pakistani law but was not recognised by the British authorities, so she was allowed in only as a fiancée. Problems in producing a death certificate for her first husband meant that there were delays in the couple marrying again under British law and within a year the marriage had broken down, without the British ceremony having taken place. Nasreen was therefore told to leave the country. At the appeal against this, the Home Office argued that there had never been a valid marriage in law, but the adjudicator was more concerned about other matters. He referred to Nasreen as a burden on the social security system and believed that 'she could not possibly have considered herself married as she let her husband beat her up and throw her out while pregnant.' His conclusion was:

> My decision to dismiss the appeal may excite a certain degree of sympathy for the appellant, but I do not think it should. It must be borne in mind — firstly that she (having two children by a previous marriage) 'married' a man (who has five children by a previous marriage) she had never seen or conversed with and secondly that she having discovered (not surprisingly) that the alliance was a disaster, is resolved to live here on social security for as long as she can. I think that to a great extent she has brought her troubles upon herself.

The Immigration Appeal Tribunal in fact accepted the validity of the proxy marriage: Nasreen should all along have been allowed in as a wife rather than as a fiancée.

Under this system of questioning, Asian women from peasant communities were expected to have the knowledge a Western wife might have about her husband's daily routines — about the nature of his job, his home in England — despite, perhaps, having been kept apart from him by immigration law for years. In fact, most people would have difficulty giving consistent or accurate answers to some of the questions asked. But it is particularly difficult in a situation of extreme stress. An interview often lasted several hours and the whole future of the family could depend on it; the woman was interviewed in an office after a day's journey when she might scarcely have left her village area before; she was interviewed by the first European man she had probably ever spoken to and his questions were relayed to her by an interpreter who might speak a dialect very different from the one she was used to. The potential for fear, error, panic and discrepancies is enormous.

Answering questions correctly was not the only requirement to be fulfilled by wives seeking to join men settled in Britain. Until comparatively recently, many of the areas of migration had very sparse documentary records, but British officials ignored this and insisted on documentary evidence of births and marriages. This led to production of forged documents for a period, a fact which has ever since been used by officials to justify discrediting the genuine documents increasingly available. As a result, many applicants were caught in a trap: without adequate documentary evidence their applications were not processed; but any documents produced were viewed with suspicion or discounted as unreliable. The use of nicknames instead of formal names, differences in methods of recording dates and times, and ignorance of entry clearance officers about customs and conventions rendered the whole exercise of trying to establish the applicant's 'truthfulness' an arrogant and racist imposition of one set of cultural practices on another.

From 1988, all women seeking to join husbands in Britain have to show that they can be supported and accommodated without recourse to public funds; before 1988 Commonwealth citizen men settled in Britain since before 1973 did not have to show they could support their wives. 'Public funds' for this purpose were first defined comprehensively in 1985, to be supplementary benefit (now income support), family income supplement (now family credit), housing benefit and being rehoused as homeless persons. Thus a husband who was claiming any of these benefits would be ineligible to bring his wife over.

Investigations are carried out in Britain to ensure that the support and accommodation are up to the Home Office's standards of adequacy. Low wages and widespread unemployment make it increasingly hard for men here to prove they meet the Home Office's requirements.

The hurdles described so far are not the only ones that wives encounter. Reference has already been made to yet another gross injustice in the entry clearance system: the substantial delays that are built into every step. It is clear that unpublished immigration quotas for the numbers of black entrants to be admitted annually have dictated the pace of entry to Britain, rather than any attempt to unify families as provided for in the law. In 1974, as previously stated, wives in Bangladesh had to wait 38 months between applying for entry clearance and being granted their first interview. Delays have been gradually reduced but were still 20 months in 1984 and 6-9 months in 1993, grossly above what would be politically acceptable if it were white couples who were being separated. (Long delays do not occur throughout the system of immigration control — people in Britain for a limited time trying to stay on may be dealt with in a matter of weeks.)

Frequently, the first interview did not lead to a decision but to further delays. The case of Amara Begum is illustrative. She

> was first interviewed on 8 February 1974, when further documents were requested. These were produced and she was interviewed again on 6 September 1974. At this interview, the entry clearance officer neither granted nor refused to grant her an entry certificate but refused to take her application further unless she gave a prior undertaking to 'tell the truth' at a further interview.

The officer concerned wrote:

> I advised her that I could not accept the family tree she had given me was an accurate record of family details. When Mrs Begum feels able to let me have *full* particulars of her family and relatives she should write and tell me so and I will arrange for her to be given a further appointment.

Although Mrs Begum had given full particulars the first time, she gave this undertaking and another appointment was fixed for May 1975, well over a year after her initial interview.[18]

If the woman's application was not resolved at the post abroad, it would be referred to the Home Office in London for 'further inquiries'. The husband would, after many months had elapsed, be interviewed by a police or immigration officer and asked questions; his answers would be compared with those given previously by his wife. If the application was refused and the wife decided to appeal, the procedure dragged on for several years more. Neither the wife nor the entry clearance officer who interviewed her could be present at the appeal because it would be heard in Britain.

The entry clearance officer, usually many months after the interview, prepared a written account of it (known, revealingly, as the 'explanatory statement') which was sent to Britain for the appeal. This document was his version of what took place at the interview and would, in any other area of law, be viewed in that light — as the evidence of an interested party. It would, for example, be unthinkable for statements prepared by police officers for criminal trials to be taken at face value as impartial explanations of the matters under consideration by magistrates, judges and juries. Yet they are directly comparable to explanatory statements of what happened at the interview which were treated as unbiased statements of fact by adjudicators. The fact that entry clearance officers were bound to construct reports which justified their decision, that — whether intentionally or not — they were likely to recall points which confirmed their view and not those which contradicted it, that they might well have made errors of understanding or interpretation, particularly given the cultural differences already mentioned, and that the cumbersome process of translation gave rise to problems of accuracy and reliability — all this was overlooked.

As a result, though the majority of applicants do eventually succeed, some wives have never been allowed to exercise their legal right to join their husbands in Britain. There has been a high rate of refusal of applications for entry from wives from the Indian subcontinent each year since 1977 with substantial fluctuations. More than half (56 per cent) of the applications from wives and children in Bangladesh were refused during 1983.

These were the worst refusal figures since 1977, representing an increase in the refusal rate of almost 25 per cent since 1981.[19] The figures also reflected the entry clearance officers' practice, until the mid-1980s, of refusing the whole family if there was any doubt about the identity of even *one* member. As the questioning by entry clearance officers became more sophisticated, more 'discrepancies' could be found. After 1985, 'split decisions' became more common — only the family members about whom there was doubt were refused and others, most commonly the wife and the younger children, were issued entry clearance. With the advent of DNA testing (see Chapter 5) refusals plummeted; the refusal rate was 17 per cent in 1991. But before such incontrovertible proof existed, some divided families applied over and over again. The case of Ijaz Begum illustrates this.

She first applied to come to join her husband Mohammed Khan in January 1973. They were interviewed at Islamabad in November, with five children, ranging in age from 16 years to 18 months and all of them were refused permission to come. They appealed and the appeal was not heard until 1975. At the appeal, Mohammed Khan explained that two of the children he wanted to bring here were the sons of his brother, who had died, and whom he had brought up as his own ever since. This meant that the whole appeal had to be withdrawn; the adjudicator would not listen to all the other evidence showing that the rest of the children were his. Ijaz and the three other children applied again, on 1 January 1976; they were interviewed in March 1977, and refused again. At their appeal in April 1978, the adjudicator said his 'faith in their credibility [was] inevitably destroyed' by the fact that they had tried to bring two nephews to the country before and because of some 'discrepancies' (about the name of a young cousin, the date of the maternal grandmother's death and whether they had one or two relatives called Mohammed Anwar). The appeal was dismissed. The family appealed still further but in September 1978 the Immigration Appeal Tribunal agreed with the adjudicator. Ijaz and her three children applied for the third time for entry clearance in July 1981 and were interviewed in September 1982. They were refused yet again, by which time the two older children were over 18. At the appeal, in September 1983, the adjudicator wanted to dismiss the case out of hand as she thought there were no new facts or circumstances, but a neighbour of Mohammed's, a university professor, wanted to give evidence about his knowledge of the family over many years, so the appeal was allowed to proceed. His evidence eventually convinced the adjudicator that Ijaz and Mohammed were indeed married, and that the three children were theirs. The Home Office decided that they would, exceptionally, grant entry to the two elder children too, although they were now 23 and 19. In December 1983, more than 10 years after their first application for entry, the family was reunited in Britain.

Some of the husbands living in Britain apart from their wives and children have formed Divided Families Campaigns to attempt to change Home Office practice. Groups have been formed in the North West, Bradford, Sheffield, Birmingham and the East End of London; they have organised marches, petitions and even, in one instance, a 48-hour fast.

The campaigns met together in Birmingham in March 1985, when over 200 people agreed a Charter for Change, long before the 1990s fashion for Charters. It called for such changes as an end to entry clearance queues, that the burden of proof should be shifted to the immigration authorities to prove that a claimed family were not related, rather than the family having to prove they were, the ending of fees for entry clearance and that family members should be able to be present at their appeals against refusal. The Divided Families Campaigns, together with the Campaign against Racist Laws and the Immigration Widows Campaign, organised a mass lobby of Parliament on 21 May 1985, calling for family reunion rights. Co-operation in campaigning work continued and, when the immigration rules on husbands and wives were made more equal, and the campaigning points thus converged, the Immigration Widows Campaign joined up with Divided Families Campaigns in London. As discussed in Chapter 3, the new group has continued to try to offer support to split families and to publicise their situation, most notably in its 1990 pamphlet *Give us a happy ending: how families are kept apart by British immigration law.*

The 'primary purpose' rule

In the early 1990s the primary purpose rule, discussed in detail on pages 78-85 and which had applied to all women seeking to join their husbands since 1988, began to be used more frequently against women abroad applying to join British husbands, mainly from Thailand and the Philippines. Frequently the couples had established initial contact as pen-friends, and developed their relationship through letters before meeting when the man travelled to the woman's country and then decided to marry. Some had met through friendship agencies, a common way of meeting in Thailand. When these women applied for entry clearance, the UK government alleged that they must have primarily economic motives for marriage and the applications were refused; in both 1990 and 1991, 200 women were allowed to come from the Philippines; 110 were refused in 1990 and 140 in 1991.[20] In the UK, men separated in this way set up a group — Anglo-Philippines Association for Real Togetherness (APART) — to offer mutual support and help, as the Immigration Widows Campaign had done. With this support and help, many appeals against refusal were successful.

Victoria and Michael married in the Philippines. They had been pen-friends before, introduced to each other through Victoria's sister, who was married to a friend of Michael's. They also wanted to live in the UK together after their marriage but Victoria was refused entry clearance. Her appeal was eventually allowed, the Tribunal accepting that just because they had been pen-friends and had considered marriage before they met did not mean that the primary purpose of the marriage was immigration and the fact that Victoria's sister was already living in the UK, happily married, suggested that it was not. Victoria and Michael had to wait well over a year after applying to start their married life in Britain.

'Jumping the queue?'

Government assurances given in 1969, when compulsory entry clearance was introduced, that it was not intended to cause delays or to deter people from exercising their rights have proved false. Wives arriving here to join their husbands without entry clearance are refused admittance and can be sent straight back even when their relationship is not in doubt. The consequences of this policy can be horrifying.

Zahira Galiara was in an advanced state of pregnancy when she and her husband Aszal flew from Bombay to London, in October 1976. He had been resident in Britain for five years, had gone back to India to marry Zahira and she intended to settle in Britain with him. They arrived at the airport with their marriage certificate and all the documents required to prove that Aszal was settled in the UK. Because Zahira did not have an entry certificate, immigration officers refused to allow her in. Despite her condition she was questioned and made to wait for 12 hours without food or water. At one o'clock at night she was sent to Harmondsworth detention centre; her husband was not allowed to accompany her even though she spoke no English. She was told she would be put on a plane back to Bombay the following morning. She started having labour pains that night. The following morning she was taken back to the airport where she asked to see a doctor. Again, her husband was not allowed to accompany her. The doctor's opinion was that she was fit to be put on a plane that afternoon. 'When she came back from the doctor,' her husband told a reporter, 'she was crying in pain, but the immigration officials and Securicor men [who then guarded all the detention centres] just laughed and said she was pretending because she didn't want to be sent back.'[21] Even when Zahira was screaming in pain, they refused to call a doctor. Aszal, who tried to call an ambulance from a public phone box, was stopped by a Securicor guard. Only when the baby's head began to emerge was a doctor sent for. 'By the time he arrived,' said Aszal, 'the baby was half-out, the only people to help were myself and an Indian cleaning woman.' Zahira and the baby were eventually taken to a hospital where staff said that the baby had been born prematurely and with severe abnormalities. It died soon after. Zahira was given permission to stay.

The insistence on prior entry clearance extended even to women who were patrial and therefore not subject to immigration control. Until the 1981 Nationality Act came into force, any Commonwealth woman marrying a patrial UK citizen became patrial automatically by virtue of that marriage. It was argued before the courts, in the case of *Phansopkar*,[22] that patrial women could not be forced to wait in a queue before exercising their absolute right of entry to Britain — and indeed the courts upheld this argument. But since most of the women entitled to exercise this right were from India and Bangladesh, administrative hurdles ensured that this potentially easy access was impeded. To start with, the majority of the women could not avoid delays because they travelled with children, who needed prior entry clearance. Other women faced the prospect of having their claims about their relationship to their husband disbelieved if they attempted to get through immigration control in Britain without entry clearance. They thus risked being refused entry and sent straight back to join the end of the queue, having wasted the cost of the fare over.

In 1983, the government invented a new passport endorsement, a 'certificate of entitlement to the right of abode', the new name for patriality, a certificate which was necessary for people with the right of abode travelling to the UK for the first time. Thus people with this status needed to go through the time-consuming immigration procedures before being able to travel to Britain. Even though a special shorter queue was set up for this category, people travelling from the Indian subcontinent have had to wait on average three months before attempting to exercise what is, in theory, an absolute right.

'Virginity tests'

Fiancées, as has already been explained, were, until 1985, the only immigrants who could be admitted to Britain for settlement without having to obtain prior entry clearance. An official explanation for this was set out in a 1977 government Think Tank Report:

> The rationale for... interviewing fiancés and not fianceés in the country of origin [for entry clearance] is that the former are more likely than the latter to be intending not to marry and it is better to stop them before rather than after they reach the port of entry.[23]

There was pressure, at different times, to introduce compulsory entry clearance for fiancées.[24] The difference in the treatment of fiancés and fiancées paralleled that for husbands and wives. Men were seen as workers and heads of household, an immigration threat for both reasons; women were seen as completing families already over here, posing no threat to the job market and usually unable to bring in further dependants.

The parallel went still further. Wives, in theory, had the right to join their husbands here but, in practice, if black, faced great difficulties. The same was true of black fiancées.

The extent to which British officialdom was prepared to translate its mechanistic, simplistic assumptions about marriage into its practice to justify excluding black people, was horrifyingly illustrated by the 'virginity-testing' scandal.

According to official British thinking, no Asian woman could ever have pre-marital sex. The factual research backing this assumption was never published or, indeed, referred to. So one can assume that none existed or was undertaken, and that British officials founded their assumption on an arrogant complacency about their knowledge of Asian customs.

It followed from this assumption that a test which purported to establish that a woman was not a virgin also established that she must be married. This was sufficient evidence to justify refusing her entry as a fiancée. (The corollary of this should have been that Asian women seeking to join men here were their wives. Clearly there was a contradiction between official assumptions of pre-marital virginity, on the one hand, and a widespread desire to settle in Britain with someone falsely claimed to be a husband, on the other.)

The test was the infamous 'virginity test'. This officially sanctioned sexual abuse was introduced without the formal approval of Parliament or any public discussion, as an entirely new, extra-statutory hurdle. Vaginal examinations were carried out at Heathrow Airport on Asian women seeking entry as fiancées of men settled here and as unmarried, dependent daughters of parents settled here. This scandalous practice had been known to people working in the field of immigration for some years. But it only became the subject of a public outcry when an Indian woman who arrived at Heathrow Airport in January 1979 to join her fiancé was brave enough to relate her experience to *The Guardian* newspaper which then carried the story blazoned across the front page. The official logic was that if she was a genuine fiancée, she must be a virgin — although, of course, there is no physical test which can prove this. In the investigation that followed the newspaper story, it came to light that these tests had also been carried out for some time at the British High Commission in New Delhi. The government of the day feigned shock and horror at the revelation. A 2,000 strong demonstration was organised by the Asian women's group AWAZ in London on 3 June,[25] and they also organised a demonstration at Heathrow. As a result of this and the massive public condemnation, the practice was stopped.

In further response, the government promised to investigate these tests and the use of medical examinations in immigration control in general. Dr N.J.B. Evans carried out the investigation, on behalf of the Chief Medical Officer, Sir Henry Yellowlees; his report[26] over a year later scarcely mentioned 'virginity testing' but discoursed at length on the dangers of the spread of tuberculosis.

The public outcry also resulted in the report by the Commission for Racial Equality on immigration control procedures, mentioned above. The CRE, set up by the merger of the Community Relations Commission and the Race Relations Board in 1976 to enforce anti-discrimination legislation, believed that the events surrounding the 'virginity test' were serious enough to warrant a formal investigation into immigration control. The Home Office at first refused to co-operate in the investigation, claiming that immigration control was outside the CRE's remit. Only after the CRE successfully challenged this assertion by way of judicial review was the Home Office compelled to co-operate with the inquiry, which was delayed for 18 months by the court proceedings.

The resulting report, published in February 1985,[27] covered the entire administration of immigration control, without discussing its political basis. It provided the most detailed overview of the immigration system and is still of current as well as historical value for the light it sheds on immigration service attitudes. A general conclusion of the report was:

> 'too great an emphasis has been placed in the operation of the procedures on the detection of bogus applicants, at an unacceptable cost to genuine families and to race relations generally.'[28]

Successive governments do not appear to have heeded this warning.

One of the 1985 immigration rule changes, following the European Court of Human Rights decision in the ABC cases (see Chapter 3) and in the name of sex equality, was to make entry clearance compulsory for female fiancées, as it had been since 1969 for husbands, wives and male fiancés. Rather than increase entry clearance staffing levels to deal with extra numbers, in the countries of the Indian subcontinent four separate entry clearance queues were created, for people with a claim to the right of abode; spouses and children; fiancés, fiancées and other family members; and reapplicants. Those in the last queue were forced to wait two or three times as long as people in the other queues, although, as discussed, the refusals often resulted from the prejudices and incompetence of entry clearance officers rather than any fault of the families concerned.

Man as head of household: the special quota voucher system

The most extreme consequence of women being treated as dependants under immigration law is that where they have an entitlement to come to Britain in their own right, this is lost on marriage. This is the situation of those women, now called British Overseas citizens, who may qualify to come to Britain under the special quota voucher system explained in Chapter 2. They are mainly women of Asian descent from East Africa who, although British nationals, lost their unqualified right of entry to Britain in 1968 and can only travel here if they first obtain vouchers from the British High Commission. When the scheme was first introduced, the Home Secretary said that vouchers would be issued to UK passport holder 'heads of households' if they could show that they were under pressure to leave their country of origin. Heads of households were specifically stated to be men, or unmarried, widowed or divorced women.

Married women cannot get vouchers in their own right. So an unmarried British woman in Kenya could obtain a quota voucher for herself; if she got married to a Kenyan citizen, however, she would lose her claim and her right of entry to Britain altogether. She would thus have been rendered even more nearly stateless than the British men in East Africa disqualified from entry by the Act. Only in particularly compelling circumstances are married women granted vouchers. In one such instance, a woman's husband had been paralysed by a stroke and for several years she had had to manage their shop and support their children; she was exceptionally considered to be the head of household and allowed to come to Britain with her family in 1977. Divorced women, who have a theoretical right to a voucher, have suffered the insinuations of British officials that their divorces were procured to enable them to come to the UK and young unmarried women have had their applications investigated in depth to ensure they really are unmarried.

Even when a woman is entitled to her own voucher, efforts may be made to delay her. Daljit Kaur was born in Kenya. When she was 22, she went to India to marry and had three children. She was not happy in her marriage and was cut off from her family who were all in Kenya or Britain. In 1978 her husband died; as she did not get on with her in-laws, she decided to return to her widowed mother in Kenya. She was not a Kenyan citizen so she was not allowed to work; but since she had always been a UK citizen, she applied for a special quota voucher to come to Britain. As a widow, she was one of the few women entitled to a voucher, but the British authorities attempted repeatedly to stop her from entering. They alleged that her normal country of residence was India and that she should apply there (where at the time there were British Overseas citizens in her situation waiting seven and a half years to exercise their right to come here). It took over three years for Daljit and her family to win their fight to get her voucher in Kenya — formative years for her children and years in which her mother was finding it harder and harder to support the family.

When women have applied for vouchers it has been very difficult for them to travel to Britain for any other purpose, and to keep up family ties. For example, Mrs Kokila Patel, a British Overseas citizen, widowed for the past 20 years, applied in India in 1984 for a voucher, to be able to live with her brothers in the UK. She listed her children as her dependants. Four years later, when she had still heard nothing about the voucher, and when she wanted to see her relatives and attend her niece's wedding, she tried to come to visit. Because of her voucher application, the immigration officers did not believe she was just a visitor, and so refused her entry but let her stay on 'temporary admission' while they made arrangements to return her to India. She was only given formal permission to stay, months later, because the Indian authorities refused to give her a visa to re-enter India until she had been given formal permission to enter Britain. But permission was only granted for a year. When she wanted to visit her sons in India, the Indian authorities still refused — they would not allow her in to live as she no longer qualified, nor to visit as they were not satisfied that she would be able to return to Britain after a visit. But her sons, under 18 in 1984, had become over-age while she was waiting for her voucher. As she had travelled to Britain before the voucher was issued, their applications were considered separately and it took another year of fighting before they were eventually permitted to join her.

When the Sex Discrimination Act came into force in 1976 attempts were made by some of the women concerned to claim that the 'head of household' policy was a violation of the Act and therefore unlawful. But these attempts failed: the Equal Opportunities Commission was not able to investigate the voucher scheme, because it was a product of a law passed before the Sex Discrimination Act and therefore exempt from it. A British woman refused a voucher also attempted to have her case reconsidered through the courts. Her case failed, though it went as far as the House of Lords where it was narrowly lost by a majority of three to two.[29]

The Home Office pressure on these British women not to come to Britain, and even to leave the country if they had managed to gain entry for a temporary purpose, intensified in the early 1990s. Formerly they had been able to come to Britain as visitors, and then changed their plans and applied to stay on in the country of their nationality. The Home Office recognised the practical difficulties of attempting to force them out; until about 1990 it usually granted extensions of stay, on a yearly basis, followed by settlement after about four years, on a similar basis to work permit holders, or business people. Recently, Home Office practice has deteriorated, so that where a married woman is in Britain, with a non-British husband living abroad, the Home Office frequently refuses applications for further leave to remain. This is especially likely if the woman requests settlement before the end of the unofficial four-year qualifying period. The intention is clearly to force her to return to her husband abroad, rather than to give the family a chance to live in Britain.

Teresa, a British Overseas citizen born in Kenya, was living in Kuwait with her Indian husband when her parents and sisters all came to the UK in the 1970s. She visited them in 1986, when her youngest son was born here. After the Iraqi invasion of Kuwait, she and her family were forced to flee through Jordan to India. To recover from this experience, Teresa and her youngest son came to visit her family in the UK in summer 1991. Her husband and older children, Indian nationals, applied for visit visas but were refused; their aunt in Kenya therefore invited them there instead, as life in India was hard. Teresa stayed on in the UK longer than intended, to care for her sick mother, and applied to settle as she could see no future for the family in India, and wanted to make a new life for them all with their relatives in Britain. The Home Office failed to respond for nearly two years, with Teresa and her daughter Anita in Kenya becoming increasingly desperate. Her husband deserted Anita and her brother in Kenya; Anita had to live alone, as she did not get on with her aunt and was asked to leave her home. She knew that, as she became closer to 18, it would be more and more difficult for her to rejoin her mother. Eventually, the Home Office refused Teresa's application for settlement and although she appealed, it was the last straw for Anita. She committed suicide in Kenya two months after her 18th birthday; Teresa rushed out to Kenya to be with her son in his distress; but as she has been refused permission to stay in the UK, she is most unlikely ever to be able to return to live in Britain in the future.

Where women have overstayed, even if inadvertently, their applications for extensions have been refused, with decisions to deport following. No deportations have yet been carried out and it is unlikely that any other country can be forced to accept a British national unwillingly deported from Britain. But it is quite clear that the Home Office attempts deportation to ensure that husbands will not be able to join the women here. In Teresa's case, the Home Office did not believe that her husband had really left her; in fact her distress at Anita's death was compounded by her inability to contact him and tell him what had happened to their daughter.

Even when there are clear compassionate reasons why a British national needs to remain in Britain to carry out family responsibilities, she is likely to be refused. Padma left her husband and three children in India when she came to visit her parents in Britain. Her father had a stroke while she was here and her mother's severe arthritis makes it impossible for her to care for him. Padma has been looking after them ever since and has explained all this to the Home Office. It has refused to allow her to stay and has even decided to deport her to India, although she is a British national and there is no-one else to care for her parents.

Wife as appendage

Women who come to join their husbands in Britain have no independent right to stay unless their husband is settled and they too are granted settlement. Their leave is literally appended to their husband's. So if the husband is a student, for example, or on a work permit, and his wife and children are here with him, their right to remain is completely dependent on him. If he decides to leave the country or just abandons them, they are forced to leave, however catastrophic the consequences for them. If he is in breach of the immigration laws and is deported, his wife and children may be deported too — to his country of origin, even if they have never lived or even been there. A case in point is that of Mr and Mrs Mustafa.

Ayse Mustafa, a Turkish woman, married her Turkish Cypriot husband in the UK in 1974. At that time, they were both overstayers. He had overstayed his leave because his brother had been killed and his family displaced by the troubles in Cyprus in 1974; she had overstayed because she wanted to remain with her husband and had nothing to return to in Turkey. In 1976, they applied for permission to stay, knowing that some displaced Cypriots had been allowed to remain. The Home Office refused their application and made decisions to deport them both — Mr Mustafa because he had overstayed, Mrs Mustafa because her husband was to be deported. Her appeal against deportation was lost and the tribunal agreed with the Home Office that the birth of two children here, and the unstable situation in Cyprus, were not strong enough compassionate reasons against deportation. They also stated:

> It is obviously desirable that a husband and wife, who are living together in harmony, should both be deported to the same country — she should be removed to the same country as her husband, viz. Cyprus, where he has close relatives living.

So Ayse was unwillingly deported to a country where she had never been and where her husband could not return to his home town.

Even when women are settled in this country, they (and their children) can be deported if the husband is deported, following a criminal conviction. This really illustrates the extent to which a wife is considered an appendage. Even if she has no immigration restrictions on her stay (which is what 'settled' means), she may still be treated as dependent on her husband's status, not a person with independent rights. Of course, no similar provision exists for deportation of a settled husband following a woman's deportation.

However, as shown earlier, a husband also will not be granted settled status in the first place if the marriage breaks down within the first year. An example is the case of Muhammad Idrish, a Bangladeshi community worker. He lived with his wife for nearly two years while the Home Office was considering his application to stay in Britain with her. Three weeks after the couple separated, the Home Office refused his application. After a long campaign he was allowed to remain exceptionally.

When deciding whether to deport members of the family along with a man being deported, the Home Secretary must, according to the Immigration Rules, consider such factors as ties with the UK other than those that family members have as dependants of the man being deported. But the rules stress the ability of the wife to maintain herself and her children or to be maintained without 'recourse to public funds'. Since the Immigration Act came into force, 74 family deportation decisions of this kind have been made of which 26 have been enforced, none since 1983.[30]

A Pakistani couple, Mr and Mrs Khan, with three children, found themselves threatened by this policy. They were all settled here, but the husband was convicted of a serious drug offence and was eventually deported; the wife Amina and children were also to be deported because of their relationship with him, even though they had been in the country for a considerable time and were in no way implicated in his criminal activities. Fortunately, Amina won her appeal to stop the Home Office from deporting them and in 1983 she and her children were given permission to stay on.

The fact that so few decisions have been made and fewer still enforced makes it the more shocking that the Home Office did not take the opportunity to discuss the repeal of this power in the 1993 consultative document of consolidated immigration rules discussed on page 3. This document did state that deportation would not 'normally' be considered when the wife had qualified for settlement in her own right, or was living apart from the man being deported, who is referred to as the 'head of the family'. Home Office protestations against sex discrimination do not run very deep!

If a marriage breaks down, or the couple separate, when the woman is not settled in Britain, she may have to leave. Women have been forced to stay in violent, dangerous and desperate circumstances to avoid deportation. Several campaigns were organised by women in this situation. The women often had small children, no money and nowhere to go if forced to leave. In many cases, they were denied state benefits by a 'welfare' state system eager to starve them out of the country.[31]

One such case is that of Maria Otomando. She came from Nigeria to study in 1978. After qualifying as a hairdresser, she returned to Nigeria, where she got married. Her husband then travelled to Britain to study, and she was allowed in as his wife. She became pregnant, but the marriage deteriorated, and her husband became violent towards her. Eventually, she left him soon after their daughter was born but he continued to threaten her and to steal and destroy her property. Her permission to stay had run out just before her daughter was born; she applied for an extension of her stay late, after the birth. The DHSS (as it then was) refused to pay her supplementary benefit; the Home Office refused to allow her to stay. Since she had no money to pay for rent or food for herself and her baby and could see no solution to her problem, she borrowed the fare back to Nigeria and fled. But she had no home there and her parents are dead. Her husband followed her to Nigeria and snatched their daughter, whom he placed with foster parents in Britain. Maria has no chance of being allowed to return to fight for custody.

Women married to men *settled* in Britain can face immigration problems if their marriage breaks down, rendering the decision to get divorced a particularly difficult one. In one case, a Turkish woman who married a settled man in 1982 and then petitioned for divorce shortly afterwards following violence from him which resulted in her having to be hospitalised within weeks of the marriage, was issued with a deportation notice: the 'genuineness' of her marriage was (retrospectively) called into question by the Home Office because it had lasted for a such a short time.

A 'change of circumstances' may also remove a wife's right to come to Britain. Afia Begum came from Bangladesh in June 1982 aged 19, with her baby daughter, Asma. Shortly before she arrived her husband, Abdul Hamid, was killed in a fire which broke out in the condemned house in Brick Lane, east London, where he was staying. Afia had been granted entry clearance to come to Britain as a wife; she lost her right of entry once she became a widow. When she arrived at Heathrow Airport she was refused the right to settle in Britain and was only allowed in temporarily to arrange her husband's affairs. Her appeals against the refusal were turned down and, in January 1983 when her removal from Britain seemed imminent, Afia went into hiding. Most of her family are resident in Britain, except for her mother who has applied for permission to join her husband here. Her fight received widespread support.

On 8 August 1983, a group of Asian women chained themselves to the railings of Home Secretary Leon Brittan's house to protest at the Home Office's treatment of Afia. The women, who called themselves the Sari Squad, were arrested and were harassed by the police while in custody. Charges against them were eventually thrown out of court. Their action attracted widespread publicity and, as a result, the campaign grew. Campaigners organised numerous activities, including a picket of the Conservative Party Conference at Blackpool in October 1983. As one participant put it: 'The Sari Squad campaigned in a way which stressed the militancy and strength of black women rather than portraying us as possible victims incapable of fighting for ourselves.'[32]

Their tactics were novel and powerful. Indeed, David Waddington, the minister responsible for immigration, was forced into publicly explaining the Home Office's conduct: he took the then unusual step for a Minister of writing a letter to *The Guardian* to counter the publicity successes of the campaign in support of Afia.

Afia and her two-year-old daughter had been in hiding for over a year when immigration officers staged a pre-dawn raid on their relatives' flat in the East End of London on 3 May 1984. They were taken to Harmondsworth detention centre and kept there for several days before being flown back to Dhaka. Although the Home Office claims that ministerial compassion and discretion mitigate the harshness of the Immigration Rules, it ruthlessly disregarded the tragic death of Afia's husband and forced Afia to return to Bangladesh.

Two hundred people staged a demonstration at the airport in protest over Afia's removal; police attacked the demonstrators, arrested 21 of them and held them for over five hours. According to a member of the Sari Squad, members of Afia's family and campaign were continually harassed after she went into hiding; several of their homes were searched, and they were subjected to other forms of surveillance such as phone tapping.[33] In May 1984 the Sari Squad toured Europe, addressing various women's and immigrants' groups and succeeding in getting the European Parliament to approve an emergency resolution condemning the British government's treatment of Afia Begum as 'callous and showing the racist and sexist nature of the UK immigration laws.'[34]

Marriage breakdown and violence

Many women have fought back publicly against their enforced dependency. For example, Najat Chaffee, a Moroccan woman who came here to join her husband in 1979. The following year she gave birth to her son Mohssim. Because her husband was consistently violent to her she left him to live in a Women's Aid refuge, together with her son. While she was living separately from her husband, the Home Office deported him after he was convicted of a criminal offence. Najat herself, as his wife, was then threatened with deportation. A campaign was set up in her support involving many different local groups. Central to the campaign were two particular features of Najat's situation. One was that the only reason for her being under threat of deportation was because she was treated as the dependant of her deported husband. The other was that Najat had suffered from her husband's violence, and would again face that threat if deported. Within the Friends of Najat Chaffee Campaign there was a continuing debate as to whether the opposition to Najat's deportation should focus on the racism and sexism of the laws under which she risked being deported or on the domestic violence she had suffered. Nevertheless, the combined efforts of groups with different views were successful and Najat was allowed to stay on in Britain.

In 1985, the changes in the immigration rules on marriage resulted in the extension of the one-year probationary period for settlement, which had applied to men since 1977, to most women. In 1988 this was further extended to apply to all women. Yet another means of oppressing and removing women from Britain was thereby introduced. Women beaten and abused by their husbands have had to choose between remaining, often with their children, in the marital home under threat of violence, or of leaving the violent husband/father and attempting to set up on their own, under threat of removal from the UK.

The immigration rules state that, before granting settlement on the grounds of marriage, the Home Office must be satisfied that 'each of the parties has the intention of living permanently with the other as his or her spouse'. Thus if the couple are not together, for whatever reason, the wife does not qualify to remain. She then has to throw herself on the Home Office's mercy by applying to remain exceptionally, outside the rules. While there are many reasons why marriages break down, violence is a particularly distressing one; yet the Home Office has refused to announce any general policy on violence within marriage. An anodyne statement on the Radio 4 programme *You and yours* in May 1991 said the Home Office was:

> always prepared to consider individual cases on their own merits in the light of any compassionate circumstances. Factors which might be relevant in such cases would include the respective strength of a woman's ties with the UK and her own country and whether she would suffer any hardship if she was to return to her own country. Any violence or threats of violence should, of course, be reported to the police who will take appropriate action.[35]

This statement ignores the lack of any protection for abused women in some countries and the acknowledged difficulties in obtaining police intervention in domestic violence cases. A woman brave enough to leave her violent husband may be faced with deportation to a country where her stand will not be understood or condoned, where she will face discrimination as a woman alone, and have no means of support. The Home Office also ignores the possibility that she might qualify for asylum, if she would not be adequately protected from violence in her home country, a concept discussed further in Chapter 8.

There have been several campaigns in support of women in this position. Leove Bongay from the Philippines, whose fiancé threw her out of their home and refused to marry her when she was four months pregnant, and Lisa Huen, deserted with a small baby, were both successful in campaigns in 1988. Mamta Chopra came from India to marry in 1988 but left her husband after a few months due to his violence. She is now a multilingual childcare worker in a Women's Aid refuge, a job to which she brings valuable expertise and experience, and where she is campaigning to remain, but she has lost all her appeals against deportation. Prakash Chavrimootoo travelled from Mauritius with her son Prem, to join her husband. The marriage deteriorated in Britain, and Prakash had to leave him to ensure hers and her son's safety. But this was within the one year period, and she was refused permission to stay. With the help of a defence campaign and her union, NUPE (now part of UNISON), Prakash fought for the next five years to remain in Britain, but at the time of writing her court case against deportation had been unsuccessful. Many more women affected have not felt able to take the courageous step of publicising their private life. Yet despite extensive pressure and campaigning, particularly from the Asian feminist group Southall Black Sisters, there is still no sign of a change of policy.[36]

Even a woman who believed herself to be a British citizen faced removal when her marriage broke down. Naheed Ejaz had come to Britain in 1985 to marry Arshad Iqbal; she was allowed to settle and later became a British citizen on the grounds of her marriage. The couple had five children and travelled between Britain and Pakistan; on one visit, their daughter died because Naheed could not get medical treatment for her. In 1992, the Home Office found that Arshad had entered the country illegally and was not entitled to British citizenship; he was arrested, detained and sent back to Pakistan. By that time the marriage had broken down because of his violence, but Naheed was told that, because she had travelled on a British passport to which she was not entitled, she and three of the children were also illegal entrants; the youngest baby, who had never travelled, was not. Naheed and her two youngest children were detained for several days at Stansted airport in September 1992. She fought for hers and her children's independent right to remain and in late 1993 the Divisional Court accepted that the Home Office was not entitled to strip her of her citizenship on the basis of her husband's actions without going through formal procedures. But the family's right to remain has not yet been confirmed.

Paradoxically, there is one situation where a woman's dependent status in immigration law may allow her to stay in this country when her husband cannot. As stated above, until the 1981 British Nationality Act came into force, a Commonwealth citizen woman marrying a patrial man became patrial and thus no longer subject to immigration control. Such women retained patrial status, even if their husbands lost it when their countries of origin became independent. This is illustrated by the case of the Thomases.

Winston and Beryl Thomas travelled together from Jamaica in 1950 and lived in Britain for 20 years before returning to Jamaica to retire. In 1960 Jamaica had become independent so they both automatically became Jamaican citizens. In 1978 they wanted to join their daughter and grandchildren in this country. Beryl was still a patrial, because she was married to a man who had once been patrial (when he lived here for more than five years as a UK and Colonies citizen). Winston was no longer a patrial because he was longer a UK citizen. So Beryl qualified to come back in her own right, but Winston did not.

When is a wife not a wife?

As discussed in earlier chapters, women's nationality rights, as much as their immigration rights, have depended on their marital status. Until the 1981 British Nationality Act came into force, women married to UK citizens had an automatic right to acquire British nationality on marriage. The 1981 Act deprived women of this right, except for those women married before 1983 who could still register as British on the basis of marriage for a transitional five-year period until the end of 1987. Under the 1981 Act, the spouse (be it husband or wife) now has to live in the UK for three years before qualifying to apply for British nationality by virtue of marriage.[37]

Even before the 1981 Act, there was, however, a large group of women married to UK citizens who were not allowed to exercise their automatic right to register as British by virtue of marriage. They were women whose marriages were deemed null and void — that is, not recognised as existing under British law, because they were polygamous or potentially polygamous.

A marriage celebrated in Britain or between people domiciled in Britain (that is, people who consider Britain their home) must be monogamous to be valid, but English law recognises as valid certain polygamous marriages celebrated abroad.[38] Until 1982, the official view was that a marriage which took place in a country permitting polygamy, where one of the parties was domiciled in Britain, was null and void in English law. This had very widespread repercussions for Pakistanis, Bangladeshis and other Muslims.

The case of Fatima Ahmed is illustrative. She was living in Pakistan at the time of her marriage to Mohammed, who had settled in Britain and obtained British nationality. She applied to join her husband and eventually, after a long delay, was interviewed by an entry clearance officer and granted entry clearance. Two years after arriving, she decided to apply for British nationality on the basis of her marriage. She was turned down and told that her marriage to Mohammed was potentially polygamous and therefore null and void in English law. She also had difficulty persuading the local social security office about the family's eligibility for benefits for the same reason. Fatima obtained British nationality only after re-marrying Mohammed in a register office in Britain. In the eyes of English law, some marriages are not marriages at all.

But if women with polygamous or potentially polygamous marriages were not wives, it follows that the Immigration Rules for wives should not have been applied to them. Logically, they should have been treated as fiancées, women given entry on condition they marry within three months. How can you both be a wife and not be a wife? But immigration authorities refused to accept this argument, because it would have conferred a substantial immigration advantage on the women affected. They would have been able to enter without prior entry clearance as fiancées, thereby avoiding the queues abroad. In fact, these women lost out both ways. For nationality purposes they were not treated as wives, thus losing the automatic right to register as British; but for immigration purposes they were, so that they had no easy means of entering Britain.

The courts helped to break the logjam of this catch-22 situation in the 1982 case of *Hussain v Hussain.*[39] This decided that de facto monogamous marriages celebrated after 31 July 1971 in a country permitting polygamy are valid in the UK, thus entitling the women concerned to join their husbands as a matter of law rather than as an exception to the Immigration Rules. The 'social problems' arising out of not treating such marriages as valid were referred to in the judgement, having been disregarded through the 1970s by all but the numerous Muslim women affected. This judgement rendered obsolete the degrading process insisted on by several government departments of couples having to legitimate their marriage by remarrying in register offices.

The judgement also ensured that women in marriages which were in fact polygamous could come to the UK to join their husbands. Although the numbers involved were always insignificant, the possibility of polygamous households being set up in the UK aroused racist and anti-Muslim feeling. Once again under the guise of eliminating sex discrimination, the government used the 1988 Immigration Act to remove this further, negligible source of migration. The Act made it impossible for more than one wife in a valid polygamous marriage to come to the UK to join her husband, clear discrimination against a particularly vulnerable group of women and their children. The longest and most tortuous section of the Act is that which tries to explain how a woman with the right of abode in the UK because of her marriage to a British citizen before 1983 is still restricted from exercising that right because another woman has come to the UK earlier.

The only way that a second wife in a polygamous marriage can join her husband, therefore, is for him to divorce his first wife and for the second wife to apply for entry clearance as a fiancée to get married under British law, and then qualify to remain as a wife. This may well produce more problems than it solves and shows a total disregard for the marriage and culture of the family involved.

Ironically, once a polygamous marriage to a British citizen is recognised as valid, any children of the marriage are British citizens by descent from their British father and therefore have the right to travel to the UK. Their mother however has no claim to accompany them. In one appeal case, an adjudicator recommended that a mother be allowed entry to prevent separation from her young children, recognising that the effects on the children of separation from their mother would be more serious than those on the country in allowing one more woman in.

Child wives

In March 1986 two instances were revealed where overseas students from the Middle East had brought their wives with them here — and the wives were 12 and 13 years old and were attending school.[40] This situation was widely condemned; the Home Office was at pains to point out that men settled in Britain would be incapable of contracting a legal marriage with a child under 16, but that entry could not be refused to a child who was legally married to a person granted leave to enter as a student. Public opinion, however, forced a change to the immigration rules only two months later in order to make it impossible for a person under 16 to be admitted as a spouse or fiancé(e). This speedy action contrasted with the lack of reaction from the government to the efforts of Mrs Miriam Ali to get help for her British-born daughters. Nadia and Zana had been taken by their father to the Yemen in 1980, ostensibly on holiday, and had been tricked into marriage with cousins there — the sisters were aged 14 and 15. Seven years later, their mother at last rejected Foreign Office advice, and spoke to the press about her daughters' situation, which was publicised at length in *The Observer*.[41] This resulted in Nadia being able to return — but Zana's husband would not allow her to take their child, and she felt she could not leave her daughter unprotected, to face a similar forced marriage.

Conclusion

The treatment of wives under immigration law reflects the conflicting pressures between assumptions about women's dependence on men and a policy of minimising the number of black entrants to Britain. Black women entitled to enter by virtue of their marriage to men settled in Britain have encountered a variety of obstacles, ranging from intrusive interviewing techniques to sexual abuse in the form of 'virginity tests'. In many cases the right to enter has proved elusive or been enforced only at great personal cost.

So for wives seeking entry, administrative practice has not matched official pronouncements about the desirability of family unity. Where the two have been much more in line is the converse situation, where wives have lost their rights to remain because their husbands leave the country, either voluntarily or under deportation. Here, the commitment to family unity has over-ridden strong compassionate claims — wives should follow their husbands abroad, if necessary by being deported with them. Where family unity takes place abroad, it is encouraged by the immigration service; where Britain is the site for reunion or when women attempt to remain independently after marriage breakdown, the rigorous enforcement of immigration control takes precedence.

Chapter 5

Childless mothers: children kept out

All British governments have paid lip-service to the concept of the family as the basic unit of society. But governments have defined the term, not the families themselves. In the government's definition, for immigration purposes families are not only based on marriage but on a Western nuclear model. They do not include extended family relationships, step-children, children over 18 or those who have worked, or elderly aunts. Families may not make their own decisions to be together, to support other members or to work together if these decisions do not fit in with British immigration regulations. When the families are black, even their relationship to each other may be doubted or denied. This does not apply just to husbands and wives — a mother may not be permitted to live with her children or a daughter may not be allowed to care for her elderly parents. The Immigration Rules keep them apart. This contrasts with EC law, which has a much wider definition of 'family' and gives families rights to be together, as discussed in Chapter 7. The effect of British immigration law is that children are often prevented from joining lone parents and that elderly people cannot generally come to spend their last years with their families in Britain. This chapter looks at the problems women have in bringing over relatives other than husbands and in taking on the responsibility of caring for their families, whether chosen or forced upon them.

What the Rules say about children

Under the Commonwealth Immigrants Act 1962, children under 16 had the right to come to join either or both parents settled in the UK. This included step-children, adopted children and 'illegitimate' children coming to join their mothers (but not their fathers, unless their exclusion would cause 'hardship'). Children between 16 and 18 were able to come if they were joining both parents or their sole surviving parent or an unmarried mother (provided she had had the sole responsibility for their upbringing). Children between 18 and 21 could be admitted if unmarried and, if sons, still fully dependent on their parents. Widowed daughters of any age could also be admitted to join their parents, if they could be financially supported. Thus, sexist assumptions about women's dependence were present from the earliest published Rules. In the Caribbean, it was not usually difficult to show parentage of a child; in the Indian subcontinent, where there was a less developed system of documentation of births and marriages, it was harder to prove that children wanting to come to the UK were in fact related to the parents here. But in both cases, the underlying assumptions of the immigration control system often militated against children being reunited with their parents. Although thousands of children have been allowed to exercise their right to join their parents, this has often been after years of delay.

In March 1968, the Rules were amended to provide that a child coming to join only one parent could not do so unless the parent here had had the sole responsibility for the child's upbringing or if there were family or other special considerations making the child's exclusion undesirable. The point of this change was to exclude boys of almost working age from coming from Pakistan to join their fathers while their mothers and sisters stayed abroad and to stop Caribbean lone parents, usually mothers, from bringing in their children.

In 1969, prior entry clearance for all dependants became compulsory; the effects of this system and the delays and harassment it produces have been described in Chapter 4. The Rules introduced with the 1971 Immigration Act in January 1973 provided for children up to the age of 18 to come to join both parents but continued the restrictions on those coming to join just one parent. They removed any claim for widowed daughters to come to join their parents and introduced a special restriction on adopted children, who could qualify only if 'there had been a genuine transfer of parental responsibility on the ground of the original parents' inability to care for the child and the adoption is not one of convenience arranged to facilitate the child's admission.' These Rules also made it necessary for a Commonwealth citizen who became settled in the UK after 1972 to provide evidence that the family coming here could be supported and accommodated 'without recourse to public funds', a requirement previously applied only to non-Commonwealth citizens.

Changes to the Immigration Rules in 1980 further tightened the regulations governing the admission of children. The reference to sons over 18 was dropped altogether and daughters between 18 and 21 now had to have 'no other close relatives in their country to turn to'. Younger children could come to join a lone parent here only if she or he had had the sole responsibility for their upbringing or if there were 'serious and compelling' other considerations making their exclusion undesirable. These requirements are still in force. The 1988 Immigration Act extended the requirement that support and accommodation be available to all families coming to settle in the UK, regardless of how long the sponsor had been settled. And in July 1993, the Home Office published a consultation document which was a draft of consolidated immigration rules. This draft removed the last vestiges of more favourable treatment for young women, in that the provision for unmarried daughters between 18 and 21 was omitted.

The same Rules apply to both men and women wanting to bring their children to join them. But because of the discrimination in other Rules, it has been harder for women. For many periods they have been prevented from bringing their husbands over, therefore their children had to qualify under the much more restrictive Rules for joining lone parents — although the mother in Britain was only on her own because of the Immigration Rules. Furthermore women are less likely to be in well-paid jobs and more likely to want to, or to have to, give them up to care for children. So, in practice, women face much greater difficulties than men in bringing over their children.

Proving identity

The entry clearance system, explained in the previous chapter in relation to wives, also works against children. The assumption is made that in many immigration applications so-called 'children' are in fact nephews or nieces, or other relatives. Entry clearance officers often refuse to believe that children are 'related as claimed' to their parents and thus exclude them. This system is used mainly against families from the Indian subcontinent, where documents such as birth and marriage certificates may not exist for events that took place many years ago. The refusal rate for applications from children from the Indian subcontinent was consistently high through the 1970s and 1980s, rising to 50 per cent in 1983. After the use of DNA testing, discussed on pages 135 et seq, the refusal rate decreased; it had gone down to 15 per cent in 1991.

A well-publicised example of a family separated in this way is that of Anwar Ditta and Shuja Uddin. Anwar, who was born in Britain, had been sent to Pakistan by her parents when they separated. She grew up and married there and had three children. She and her husband then decided to live in Britain and came here in 1975; their fourth child was born the following year. When their other children applied to come to join them, they were refused entry. Anwar then pioneered the practice of forming a campaign around a particular family to highlight the injustice of the system. She spent five years campaigning for her children to come to join her. At the first interview after the children applied to come to Britain the entry clearance officer alleged numerous 'discrepancies' in the children's and other relatives' statements about dates, names and whereabouts of particular people. Their application was therefore refused and although they provided explanations for the discrepancies at their appeal against the refusal, this made no difference.

A long and concerted campaign followed, to 'Bring Anwar's children home'.[1] It began in their home town of Rochdale and spread — from Leeds to Birmingham, to Manchester and London. It became not just a fight to bring Anwar's children home, but a political campaign highlighting the injustice of the law and its practice. Anwar spoke at hundreds of meetings describing her particular situation, but also openly attacking the Labour government for racist immigration policies which split black families, harassed them and treated them as liars. Eventually, the publicity surrounding her case led Granada Television to make a *World in Action* programme about her. The television company paid for blood samples from the children to be flown from Pakistan to laboratories in the UK for tests, which proved, as conclusively as could be done before the advent of DNA testing, that the children were hers. The extensive public support and sympathy that this publicity generated forced the Home Office to give in and Anwar's children finally arrived in Britain in April 1981. Other separated families have been compelled to copy this blood-testing tactic, flying blood taken from children in the Indian subcontinent to British laboratories for testing.

It is particularly common for doubts to be cast on the identity of older children, nearing working or marriage age. When such children are refused entry, there is often no justification given for the refusal but the fact that the mother 'looks too young' or there are some differences in answers given to questions asked about distant family members. A gap between the birth of children may also be seen as suspicious; the CRE report quotes a letter from an entry clearance officer:

> Ask the sponsor if he can explain the gap in his child fathering between (first child) and (second child). It was during this period he first went to the UK but he made a visit back to Bangladesh from 27 October 1966 to 22 July 1967 yet no children were born as a result of that visit.[2]

These trivial excuses separated children from their parents for ever, or for years while their cases went through the immigration appeals system.

Abuse of medical techniques

Some of the indignities which women and children have had to suffer in attempting to come here are illustrated in the story of Selina Begum and her family. In December 1973 she and her sons, then aged 12 and 10, applied to come to Britain from Bangladesh. They were interviewed in September 1975 at the British High Commission in Dhaka and asked detailed questions about the family. Selina's husband had two brothers and a sister; she herself was an only child. The entry clearance officer

> observed that these family details were extremely sparse by local standards, so sparse that he could not accept that Selina Begum had given a full account of her relatives. 'Pruned' family trees seem to be becoming an increasingly common feature of applications dealt with at this office and one can only assume in such cases that the applicants are concealing material facts.[3]

Selina had been warned about the kind of problems she might expect. A common one is that a child who looks older or younger than the age on his or her passport will arouse the suspicions of entry clearance officers, particularly where teenage boys are concerned. So Selina had gone to the trouble of having X-rays taken of herself and her sons, to be used to estimate their ages. Not content with these, the entry clearance officer sent her to the Dhaka High Commission's medical adviser for further X-rays when the family was interviewed again in August 1978. According to the medical adviser, the age estimates based on these X-rays showed that her elder son was five years older than the age on his passport and the family was refused entry. The family's appeal against the refusal was not arranged until 1980 — by which time Selina's husband had decided to return to Bangladesh to live.

The use of X-rays for this entirely non-medical purpose has been endorsed by doctors at British High Commissions. Age estimation through bone X-rays was used quite unscientifically by entry clearance officers. In the UK and USA the main use of the technique has been to show the different rates of bone development of children known to be the same chronological age and it is known medically that there is frequently a variation of up to 18 months either way. In Bangladesh, Pakistan and, to a lesser extent, in India, these X-rays were used to try to date children's births. They were also used on adults to try to validate decisions about whether a woman was old enough to be the mother of her children — a practice that has been medically discredited for many years. No attempt was made to explain the danger of frequent X-rays, particularly to growing children or to pregnant women. A 'lady who thought she might be pregnant', according to an entry clearance officer, was X-rayed only on the skull in the mistaken belief that this would not affect the foetus.

X-rays were employed more and more frequently at British posts in the Indian subcontinent after 1973. There was increasing disquiet at their use for this administrative purpose. So when the inquiry into the medical examination of immigrants was set up following the 'virginity-testing' scandal in 1979, the use of X-rays was included in its terms of reference. The ensuing report,[4] mentioned on page 112, was eventually published in December 1980 and contained only an appendix on the use of X-rays. The report did, however, confirm that X-raying adults did not give any useful information about their age and subsequently this practice was stopped. Nevertheless, the practice of X-raying children continued — during 1981, 420 children were X-rayed in Islamabad and 262 in Dhaka.[5] Further pressure and a report highlighting the dangers of X-rays and their unreliability in proving age[6] eventually led to the announcement, on 22 February 1982[7] that all X-rays for age estimation would stop.

Other medical age estimates, usually obtained from a visual examination, continued to be used regularly until the mid-1980s; the CRE report recommended that they should be stopped, as they 'may be unacceptably dangerous and unethical when used for non-medical reasons...in particular, the use of medical age assessments should now be ended altogether...'.[8] They are now rarely used.

Scientific proof

The invention of DNA fingerprint testing in 1985 has greatly changed the operation of immigration control on black families. Dr Alec Jeffreys and his colleagues at Leicester University found a technique to isolate the unique banding structure of an individual's DNA from a small sample of the person's body, such as blood, skin or semen. This discovery was first used by the police to link suspects to evidence left at the scene of the crime. Later, the technique proved valuable in immigration cases: people who are related share more DNA bands than unrelated people and the DNA testing of blood samples from a child and his or her parents shows, on a probability of several million to one, that the child is related to the parents. This technique could therefore prove the relationship between two living parents and their child beyond reasonable doubt. The whole paraphernalia of questioning and suspicion built up by entry clearance officers had become redundant.

There was considerable controversy in the UK about the desirability of DNA testing, particularly within the Bangladeshi community, then most affected by family immigration refusals. Many people saw its possible routine use by the immigration authorities as an insult, a denial of the veracity of a whole community. Others, mainly those who had been separated from their families for years, thought that such scientific testing could mean a speedy end to their misery. Yet others were concerned about the effects on families if DNA testing revealed a child to have been fathered by someone other than the putative father. In a society where men are away for long periods working in Britain and where there are strong religious and cultural views on extra-marital sex, particularly for women, such women could face serious problems in both agreeing to or refusing the test.

The government took a long time to decide whether, or how, to use this technique. It carried out a survey in Bangladesh in April 1986, to see if the procedures worked, against the wishes of the Bangladeshi government which resented Bangladesh being singled out in this way. The survey results[9] were not published until July 1988; they showed that of 103 children tested, 86 were the children of both their parents and 4 were related to one parent only. This was a much higher percentage rate of genuine applicants than the entry clearance officers had ever accepted; only 44 per cent of wives and children applying in Dhaka had been granted entry clearance in 1983. Despite this evidence of faulty decision-making in the past, the Home Office delayed setting up a system, ostensibly to work out a foolproof way of ensuring that blood taken was from the correct people. Only doctors approved by the British High Commission could take blood overseas, and the Home Office checked and verified all the tests.

It was not until June 1989 that the Home Office finally announced that there would be a government scheme to provide DNA testing for certain families. Even then, the scheme did not come into force until 1 January 1991. Two weeks later, entry clearance application fees throughout the world were more than trebled, from £25 to £80, for all settlement applications. The Home Office had promised that the charges for these DNA tests would not fall on the taxpayer. It approved only two companies in the UK for doing the tests. Only families applying for the first time, and who entry clearance officers were considering refusing, were eligible for government-funded tests. Other applicants would have to pay a commercial rate (£145 per blood sample at the time of writing).[10]

Since the invention of DNA testing techniques, the refusal rate for wives and children has fallen drastically. It was 25 per cent in the Indian subcontinent in 1992; 82 per cent of DNA tests results obtained in that year showed the child was related to both parents. It is clear that the subjective grounds used by entry clearance officers in the past to refuse people and keep families apart had led to many wrong refusals.

Over-age children

The government has not rectified this injustice. The hardship of children who had unsuccessfully appealed against entry clearance refusal but became 18 and therefore ineligible to apply for entry to join their parents before the advent of DNA testing persisted. Many families had refused to accept these unjust decisions; when a form of scientific proof became available, they paid for the test privately to prove their children were related as claimed. But even a successful test did not entitle the children to join their families, as the government did not rush to reverse its wrong entry clearance refusals. Instead it delayed its policy announcement until June 1989.

When finally published, the government policy was ungenerous in the extreme.[11] Young people were only to be considered for entry clearance in the most exceptional compassionate circumstances — the mere unjust refusal in the past not being such a compassionate circumstance. Thus families remained apart and their suffering continued. Only 126 of the 701 children now proved to have been wrongly refused in the past, and who applied again to join their families, have been belatedly allowed to do so.[12]

The extreme consequences of this policy are shown by the fate of Shorif Uddin. He killed himself by lying on a railway track in front of a train on 12 November 1987, because he expected to be returned to Bangladesh away from his family. He and his three younger brothers had first applied to come to the UK with their mother in 1974, when he was 13. The mother and two youngest boys were allowed to come; Shorif and his brother Mozir were refused. They lost their appeals, but reapplied in 1980. All the evidence available at that time — conventional blood tests, independent village visits — suggested they were part of the family, but they lost their appeal again. In desperation, they travelled here to visit their parents and brothers whom they had not seen for 12 years. They were refused entry, but given temporary admission and were able to stay in order to have DNA tests — which proved they were related. But the Home Office told their solicitors that they would be returned to Bangladesh to apply for entry clearance there — knowing that, being over 18, they would be ineligible. At this point Shorif, who had been a voluntary patient in a mental hospital because of the strain, walked out of the hospital grounds and killed himself. It was months after his death before the Home Office eventually allowed Mozir to remain, his mother also having had medical treatment for depression.

Older children

Children under 18 will be able to join their parents in Britain if support and accommodation are available. Until 1980 children under 21 were allowed to join their parents provided the children were unmarried, the whole family was coming here together and, in the case of sons, they were still financially dependent. In the case of daughters, it was apparently assumed that until they were married they would always be financially dependent on their parents.

Firoza and Sultana Khan were 21 and 19 when they, their mother and their younger brother and sister applied to join their father in 1976. He had come from Pakistan with an employment voucher as a teacher 11 years earlier, but had been unable to find a teaching job. Accordingly, it had taken him a long time to be able to save up enough for a home and the fares for his family. When they were interviewed, the mother and younger children were allowed to come, but Firoza was refused because she was over-age, Sultana because the whole family would not be coming to the UK (as Firoza had been refused). When their appeal was heard, the adjudicator would not listen to reasons why the application had not been made sooner, saying this was 'irrelevant'. The two young women were not able to come to Britain. Changes to the Immigration Rules in 1980 made it even harder for older children to attempt to come to Britain. Sons over 18 were excluded altogether, reflecting the ever-increasing preoccupation with young men of working age entering the UK. Older children were normally considered for entry only if they were living alone in the most exceptional compassionate circumstances, with a standard of living substantially below that of their own country and mainly dependent on relatives in Britain.

This provision was practically impossible to fulfil for people living in a country where the average standard of living was lower than in Britain, as remittances from their family abroad meant that their standard of living was automatically raised above the average. The courts agreed that this provision was unreasonable in the case of Manshoora Begum,[13] a partially-paralysed 48-year-old Pakistani woman who applied to come to join her brother in Britain in 1984. He sent money to her and arranged for her to have a regular share of the crops on his land, so her standard of living was not below average. She was refused permission to come and lost her immigration appeals; the Divisional Court agreed in July 1986 that the rule was a 'mirage' which could not be reached and the requirement about standard of living was invalid. The Home Office was therefore forced to omit it when the rules were next changed.

When children reach the age of 18 many parents think that, as the opportunity for them to come to live in Britain has now passed, the immigration authorities will not object to their coming to visit. But this is not the case; it is in fact extremely difficult, if not impossible, for a child who has once applied to live in Britain to come to visit. Immigration officers generally suspect the child of wanting to live here and do not believe that a mother would let her child go back again, once allowed in. The result is that children in this situation are usually not allowed in at all and many of their appeals against refusal are also unsuccessful.

Firoza and Sultana were refused entry when they tried to come to visit the rest of their family in 1981, two years after their appeal to live in Britain was turned down. They were sent straight back to Pakistan. From 1986, visitors from the Indian subcontinent, along with those from many other countries, have had to surmount the extra hurdle of obtaining visas in advance of travelling. The combined effects of these measures has meant that children refused entry clearance have been permanently separated from their parents. And in July 1993 the right of appeal against refusal of a visit visa was removed, leaving families with no legal remedy against unjust refusals.

'Adequate' accommodation

Another hurdle that all parents now have to overcome before bringing their children to Britain is proving that they can support and accommodate them 'in accommodation of their own and which they occupy themselves'. Coupled with the recession and the decline in council accommodation, this requirement has resulted in a substantial number of families being refused in recent years. Although parents send details of the available accommodation to the British High Commission or Embassy where the child has applied, investigations are also frequently carried out by the Home Office to ensure that the accommodation is up to Home Office standards, rather than what the family itself believes is adequate. If the

Home Office is not satisfied, the children are refused. So the family is kept apart even though the children abroad may be living in worse conditions than they would be in the parental home. For example, Concepcion Mejia, a Colombian waitress living in two rented rooms in London, wanted her 16-year-old daughter and 12-year-old son with her; they had recently been abandoned by their father and were staying with Concepcion's mother in a one-room shack in the slums of Cali. Even if the accommodation in Colombia were adequate, Concepcion felt that her mother was too old to take on this extra responsibility. She had been told by her local council that rehousing would be considered when her children joined her, as she would then be statutorily overcrowded — but the children were not allowed to come until she could show that she had 'adequate' accommodation for them. Catch-22. In some cases, a firm offer of housing from a local authority is accepted by the Home Office as adequate, so children are allowed to come. More often, the entry of children is delayed until accommodation is actually available.

As in other areas, the Immigration Rules evaluate accommodation by enlisting the model of conventional nuclear family living arrangements. Mr Riaz Sheikh shared a large house with a friend and his family. He was not allowed to bring his own family to Britain because his 8-year-old daughter would be sharing a room with his friend's 11-year-old daughter, so the accommodation for his family would not be 'under his own control or occupied solely by his family.'

Decisions of the Immigration Appeal Tribunal have contributed to this problem. They have established that being able to provide financial support at the level of income support is not enough. Decisions on accommodation have been contradictory, with some Tribunals finding that the accommodation must be self-contained, while others accept that this fails to maximise the use of housing stock.

The housing departments of some local councils have also rendered the support and accommodation requirement more onerous by attempting to minimise their responsibilities towards families from abroad. Tower Hamlets, a London borough with 35.5 per cent of families from ethnic minorities, 22.3 per cent from Bangladesh, according to the 1991 census, has attempted to alleviate its acute housing shortage at the expense of people from abroad. In 1986 the council's Homeless Persons' Unit declared 56 families from Bangladesh to be 'intentionally homeless' and therefore not eligible for housing under Part III of the 1985 Housing Act, dealing with homeless families. These were families of long-settled men from Bangladesh, who, under the rules then in force, did not have to show support and accommodation was available before bringing in their families. As the men had previously been alone in the UK they only sought council housing large enough for the families once they arrived. The local authority's argument was that the families had abandoned accommodation in Bangladesh, which it was reasonable for them to occupy, considering also the fact that the men had joined them there for lengthy periods and they did not therefore require housing by the council. Although the Court of Appeal eventually reversed these decisions and held that accommodation abroad should not be relied on in this way, the damage had been done and many people were deterred from applying for housing.

The 'sole responsibility' Rule

In 1965, International Social Service, a body consisting mainly of social workers specialising in intercultural and migration problems, was asked by the Home Office to set up and report on 'a pilot scheme to explore the welfare and social needs of immigrants arriving at Heathrow', the particular concern expressed being with children nearing the age of 16. The main focus of the report[14] was on Pakistani boys coming to join their fathers in all-male households in the north of England. The report described this situation as 'no family life in the sense that we think of it. Just a group of men living together and going out to work — a rough existence' and, by contrast, noted with approval 'the striking difference in the whole atmosphere and in the comforts provided in one household where there was a woman to take care of the children.' The report recommended that local authorities should be notified of the arrival of immigrants and that entry certificates should be compulsory for children under 16 coming to join one parent here and should be issued only after consideration of a social worker's report on the situation in the UK to which the children would be coming. It was suggested that children should not be allowed to come if a social worker thought this undesirable. For example, to quote from the report,

> A., a girl of 12 (a cripple), was left by her mother in an institution in Jamaica while her mother came to England, promising that A. should

> follow her to England in a few months. Mother stopped writing and contact was broken. Two years later there was a request from a Jamaican children's agency to ISS to know if the mother still intended to bring A. to the UK as she very much wanted to come. The Children's Officer discovered that the mother had just had twins and her older daughter had just had a baby and all were living together in one room. After full discussion of the situation, the mother realised that she would not be able to provide a suitable home for the crippled A. Although this was a hard decision for A. to accept, it was preferable to the damaging experience of a possible rejection on arrival here.

The solution was thus to exclude a child from Britain rather than attempt to help her family find more suitable accommodation and to advise on facilities available for people with disabilities.

The Labour government took the opportunity provided by the Commonwealth Immigrants Act 1968 to introduce new Immigration Rules about the admission of such children. These allowed children in only if the parent in Britain had had the 'sole responsibility' for the child's upbringing or if there were 'family or other considerations making the child's exclusion undesirable'. After entry clearance became compulsory in May 1969, more children were prevented from joining lone parents in the UK.

Although the 'sole responsibility' Rule was designed to prevent Pakistani boys from joining their fathers, in practice it particularly affected single women from the Caribbean wanting to bring their children to join them, once they had been able to make homes here. This was explained by a Home Office official in 1976, giving evidence to the Select Committee on Race Relations and Immigration:

> the origins of this rule were... not in the context of a specifically West Indian problem, but in the context of all-male households of Asians who were bringing over boys just of working age who had parents in the home country... I think it has had an impact on the specific problem which it was originally aimed at. There is no doubt that it has had a substantial impact on immigration of children from the West Indies.[15]

The clear implication was that the entry of black children was a problem and their exclusion a positive effect of the Rule. British concepts of the nuclear family were deliberately used in order to exclude children.

The Rule was universally recognised as unjust in the Caribbean. Women had often left their children with a maternal grandmother or aunt while working, both before and after coming to the UK. It was therefore very difficult, if not impossible, for them to prove that they had had the 'sole responsibility' for the upbringing of the child. In no other area of the law do unmarried mothers have to prove this.

Even two immigration appeal adjudicators, travelling to the Caribbean in January-February 1974, recognised

> Our 'sole responsibility' rule appears to baffle even the social workers and it would be very difficult to find a single West Indian who thinks that this rule is fair or even logical. To admit children on the basis of the 'sole responsibility' of the parent may appear as illogical and unfair to a West Indian as to admit the child on the basis of the size of his feet. The West Indian working-class feeling is that at the end of the day the mother ought to win, in contrast with the middle-class feeling that the interests of the child ought to be paramount... they see the 'sole responsibility' rule as a monstrous injustice, a rule which apparently applies British standards of morality to a West Indian society which is totally different.[16]

This report also stressed the importance of social workers' reports on the situation of the child in the Caribbean and recommended that these should be compulsory, as well as that 'illegitimate' children should have a right to join their mothers in the UK. Its authors felt that this change would go a long way towards eliminating the worst perceived injustice in the Rules.

No alterations have been made to the Immigration Rules in order to implement this recommendation. In 1974, for example, half the applications for entry clearance for settlement from the Caribbean were refused.

An illustration is the story of Hazel Cox, whose parents were not married and had never lived together and who was brought up by her great-aunt in Jamaica after her mother came to the UK. For the first three months of Hazel's life her father had made some financial contribution towards her support but he was then forced by court order to pay out maintenance for another child of his by a different woman and so ceased any payments for Hazel. He later married and had six children from his marriage; the family lived 80 miles away from Hazel and her great-aunt. When Hazel was 13, her mother tried to bring her to Britain and applied to the British High Commission. They told Hazel to bring her father with her when she came for interview, so she wrote to him — the first contact she had had with him for years. When he came for the interview, he gave the impression that he had supported Hazel, having been sued once for maintenance. Hazel was therefore refused permission to come to join her mother.

In 1975 the Home Office stated that it would operate a 'concession' for children under 11, permitting them 'fairly freely' to join a lone parent settled in this country 'provided there is suitable accommodation and, if the parent is the father, there is a female relative resident in the household who is willing to look after the child and is capable of doing so.'[17] Inadequate as this 'concession' was, no efforts were made to give it publicity and nothing was done to remedy the situation of children already refused and over-age, so it had little positive effect.

The Select Committee's 1976 report on the West Indian community[18] recommended that the 'concession' should be extended by one year to children under 12, but members 'strongly believe[d] the amendment they propose[d] should be limited to those below secondary school age. In the case of older children the character and interests of the child should be major considerations.' No definition was given of these or of who should assess them or on what basis. The government's comments on the report,[19] published in April 1978, accepted the recommendation on children under 12 but made no mention of other restrictions on older children, as the system already effectively excluded them.

The 'under-12 concession' has never been incorporated into the Immigration Rules, thus allowing unscrupulous entry clearance officers the freedom to ignore it. In Ghana in the 1980s the senior entry clearance officer made it quite clear that she did not agree with this policy and refused to issue entry clearance to children who fitted within the terms of the 'concession'.

This was shown by the story of Esther, who travelled to Britain in 1978 with her husband, who wanted to make a new start in the UK, unwillingly leaving her two small sons with her mother in Ghana. Her husband had treated her badly throughout their marriage and his violence became worse in the UK; eventually she left him and formed a new relationship. Neither she nor her husband were legally in the UK; when he was arrested, he told the Home Office about her and she left the country as soon as she was able to take her new baby with her. After her divorce, she was able to return as a fiancée to marry her second husband. She wanted to bring her sons from her first marriage, as her mother was becoming too old to care for them properly but as she and her husband were living in a bedsit, she had no accommodation for them. By 1986, she had accommodation, a three-bedroomed flat where she and her husband and their two British-born children lived. Then she heard that her mother was very ill, and managed to go to Ghana to see her before she died.

During that visit, she applied for entry clearance for Kofi and Kwaku, by then aged 11 and 9, but had to return to her job before it was granted. She left the boys with their 19-year-old cousin, assuming that it would be for a short time. But the applications were refused, even though the children were under 12, the entry clearance officer stating that she did not intend to operate the policy. The children appealed in May 1987, and arguments raged between the Home Office and the High Commission about admitting them. In the meantime their cousin had begun a course of studies and was only able to be with the children at weekends; during the week they lived alone and had to fend for themselves. The British High Commission knew all this but did not issue entry clearance; when the officer dealing with the case was transferred to another post, her successor was unable to find the file. Eventually, new application forms had to be completed before the boys were finally allowed to come to join their mother in August 1988.

One further effect of the 'sole responsibility' Rule was that British officials in the Indian subcontinent invented the concept of 'courier wives'. When boys who had lived with their mothers in Pakistan and Bangladesh were prevented from joining their fathers here, on the grounds that they had not had sole responsibility for them, unless their mothers came too, family plans were changed and mothers also applied to come. Some did not remain in the UK for long, either from choice or because their husbands did not want them here. But the majority were coming to the UK to live with their families and were unjustly suspected by entry clearance officers.

A new series of questions was developed to determine the mother's intentions after reaching the UK; if it was believed that she did not intend to stay, she would be offered entry clearance as a visitor and the children refused on the grounds that both parents were not planning to stay in the

UK. Notes on an immigration officer's file at Islamabad of a woman applying in 1973 to come to join her husband are illuminating. In a re-interview in September 1976 he states:

> Story as before. Insists she is going to *settle* in UK with Zafar and Iqbal. I am certain she is a courier wife but in the absence of an admission from her or the kids... I feel we have no alternative but to issue. And as the case has dragged on for three years now we are likely to find ourselves criticised if we delay further. A reluctant issue.

'Exclusion undesirable'

The other part of the Immigration Rules about children coming to join only one parent stated, until 1980, that this may be done when 'family or other considerations make exclusion undesirable — for example, when the other parent is physically or mentally incapable of looking after the child — and suitable arrangements have been made for the child's care.' In unusual circumstances this may also allow a child to join another relative — for example, an older sister or a grandmother. As with the 'sole responsibility' Rule, a very high standard of proof is demanded and the circumstances in which a child is living have to be particularly terrible for that child to be able to come here. Many children who should qualify are not in fact able to come.

Amelia Rees and her twin brothers Keith and Kevin were left with their father and paternal grandmother in Trinidad when their mother came to the UK in 1963. She sent money back to support the whole family, as the children's father only occasionally found work. She wanted to bring the children here, but her husband, whom she married in 1965, was in the army and they were posted abroad, so no application was filed until 1975. This was refused and although all three children appealed, their appeals were dismissed. Evidence was produced to show that the children were unhappy and that their father beat them severely and could not be restrained by their grandmother, but this was not deemed to be a sufficiently strong reason to make their exclusion undesirable. So in 1977 their mother returned to visit them, the first time she had been able to afford this. She was horrified to learn from her children that their father had sexually assaulted Amelia, first raping her when she was eight years old and continuing throughout her life. Immediately Amelia's mother applied to the British High Commission to bring the children back with her, explaining why she now knew how urgent this was. But the children were again refused in March 1978. Only Amelia appealed against this and her second appeal was eventually allowed in September 1979 after consideration of two separate social workers' reports of her unhappy and dangerous situation.

Although stories like Amelia's and the consequent heartbreak for mothers and children kept apart were not uncommon, when the Immigration Rules were changed in 1980 this Rule was made even more restrictive. It was amended to require 'serious and compelling' family or other considerations pertaining in the country of origin before entry clearance would be granted to children. This was a deliberate attack on the rights of Caribbean women, the largest group of women affected by the Rule, to be joined by their children.

Since the majority of women from the Caribbean came to Britain in the 1950s and early 1960s as workers or to join husbands who had come here a few years earlier, few still have children under 18, let alone under 12, waiting to come to Britain. Thus the people affected by the rule have changed; by the early 1980s, the group of women and children most affected by the Rules about joining only one parent were Filipinos. Most of the women came to Britain on work permits during the 1970s and were later allowed to settle. Not so their families. It was impossible for these women to be joined by their families because, as shown in Chapter 3, the Immigration Rules did not allow the husbands of non-British women to come until 1985; also if husbands abroad had cared for their children, the mother could not prove 'sole responsibility'.

Clarita Torres is an example. She came to Britain to work as a waitress in 1976, leaving her six children, then aged from 5 to 14, with her husband in the Philippines. For a long time he had been unable to find work, so Clarita was the main family breadwinner. In 1981, soon after she became settled here, Clarita's family applied to come to join her. They were all refused, since she was not a British citizen born here or with a parent born here. The family saw no point in appealing against this, as birthplaces could not be altered. After the Rules about husbands were changed, Clarita considered applying for British citizenship but her two older children were already over 18, so even when she became a British citizen, the family was unable to be together in Britain.

Norma Casuga's children were not able to join her either. She came to work in Britain in 1974 and left her children with her own parents as her husband had left her. When she was in a position to bring the children here in 1983, they were interviewed in detail about their family relationships. Their father's elder sister lived close to them; she was fond of them and angry with her brother for abandoning his responsibilities towards them. They called her their 'other grandmother', though the eldest child knew her real relationship to them. When he said that his paternal grandmother was dead and the others talked about their frequent visits to her, this planted a seed of suspicion in the interviewing officer's mind. When he asked the whole family about their knowledge of Norma's boyfriend here, further confusion reigned; Norma had not dared to tell her parents, devout Catholics, of her new relationship, so it was believed that she did not communicate with them often and had not taken the sole responsibility for her children. Her children were refused visas to come to join her.

Child tax allowances

Immigrant and migrant workers are further penalised through the child benefit system. At its inception in 1977 this system was generally welcomed because it gave more money to the adult usually looking after a child, the mother, rather than giving tax relief to the father which might not benefit the child. However, it made many black families worse off. When children were not permitted to come here or were waiting in the entry clearance queue in the Indian subcontinent, at least their parents had the benefit of tax relief in recognition of the money sent back to support them. They did, of course, still have to continue to contribute through their taxes for education and health-care that their children were not getting in this country. When child benefit was originally proposed, it was intended that income tax relief would immediately stop (child benefit is payable only for children living in the UK), so that children still abroad — often because they had been prevented from coming here by the operation of the Immigration Rules — were to be doubly penalised. However, a sustained and vigorous campaign[20] forced governments to change their plans and to continue to pay child tax allowances to parents with children abroad for a transitional period after child benefit was introduced in 1977. They were finally phased out in 1982.

Adopted children

Hard though it may be for a woman to bring her own child to join her in this country, it is even harder to bring an adopted child. Generally, when an adoption takes place, the law regards the child in all respects as the natural child of the adopting parents. Only in immigration law are there further restrictions. As previously explained, the Immigration Rules state that an adopted child may be granted entry clearance to come here only 'where there has been a genuine transfer of parental responsibility on the grounds of the original parents' inability to care for the child and the adoption is not one of convenience arranged to facilitate the child's admission.'

Mr and Mrs Patel, a childless couple living in Britain and rejected as too old by adoption agencies, wanted to bring up the seventh child of relatives in India. But the baby was not allowed to come here, even though family arrangements for its adoption had been made before its birth. Another example is the story of Andrea, who was born in September 1976 in Jamaica. Her mother, Shirley Jones, had two older children, the first of whom had been born when Shirley was only 14, and no regular income. Shirley's sister in the UK, Carmen Robertson, who was 38 and had been married for 20 years without any children, wanted to adopt Andrea and bring her up herself. Carmen first discussed this with her sister when she visited Jamaica when Andrea was a few months old and this was agreed between the two sisters. Carmen sent money to her sister for Andrea while the adoption formalities were being completed. Then she applied to bring Andrea to Britain. The application was refused because the entry clearance officer was not satisfied that Shirley was unable to care for Andrea, since she had been able to care for her other children. The officer thought that it was an 'adoption of convenience' to bring Andrea here. Andrea's appeal was not heard until 1981, when it was dismissed; Carmen decided that she would return to Jamaica rather than remain parted from her daughter.

Although inter-country adoption within families has remained difficult and officially discouraged, the adoption of unrelated children from abroad may encounter fewer hurdles. With increased use of contraception, and wider acceptance of lone mothers caring for children, there are not so many babies available for adoption in the UK, so childless couples have been looking abroad, mainly to countries in central and south America, for children to adopt. Although these children should theoretically go through the entry clearance procedure, the mainly white and middle-class adoptive parents, intolerant of the delays and humiliations involved, have often just travelled back to the UK with the children, daring the immigration service to refuse them. This is not possible for children who are visa nationals; airlines refuse to carry people who require visas but do not have them, for fear of the fines which can be imposed on them for bringing in passengers without the correct documents.

In 1988-89, the plight of children in Romanian orphanages attracted considerable Western publicity. Romanian government policy prior to the overthrow of President Ceausescu encouraged the birth of children, forbidding abortion but providing no assistance in raising children. Large numbers of children had been abandoned by parents unable to support them, and faced a life in badly-resourced institutions. Many couples travelled from the West to adopt such children; the resultant publicity about the delays in British bureaucratic procedures accelerated an inter-departmental review of adoption law, with particular reference to adoptions from abroad. Eventually more safeguards for children leaving the country were imposed by the new Romanian government, thus reducing the supply of babies. Few were adopted after 1991. But the episode highlighted the shock and disbelief of the majority population in response to the immigration authorities' restrictiveness and unhelpfulness, practices which many adoptive parents from minority communities had begun to take for granted. The 1993 draft consolidated immigration rules reinforced Home Office views on adoption, by stating that adoption must not be 'solely or principally' for the purpose of bringing a child to the UK and stressing that the child's links with his or her birth parents must have been 'lost or broken', thus going against modern adoption practice.

Children and nationality

Since the 1981 British Nationality Act came into force, children born to British women are themselves British citizens regardless of the father's nationality. So are children adopted by British mothers if the adoption took place in the UK. The Act thus ended centuries of discrimination against women in nationality law. But it brought new problems for women arising out of the uncertain status of children born in Britain to non-British women. This is because the Act removed the automatic right of children born in the UK to British citizenship by birth.

From 1 January 1983 a child born in the UK is British only if either of its parents are British or are settled (allowed to stay permanently) in the UK. If the parents are not married, only the mother's status counts towards the child's nationality. Whether the child will be able to inherit a nationality or be born stateless will thus depend on the nationality law of the country of origin of the parent(s). This problem affects only a small number of people, but has potentially very serious consequences.

For example, take the case of Anna Nujomo, a Namibian student married to a South African refugee who was studying in Canada. She gave birth to their baby in February 1983, when she was in the final year of her course in London. She wanted to join her husband as soon as possible, but could not obtain any document on which the baby could travel with her. The South African authorities, then illegally ruling Namibia, would not recognise him as a citizen because of his father's refugee status; the baby was not born British and the British authorities did not want to give him a stateless travel document because this would imply he had the right to return to Britain (although the family had no intention of doing this). The one-way travel document they offered was not acceptable to the Canadian authorities. Eventually, after a great deal of pressure highlighting the absurdity of the situation, the only solution the Home Office could find was to allow Anna to settle here, so that she had a right to register her son as British and obtain a British passport for him so they could both leave.

Children born in Britain who are not British are subject to immigration control. In general, their status follows that of their parents. Children born in the UK do not need permission to remain here, but there is no guarantee that such children who leave — to go on holiday, for example — will be allowed back in. Children so affected are now still young, but as they grow up and are asked to prove their status here — for example, in order to be admitted to school or go on school trips abroad — more problems may arise. Already, children are being asked to prove their status. A local education authority does not have an obligation to provide education for a child who may not be in this country for long. Some authorities demand to see a child's passport as proof of his or her status. In one instance, a black mother was asked to produce her daughter's passport even though she had already supplied her birth certificate, showing the child had been born in the UK. The only possible reason for this request would be a racist assumption that, as a black woman, she and her family might not have the right to be in Britain. Although some authorities have a policy of not requesting passports, such requests continue throughout the country.

The older generation

The Immigration Rules relating to children have already been discussed. The Rules about parents wanting to join their adult children living in Britain are even more restrictive and it is virtually impossible for other extended family members to come. To obtain entry clearance, parents must be wholly or mainly financially dependent on their children living here and without other close relatives to turn to for support in their own country. Different Rules apply to elderly fathers and elderly mothers. A widower cannot qualify to come until he is 65, but a widowed mother may be able to at any age, provided the other requirements are met. The assumption once again is that a woman of any age may be regarded as dependent, but a man may not until he has reached an age at which he is not able to work. The secret Instructions to immigration officers clarify the pre-eminence of the relationship with a man, stating that a woman who had lived in a 'permanent association' with a man who is now dead may be treated in the same way as a widow, but a woman who is divorced, separated, or who has never married has to wait until she is 65 if the ex-partner is still alive. A woman who has been deserted by her husband but cannot prove he is dead also does not qualify to come and will have to wait until she is 65 before being eligible to apply.

For example, Jennifer Rose came from Jamaica to visit her daughter Eloise Graham in 1982. She was 63 and had never married; she was also nearly deaf. She had been living with her 20-year-old grandson, Clive, but he wanted to have his own independent life. So Jennifer Rose came to see her daughter, who had lived here for the past 20 years. She was closer to Eloise than to her other two children in Jamaica, as they had been brought up by relatives of their father's, not by her, and she had little to do with them. But the Home Office refused her permission to settle with Eloise because she was not yet 65 and because it believed that she should turn to her relatives in Jamaica for support and help. Jennifer Rose lost her appeal and was told to leave. By then she had no home in Jamaica as Clive was living with his girlfriend and their baby.

Even when a woman is a widow, the Home Office may not act generously. Gloria Cavite, a widow since 1961, came from the Philippines to visit her daughter Isabelita in November 1984. She had wanted to come in July 1983, when Isabelita was expecting her first baby, but had been refused a visa, and her appeal was not heard until the next year. Originally the family had planned for Mrs Cavite to take the baby back to the Philippines with her and look after her there for some time, so that Isabelita could continue work secure in the knowledge that her baby was well cared for. Later, she realised that she could not bear to be separated from her child, so an application was made for Mrs Cavite to stay. This was refused because the Home Office believed that her earnings from a market stall had been more significant than the money Isabelita sent, and because she has another son in the Philippines. However he is unemployed and has three children of his own to support. Mrs Cavite lost her appeal, and attempted to persuade the Home Office to allow her to stay. She continued to care for her grandchildren while Isabelita and her husband ran a small café, making this work possible. In spite of all this, she was deported in April 1993, causing disruption to her life and to her daughter and son-in-law's business in the UK, inconvenience to her son and daughter-in-law in the Philippines and acute distress to the whole family.

Emphasising its restrictive views on removing sex discrimination, in the July 1993 consultative document of draft consolidated immigration rules, the age limit is raised to 65 for all widowed parents. Again, an area in which women were treated more favourably than men has been removed.

Visiting the family

As has been pointed out, the British Immigration Rules (in sharp contrast to EC law) do not recognise any family relationships more distant than those of parents and children, other than in the most exceptional circumstances. They also do not recognise that people want to be with relatives in the UK for any reason other than settlement or a holiday visit. In 1980 a time limit of a year was placed on visits; in February 1988 this was halved to six months. There is thus no provision for the extended family to be together or to come for long visits when family circumstances warrant this, such as a mother coming to help her daughter through a pregnancy and immediately after the birth, or an aunt coming to look after children while their parents work. Black and Third World women are particularly likely to be refused permission to come here for these purposes. Statistics showed that, for example, a passenger from Ghana had a 1 in 30 chance of being refused entry in 1983, whereas one from Canada had a 1 in 7,800 chance. When visas were imposed on citizens of some Commonwealth countries, the contrast was even sharper. In 1991, one in five applicants in Ghana and in Bangladesh were refused visit visas, whereas one in 2,593 Canadian and one in 1,869 Swedish visitors were refused entry. Women are thus frequently prevented from spending time with their families and taking on family responsibilities. Yet at the same time British government policies such as 'care in the community' assume women's availability for precisely such roles.

The common Caribbean pattern of older female relatives caring for young children while their mother goes out to work has been disrupted by these immigration regulations. Children who remained in the Caribbean, for example with their grandmothers, have often been permanently separated from their mothers in Britain. Conversely, the grandmothers of children who have come to Britain, or were born in Britain, have been prevented from coming to care for them, except perhaps for short visits.

Suspicions that visitors, especially black visitors, may want to stay permanently can outweigh even the most pressing family reasons. Evelyn Booth applied to come as a visitor to look after her mother, who had suffered a stroke, as her step-father did not want to give up his job. Because she did not know how long she would be needed and because she would have been bringing her 3-week-old baby with her, the entry clearance officer did not believe that she wanted simply to visit but thought she wanted to stay in Britain. Instead of being allowed to come anyway, because her mother needed her, she was refused. Her appeal was not heard until nine months later and was then adjourned to get up-to-date medical evidence about her mother's condition. Four days later her mother died. The appeal was dismissed, so Evelyn could not even come to comfort her step-father.

Visa restrictions

Over the past decade there has been a trend towards the imposition of a visa requirement on citizens of countries from which the government seeks to restrict migration. The Home Office explained to the Commission for Racial Equality in May 1981 its view that

> a visa requirement is broadly the more appropriate the greater the pressure of immigration from the country concerned. It becomes the less appropriate the higher the proportion of genuine tourists and other short term visitors to would-be long term immigrants.[21]

In October 1986, after a concerted campaign by immigration officers over the summer about the difficulties they faced at Heathrow and the conditions in which people were kept as their cases were considered, visas were imposed on India, Pakistan and Bangladesh; Sri Lanka had already been a visa country since April 1985 (see Chapter 8). Ghana and Nigeria followed in the next months, Turkey in 1989 and Uganda in 1991. Conversely, visas were lifted from many countries of eastern Europe after 1989 — Czechoslovakia, Hungary, Poland — and imposed on most of former Yugoslavia in 1992. While the government has continued to stress that the immigration rules are the same wherever people apply, it is clear that different standards operate. In Ghana and Bangladesh, for example, the refusal rates for visit visas in 1992 were one in 2.42 and one in 3.76 respectively, a vast increase in the already-high refusal rates at ports of entry. When a Pakistani woman was refused a visit visa to come to the UK for the double wedding of her sons, who were marrying their cousins in Bradford, the case was only reported because the brides were daughters of Mohammed Ajeeb, the deputy leader of Bradford council, who was able to interest the media in the all-too-common story.[22]

The government made an unexpected addition to its Asylum and Immigration Appeals Bill of November 1992, which removed the right of appeal for visitors refused visas or other entry clearance abroad and visitors refused entry at British ports or airports if they had not obtained entry clearance in advance. This came into force in July 1993. Thus immigration officials are given unfettered powers to decide on visit applications and there is no independent scrutiny of their decisions, increasing the chances of wrong decisions remaining unchecked. In 1991, as many as 1,495 appeals against short-term visa refusals were successful, even though many people would not have bothered to appeal because of the delays in the appeal system removing the purpose of the visit. An adjudicator vividly stressed the dangers of the loss of this right, in one of the last visit appeals to be decided before the Act came into force. A recently-widowed Pakistani woman living in Britain had been advised medically not to travel and desperately wished to see her mother. In spite of medical evidence, her mother was refused a visit visa and she appealed against this. The adjudicator stated:

> This case is an illustration, if one were needed, of the dangers of taking away the right of appeal in visit applications. The entry clearance officer denied this mother a visit to her daughter whom she has not seen since her husband died, in the face of evidence that the sponsor has leukaemia. He was provided with proper evidence of that illness and because it mentioned in one letter that she was in remission he thought the visit was not urgent. This mother has a perfect right to visit her daughter whether or not she is ill and whether or not it is urgent...I incline to the view that the ECO has been too suspicious. The papers suggest that the decision was made on the day of application on the basis of a very short interview...the appeal is allowed.

Inflexibility

The inflexibility of other provisions in the Rules has also caused problems for women, as is shown by the story of Josey Thomas. She came to Britain from Grenada in 1964 and lived here until 1976. She had three sons born here, but sent them back to her mother in Grenada in 1971, intending this to be only for a temporary period. But then their father died and Josey's mother was ill, so she had to return to Grenada to look after her parent and the boys. She stayed in Grenada for two years and five months — longer than the two years allowed in the Immigration Rules to residents wanting to return in Britain to live. Josey was allowed in again only as a visitor in April 1979; until July 1984 she was fighting with the Home Office for her right to live here again. It took her five years to win her appeal against the Home Office's decision to deport her and to regain her right to stay permanently.

Josey had support in her fight from many local organisations including the church she attended and the Leeds-based Women's Campaign Against

Deportations, which grew from a series of campaigns about individuals to generalised opposition to deportation. There were meetings, petitions and demonstrations in Josey's support. Much of this support recognised that it was because she had seen her family responsibilities as overriding that she had stayed away longer than permitted. Women are most likely to do this despite being penalised for it by a male-dominated legal system.

Abeke Ajani lived in Britain for well over 15 years and her daughter Funmi was born here. The family went back to Nigeria when Funmi was a child but she and her mother returned when the parents' marriage broke down and it was clear that Funmi's sickle cell disease needed treatment in Britain. Funmi is a British citizen by birth, but her mother had been away for more than two years so Mrs Ajani was not allowed to re-enter to settle. She is now threatened with deportation and may have to leave her daughter alone to continue her life-saving medical treatment.[23]

Immigration officers generally consider a woman's family ties and responsibilities more than a man's in deciding whether she is genuinely coming for a visit. But assumptions can be made both ways: a woman who does not have children or other family responsibilities may be refused because she does not appear to have any incentive to want to return, while a woman with young children may be refused because she will have an incentive to stay abroad to work to support them. Liew Soon Lim travelled to Britain from Malaysia on holiday and to visit a British friend. In Malaysia, she had not been asked if she had any children but merely about how long she planned to stay in Britain. At Heathrow, officials searched her baggage and read her diary, which referred to her children. Immediately, the whole basis of her application was changed as the immigration officers believed that she wanted to stay out of Malaysia in order to provide for her children. She was refused entry and lost her appeal against this.

When there are no clear-cut and definite reasons for a visit, it is very hard for a family to remain together as they need. For example, Gurcharan Kaur travelled to Britain to visit her daughter, Satwinder, and her two grandchildren. Satwinder had come as a fiancée and had not seen any of her family since her marriage. The marriage had not been happy, but with her mother there, Satwinder felt better. Her husband was less violent in his mother-in-law's presence and she was also very helpful with the children. Mrs Kaur applied for permission to remain longer than a year but this was refused and her appeal was dismissed. She and Satwinder understood, with regret, that she would not be able to stay permanently, but by this time her own husband's application to go to Canada to live with two of their sons was already far advanced. She explained to the Home Office how helpful it was for Satwinder to have her around and asked at least to be able to stay until she could rejoin her husband in Canada. This, too, was refused.

As indicated earlier, since 1 February 1988 the permitted duration of a visit has been halved to six months. Applications for extensions, however compelling the circumstances, are therefore routinely refused. The Asylum and Immigration Appeals Act 1993 also removed the right of appeal against any refusal which is mandatory under the immigration rules. Thus even where there are exceptional features, a case cannot be reviewed nor the duration of a visit be extended.

Death under deportation

Joy Burke came from Jamaica to visit her mother and other relatives in July 1987, when she was 35. Her mother, Myrna Donegan, had travelled to Britain when Joy was seven, leaving her with her grandmother. This arrangement worked well, and Myrna visited Joy in Jamaica and supported her financially but there were no plans for her to leave her grandmother and come to live in Britain. Joy had a daughter in Jamaica and was settled there when she came to visit her mother, who had married and had a new family in Britain. Then she found that she was pregnant and remained in order to give birth to her son, Graeme — becoming an overstayer as a result. She had no intention of remaining until she met and married Joseph Gardner and he applied for her to stay with him. The marriage broke down, but her solicitors applied for her to remain because of the large number of relatives she had here and the studies she was pursuing. The application was refused and she lost her appeals against this and against the subsequent decision to deport her.

Joy was at home with Graeme on the morning of 28 July 1993 when five police officers and an immigration officer came unexpectedly to her home. Only Graeme, aged five, saw what happened next — but it is known that Joy was gagged with sticky tape and was restrained with a device including a leather belt with handcuffs attached. She collapsed at home and after the police made unsuccessful attempts at resuscitation, she was taken to the Whittington Hospital, where she was pronounced dead on 1 August. The post-mortem stated that she died of asphyxiation; her mother states she also had bruises on her wrists, arms and neck.[24]

Joy Gardner died because she challenged the immigration laws that did not allow her to remain with the majority of her family, even though she was fully self-supporting, she was studying and she had a son born in Britain. None of these matters concerned the immigration authorities; the Home Office decided to deport her at any cost and had deliberately arranged for the police to call on her at 7 am; its letter to her solicitor, stating that further representations had been refused, had been posted only the evening before, so she could make no preparations to leave. The police officers involved were immediately suspended and the Metropolitan Police announced an internal inquiry. Her death resulted in calls for a full and independent inquiry into the operation of the enforcement of immigration control. It also exposed a similar instance on 9 July 1993, when Dorothy Nwokedi had been deported to Nigeria with her daughter before her solicitors had been informed. Ms Nwokedi wrote from Nigeria to say that she had been forcibly deported after being arrested by eight officers who handcuffed her, sat on her in a police van, and used sticky tape to bind her legs and to gag her; her thumbs had been broken in her attempts to leave with dignity.[25]

The breakup of families through deportation is becoming ever more common as the immigration laws are interpreted increasingly inflexibly. Some women have tried other legal strategies to counter the immigration law which forces their families apart. A Sikh family, with five children, travelled to the UK in 1984 for a family wedding. While they were here, Indira Gandhi was murdered and there was widespread inter-communal violence in India, so they applied for asylum. The Home Office only interviewed the father about the asylum case, treating the rest of the family as his dependants. The asylum application was refused and appeals against this and subsequent decisions to deport the parents were lost. In January 1991 the father was arrested and detained and the mother required to report daily to the police station. In July 1991, when the eldest daughter Dalvinder was 18, a wardship application was made for her to care for the children in the UK if the parents were deported. On the date set for the hearing of the wardship application, the father was deported; the application was unsuccessful at first instance but granted on appeal.

Further representations were made to the Home Office, on the basis of the importance of keeping the remaining family together, and the mother's depressed mental state; when it appeared that these representations were unsuccessful, the mother attempted suicide, in June 1992. She continued her daily reporting to the police station; on 17 September 1992 she was arrested while reporting, with her youngest, three-year-old daughter. The child was detained for a further four hours with her mother and two hours separately before arrangements could be made to take her home; the mother was deported to India the same day. The child was traumatised by the experience; for nearly a year afterwards she screamed when her mother was mentioned, ran away to hide when she heard her mother's voice on the telephone, and trembled for hours afterwards.[26] The parents have not been able to settle in India; the father has no work and the mother's mental and physical health is precarious and they are reliant on a Sikh temple for shelter. But in 1993 the Home Office made a decision to deport Dalvinder too, thus continuing its efforts to split up a family who have lived here for almost 10 years, and who have no recollection of India. The case has been taken to the European Commission of Human Rights.[27]

Conclusion

The entry of dependants and other relatives has provoked political debate over the past 25 years. Governments have given in to different pressures at different times, walking a tightrope between calls for the denial of entry to black families from right-wingers and for family unity from human rights campaigners. In 1978, the Parliamentary Select Committee on Race Relations and Immigration was infected with prevailing views about keeping out black families and recommended, with regard to children, that future admissions of mothers with children should be limited to children under 12, except in special circumstances. It suggested that 'it may well be necessary on social grounds to adjust the Immigration Rules in the future to ensure children are only admitted if they are below school age.[28]

Another proposal for restriction — to compile a register of dependants — was suggested on many occasions from 1965 onwards. The reason for this proposal was to allay (white racist) fears about the supposed large numbers of black people waiting to come to Britain; but it was also a device for excluding those not listed. Proposals for a register were included as late as 1979 in the Conservative election manifesto. There was an outcry in the black communities against such measures and no attempts were made to put them into practice.

The 1985 report of the Commission for Racial Equality, *Immigration control procedures*,[29] showed in detail the attitudes of immigration officials and the effects these had on policies. These attitudes were taken to a horrific extreme in the circumstances surrounding Joy Gardner's death. The government dilatoriness in implementing improvements, such as approving DNA testing, which could have helped families, accelerating migrant entry to the UK, demonstrates how delay and informal entry quotas are part of government policy. The stark contrast between the family reunion rights of EC citizens and the hurdles placed in the way of non-EC long-term residents highlights the government's continuing disregard of the latter group's right to enjoyment of family life.

Chapter 6

Hard labour: migrant women workers

Previous chapters have discussed how the immigration laws have dealt with women as members of families, particularly in relation to their husbands. Popular mythology and the way laws and rules have been framed ignore the large numbers of women who have travelled to Britain independently in order to work and to support themselves and their families, following what has been seen as a 'male' pattern of migration. This chapter looks at such women and how they are dealt with under Home Office and Department of Employment regulations. Chapter 2 has shown how, after the Second World War, when Britain required more workers, recruitment took place in many different areas. Aliens required work permits to come, but the European Voluntary Workers Scheme was introduced outside the work permit scheme to fill the need for labour. The immigration of Commonwealth citizens was not restricted until 1962, so before that date people from the Commonwealth were free to come to work and settle in Britain. Because of this different legal status in the past, giving them immediate rights of settlement, Commonwealth citizens are generally referred to as immigrants, rather than as migrant workers, even though they came here to work. Those who travelled with work permits were not expected to make their homes in Britain but to leave when the work for which they were required was finished.

Over the years, the work permit scheme has altered in line with the government's view of the changing needs of the British economy. Work permits have been issued more and more restrictively and concentrated at the higher end of the job market. Citizens of the USA, Japan, Australia, India and Canada have consistently been given the largest numbers of work permits in the past five years.[1] Permits may still be issued for highly-skilled professional jobs (like people with specialised computer knowledge) or occasionally for what is seen as a short-term shortage (school teachers in some inner-London boroughs) but they are easiest to obtain at the level of board members of trans-national companies and investors bringing in millions of pounds to set up business projects.

Because the British economy also requires a large workforce in the service sector, often paid at a level which means that indigenous workers will not take the jobs, there is a tacitly-accepted pool of workers from abroad, technically working without permission, but essential for the functioning of restaurants, hotels and small factories. Besides this, there is officially-sanctioned unskilled work — the thousands of domestic workers admitted each year, working for rich foreign or expatriate families. These, mainly female, workers are doubly exploited — in their employment conditions and in their lack of access to the most elementary social rights in the UK. As the focus of this book is on the immigration laws, this chapter does not discuss the general experiences of migrant and immigrant women at work; its concern is purely with their experience in relation to the immigration laws.[2] This includes their experience of internal immigration controls in Britain because these are likely to affect women more closely in their working than in their family life.

Caribbean women workers

Until the 1970s, different systems governed the entry of Commonwealth and non-Commonwealth workers. In the 1950s and 1960s women came to Britain to work from many Commonwealth countries but mainly from the Caribbean. The Caribbean economy, geared to the production of raw materials for British manufactured goods and food for British markets, had been hard-hit by the dislocation of British industry in the Second World War. The development of local industry had been forbidden or stifled in order to keep the colonies economically dependent on Britain and to keep the valuable raw materials — such as bauxite in Jamaica and oil and bitumen in Trinidad — in the hands of the colonialists. This encouraged emigration in search of work, usually intended to be temporary, a means of saving enough money to improve life back home.

Caribbean workers established communities in the United States and Panama and, to a small extent, in Britain in the early 1900s; most people who travelled were men in search of seasonal work. After the Second World War, the numbers entering Britain rapidly increased, coinciding with an acute shortage of labour and the McCarran-Walter Act of 1952 which severely restricted travel to the United States. Britain's active recruitment of labour was to change the pattern of Caribbean migration and introduce a new dimension into Caribbean family life.

Some servicemen from the Caribbean stayed in Britain after demobilisation to work. Other people were attracted by advertising and recruitment campaigns in the Caribbean: in Barbados, mainly for transport workers and hotel staff, in Jamaica, for nursing staff and factory workers. These recruiting drives were organised or actively supported by the British government. For the first time people from British colonies were being encouraged to come to Britain to work. This included women, although they were mainly restricted to nursing and other low-paid servicing jobs. The tradition of women's powerful role within the family in the Caribbean made it possible for them to come here on their own. They travelled independently to find work and faced similar problems of racism and discrimination as men. Of course, women also came to be with their husbands but when they did so, they still needed to work to be able to support their families back home.

Gradually, the nature of the migration changed. Britain was much further away than America and it was not possible to return home for frequent visits. Caribbean women remained stuck in low-status, badly paid service jobs in hospitals, factories and canteens. Those who were trained as nurses had a little more status, but their dedication was still exploited. Life was more expensive and more difficult than expected and it was hard to save enough to send money home.

Thus women began to see their time in Britain as more long term and had to consider settling and bringing their children to join them, with all the other adjustments in their lives that this entailed. They were deprived of the support of the extended family on which they had always relied to look after children. Very few employers provided any kind of childcare. There had been increased awareness of this need in wartime, but peace had brought a reversion to the status quo. As British women were encouraged to return home, stop working and carry on with family life, workers from abroad were recruited with no social provision having been made for them. Caribbean mothers had to work to survive and to support their children, both in Britain and in the Caribbean; they therefore had to make their own individual arrangements for childcare. Private fostering and day-care were the only options available once many local authority and workplace nurseries were shut down. The authorities clearly gave no thought to the problems faced by the people they had recruited.

As has been shown, the passing of the 1962 Commonwealth Immigrants Act prevented Commonwealth workers from coming to Britain unless they had a specific skill that was in demand or a specific job to come to. The number who had such skills, or contacts who could find them jobs, was relatively small. Nurses again were an exception as there were still vacancies for training places and the training entailed working (for long hours and exploitative wages) for two or three years with the possibility of a job afterwards. The National Health Service could not have continued to function without the labour of black women as nurses, auxiliaries and doctors.

As time went on, it became more and more difficult to obtain employment vouchers, particularly after the Labour government's White Paper of 1965 sharply restricted vouchers to skilled jobs and limited the total number to 8,500, 1,000 of which were reserved for Malta. Throughout the 1960s, over 20,000 non-Commonwealth workers — mainly Europeans — were allowed to come to the UK each year. Although workers were clearly still required, racist policies meant that mainly white workers were recruited. Of course, as discussed in Chapter 2, these figures exclude the numbers of women who came to join their husbands but who also worked once they arrived in Britain. Restrictions on the numbers of Commonwealth workers were increased, until under the 1971 Immigration Act they were reduced to the status of migrant workers by means of the work permit system.

Migrant workers

The work permit system has existed since the Aliens Order of 1920; however, it was only after the coming into force of the 1971 Immigration Act, in January 1973, that it applied to Commonwealth citizens as well as to aliens. The object of the scheme has always been to restrict the entry of workers and to tie their admission as closely as possible to the needs of the British economy. Work permits are granted to *employers*, not to workers. The employer has to show the Department of Employment that the worker concerned has the skills, qualifications and experience to fit him or her for the job in question and that there is nobody already in the country who could do or be trained to do the job. If these conditions are satisfied, a work permit is issued for the named worker to do the particular job and she or he can then travel to Britain to take it up. Until 1990, the worker was allowed to stay for a year initially and then had to apply annually to the Home Office for further extensions of stay. After four years of such annual permits, permission to settle permanently (often known by permit holders as 'being free in the country') was granted. It was only at that point that the worker became free to change jobs without the prior permission of the Department of Employment.

Work permit holders are thus subject to a greater degree of uncertainty than others coming to settle, since the latter are usually allowed to stay permanently after their first year in Britain. The position of work permit holders is also dependent on their employers — as well as on the government — for permission to enter or remain. Although the permit system itself does not directly discriminate on grounds of sex, the Immigration Rules until 1989 did. A male work permit holder could bring his wife and children under 18 with him, provided he could support and accommodate them; they would be allowed to stay for the same length of time that he was. A female work permit holder could not be joined by her husband. As explained in Chapter 2, this had always been the case although there were no published rules about such a restriction until 1970. Her children could not join her either, unless they qualified under the rules explained in Chapter 5 about children joining only one parent. Thus, migrant women were placed in a position similar to European 'guestworkers'. They were deprived of family life and could be forced to leave when their services were no longer required.

An immigration rule change in July 1989 removed the sex discrimination with regard to the partners of work permit holders, business people and people of independent means joining them, replacing the word 'wife' with 'spouse'. Since then, husbands and wives have been subject to the same rules. This change was seen as the tidying-up of an administrative anomaly; it had only limited practical impact. This was because it coincided with changes in the nature of the work permit scheme. The Department of Employment published a review of the scheme in May 1989, which suggested a two-tier system. Intra-company transfers, normally for a fixed period, and people bringing in 'substantial investment and job creation' were in the top tier, where permits would easily be issued, and other skilled workers were in a second tier where more stringent checks would be made. If permits were issued, the people would be granted leave to remain for a full four-year period initially. In May 1990, these proposals were implemented. By that time, only 12-14 per cent of work permit holders entering the country applied for settlement four years later.[3]

Statistics of those travelling to Britain to work belie the popular notion that men came to work and women did not. Tables 3 and 4 show that in the decade 1963-72 nearly half the non-Commonwealth workers who came to Britain on work permits were women, as were nearly 20 per cent of Commonwealth workers. In the next decade nearly a third of work permits issued were to women (see Table 5). Table 6 shows that the proportion declined to 21 per cent during the 1980s, as the work permit system no longer catered for migration for work, but for short-term career moves. Until the 1970s, most women coming to work in Britain were from Southern European countries. There were consistently more women than men coming from Portugal to work, and until 1965 the same was true of Spain. The majority of men were married, the majority of women single or widowed.[4] The jobs that they came to do were mainly service jobs — domestic work in homes and hospitals, work in the hotel and catering industry. The 1961 census shows, for example, that one-third of the Italian women in Britain were working in service jobs (49 per cent in domestic service, 39 per cent in the hotel and catering industry) and over half of the Spanish women were so employed (75 per cent in domestic service).

Table 3 Commonwealth workers admitted on Ministry of Labour vouchers, 1963–72

Territory issuing passport: selected countries	1963		1964		1965		1966		1967		1968		1969		1970		1971		1972	
	Men	Women	Men	Women	Men	Women	Men	Women	Men	Women	Men	Women	Men	Women	Men	Women	Men	Women	Men	Women
Asian sub-continent[a]	21,546	346	6,603	521	5,275	589	2,771	383	2,600	329	2,239	297	1,614	279	1,032	140	807	123	215	72
Cyprus	431	179	347	192	137	137	40	40	49	47	55	37	47	52	49	105	38	47	15	5
East Africa[b]	90	15	70	9	31	14	13	3	13	5	11	3	24	10	49	8	62	19	31	12
Hongkong	775	59	613	51	390	51	87	19	120	13	185	22	211	29	229	38	190	37	137	30
Malaysia	49	56	58	75	59	97	32	27	19	15	17	10	19	14	44	36	32	41	15	34
West Africa[c]	1,302	76	782	32	251	20	54	14	26	4	26	10	34	16	64	17	48	29	26	11
Caribbean[d]	1,028	718	1,278	916	1,357	1,114	233	231	268	174	335	57	192	112	200	122	63	47	7	20
All Commonwealth countries	27,371	2,754	11,784	2,921	9,710	3,170	4,365	1,096	4,000	978	3,828	863	3,144	877	3,095	1,003	2,631	846	1,305	498
Totals: Men and women	**30,125**		**14,705**		**12,880**		**5,461**		**4,978**		**4,691**		**4,021**		**4,098**		**3,447**		**1,803**	

Source: Home Office, *Control of Immigration: Statistics*, London: HMSO

Notes:

a. India and Pakistan.

b. Kenya, Tanzania and Uganda.

c. Ghana and Nigeria.

d. Barbados, Jamaica, Trinidad and Tobago.

Table 4 Foreign workers admitted for 12 months on a work permit, 1963–72

Country	1963		1964		1965		1966		1967		1968		1969		1970		1971		1972	
	Men	Women	Men	Women	Men	Women	Men	Women	Men	Women	Men	Women	Men	Women	Men	Women	Men	Women	Men	Women
Portugal	156	286	193	363	329	463	336	490	294	381	252	280	314	411	574	654	510	536	338	426
Spain	1,650	3,405	2,386	3,234	2,717	2,617	2,640	2,178	2,183	1,677	2,684	1,740	2,972	1,785	3,074	1,704	2,788	1,511	1,935	1,132
Turkey	19	41	45	24	52	17	113	16	115	18	156	21	171	64	379	85	872	109	82	15
All non-Commonwealth countries	8,612	13,248	10,961	12,703	14,891	12,992	14,244	12,362	12,267	10,847	12,383	10,262	12,779	10,098	13,845	10,745	12,094	9,710	9,489	9,480
Totals: Men and Women	**21,860**		**23,664**		**27,883**		**26,606**		**23,114**		**22,645**		**22,877**		**24,590**		**21,804**		**18,969**	

Source: Home Office, *Control of Immigration: Statistics*, London: HMSO

Table 5 Work permits issued to Commonwealth and non-Commonwealth workers, 1973–83[a]

Country issuing passport: selected countries	1973		1974		1975		1976		1977		1978		1979		1980		1981		1982		1983	
	Men	Women	Men	Women	Men	Women	Men	Women	Men	Women	Men	Women	Men	Women	Men	Women	Men	Women	Men	Women	Men	Women
Caribbean	183	542	269	793	175	637	134	427	140	329	142	318	NA	NA	NA	NA	NA	NA	NA	NA	NA	NA
Cyprus	94	14	90	29	172	69	53	18	48	17	52	17	NA	NA	NA	NA	NA	NA	NA	NA	NA	NA
Hong Kong	237	75	304	126	862	163	563	93	395	82	423	75	388	81	145	43	172	62	275	39	235	258
India	505	122	623	157	469	128	347	69	299	51	465	64	490	84	419	60	NA	NA	NA	NA	NA	NA
Philippines	368	2,327	246	745	428	1,558	432	1,618	316	1,488	203	409	NA	NA	9	13	8	17	42	17	6	9
Portugal	510	531	474	342	592	309	372	150	214	93	NA	NA	NA	NA	46	18	31	13	25	19	68	24
Spain	2,609	1,596	2,139	1,268	1,737	991	635	300	356	136	372	84	NA	NA	87	25	110	37	94	27	162	38
All countries: Commonwealth and non-Commonwealth	18,915	13,879	20,548	12,497	18,667	11,411	13,307	7,163	12,527	5,887	14,535	4,614	13,183	3,759	11,927	2,734	13,028	2,823	12,962	2,492	13,175	2,732
Totals: Men and Women	**32,794**		**33,045**		**30,078**		**20,470**		**18,414**		**19,149**		**16,942**		**14,031**		**15,851**		**15,454**		**15,907**	

Source: Department of Employment Statistics, 1973–83

Note:

a. Home Office statistics for entry of workers do not distinguish between men and women after 1972. Department of Employment statistics are for permits issued only, not for numbers actually admitted. These figures include long- and short-term permits and permissions given to workers already in Britain.

Table 6 Work permits issued to non-EC workers, 1984-92

Country issuing passport (selected countries)	1984 Men	1984 Women	1985 Men	1985 Women	1986 Men	1986 Women
USA	3,816	693	5,124	967	5,783	1,073
Japan	788	62	1,159	89	1,473	116
India	291	54	408	69	467	61
Australia	266	47	385	96	445	105
Canada	273	39	398	73	429	121
Sweden	264	48	310	49	379	73
All countries	8,204	1,644	11,479	2,159	13,316	2,546
Grand totals (men and women)	9,848		13,638		15,862	

Country	1987 Men	1987 Women	1988 Men	1988 Women	1989 Men	1989 Women
USA	6,489	1,334	7,879	1,960	8,639	2,068
Japan	1,530	151	1,822	234	1,949	236
India	693	121	800	119	823	137
Australia	536	116	785	214	820	241
Canada	425	98	615	189	720	199
Sweden	370	59	471	80	526	108
All countries	14,576	2,872	18,014	4,170	20,530	4,972
Grand totals	17,448		22,184		25,502	

Country	1990 Men	1990 Women	1991 Men	1991 Women	1992 Men	1992 Women
USA	9,859	2,234	8,925	1,926	9,593	2,024
Japan	2,206	335	2,113	210	1,809	221
India	1,121	117	1,077	233	1,378	282
Australia	952	361	794	284	776	291
Canada	739	213	596	146	747	169
Sweden	525	150	432	115	462	106
All countries	23,941	6,002	21,089	5,377	21,993	5,461
Grand totals	29,943		26,466		27,454	

Source: Department of Employment Overseas Labour Section

The Rochdale case

Female migrant workers first became an important public issue in 1973, when revelations about the living and working conditions of a group of Filipino women in Rochdale resulted in government investigations and then in a ban on unskilled work permits for Filipinos. Filipino immigration to Britain was relatively new. It was only in the late 1960s, after Commonwealth immigration had been severely restricted, that British employers turned to the Philippines as a source of cheap labour. A total of 252 work permits were issued to Filipinos in 1968 and 367 in 1969; this rose to 2,677 in 1972. Over 80 per cent of Filipinos coming to work were women, recruited to fill jobs traditionally done by poorly paid indigenous female labour.

During the late 1960s, employers in the clothing industry began to recruit Filipino women. In 1971, the Alderglen factory, which made quilted housecoats and bedspreads, started recruiting in the Philippines.[5] It had transferred its operations from London and Hampshire to Rochdale to save labour costs but, because of the level of wages paid, had been unable to keep workers for more than a few weeks on average, with 180 per cent annual staff turnover. Eighty-five per cent of employees in the clothing trade in Rochdale were women, a high proportion young school-leavers. Men in the industry earned 45 per cent more than women and the average pay for women in 1971 was £17.50 per week compared to the average pay for women in manufacturing industry of £19.60.

The Filipino women who were brought to Rochdale had come in response to advertisements placed by the company in Manila offering to fly women over here to jobs at £40 per week — but not mentioning that only a very skilled machinist, on piecework conditions, would be able to earn this. The women travelled to Britain in two groups, one of 60 women in October 1971 and another of 66 in November 1972. They earned a basic wage of £12. As some of the first group had left the factory when they found this out, the second group had £1 stopped from their wages each week in order to pay back the money for their air tickets. The company had provided housing for them, but it was very overcrowded and inadequate. As most of the women were young and single, there was a public outcry when their story was revealed. Its paternalism ranged from the continued references to the Filipinos as 'girls' to the concern of the then community relations officer in Rochdale that many of them had found accommodation with single Pakistani men. But the fact that the women had travelled across the world to work was not questioned; the company's floor manager stated that 'they were no problem. They were the best girls we have ever had — keen, hard-working, early-to-bed, early-to-rise types.'[6]

In the wake of the publicity around Alderglen, the government announced a ban on work permits for such workers from the Philippines on 11 January 1973. This was intended to give the governments of the UK and the Philippines time to work out some compromise, as both wanted the export of workers to continue but could not officially support the exploitation that had taken place. The benefits for the British economy have already been discussed. For the Philippines, the arrangement was advantageous because of the economy's dependence on remittances sent back by migrant workers. When there were further revelations about the exploitation of Filipino domestic workers in January 1974 there was yet another ban on work permits for Filipinos, until safeguards for their employment could be instituted. In February 1975 the ban was lifted, though the only 'safeguards' agreed were that the lower age limit for permits was raised to 20 and workers had to provide evidence of at least a year's work in a similar job abroad. These changes made no difference to the working conditions of those allowed in. This was because the economic situation had not changed since 1972. According to a newspaper article, the need for labour in service industries had outweighed fears of the 'social consequences of introducing a new racial group, especially of young girls, into areas where housing is scarce and unemployment high.'[7]

Quotas for workers

By the end of the 1960s, the number of workers still able to enter Britain gave rise to concern at the Department of Employment. Restrictions were therefore placed on non-Commonwealth workers which were similar to those imposed on Commonwealth workers since 1965. On 11 November 1971 it was announced that, as from 1 January 1972, no more unskilled men would get work permits. An exception was made for the hotel and catering industry, which was still allowed to recruit a small quota of overseas workers, 5,500 work permits in 1972 and only 3,500 in 1973. This was 'intended to give the industry time to recruit and train additional indigenous labour to meet its needs,'[8] but was in direct conflict with racist demands being voiced at the time to stop immigration altogether. As Robert Carr, the Home Secretary, expressed it

> We cannot have it all ways... I have no doubt that because of the social problems in this country and the need to maintain good community relations it is right that we should now limit immigration to the inescapable minimum and that is a very small number. But we cannot do that and then wonder why we are running into trouble with many services — because it is not only buses and trains; it is hospitals and everything in between — when in the last long period of full employment in this country this is how we met the need.[9]

In a press release issued on 10 February 1975, the Department of Employment announced that women were to be included in the hotel and catering quota and that a quota would also be introduced to limit the numbers of resident domestic workers. In August 1977, in an explicitly racist change, it was announced in Parliament that non-European women were no longer permitted to come as resident domestics.[10] The quotas were progressively reduced, until the hotel and catering one was ended in March 1979 and the resident domestic one at the end of the year.

This was a result of the Department of Employment's belief that employers should be able to attract local labour, at a time of rising unemployment. Employers had opposed the reductions in the quota, because of the difficulties of recruiting local labour to work in generally unacceptable conditions. The unions had initially opposed the continuing entry of unskilled migrant workers altogether, on the ground that they depressed conditions for other workers by accepting lower rates of pay.

After the ending of the special quota of work permits the number of women coming to Britain to work declined. In 1976, 35 per cent of permits issued were to women; by 1980 the figure was only 19 per cent. According to the Department of Employment, this

> reflects occupational changes in permit issues away from semi-skilled work in the hotel and catering industry or as resident domestic workers towards professional and highly skilled occupations, in which female workers form a comparatively small proportion.[11]

By 1982 the only sector where a significant number of women were still being granted permits was the National Health Services usually as professional workers.

Thus, the work permit system had effectively blocked the entry of all non-professional workers from outside the EC. But this no longer sufficed. Economic recession in Britain led to a situation where racist calls for repatriation and the needs of industry no longer conflicted; workers from abroad were increasingly redundant. By now, though, the only way of reducing their numbers still further was by getting rid of those already in Britain.

On the road to repatriation

The main group of migrant workers thus targeted were resident domestics in private homes, hospitals and hotels. The majority were single women from the Philippines, though Latin American, Moroccan, Portuguese and Turkish workers were also affected. Because of the relatively small size of the Filipino community in Britain (estimated at about 20,000) and the large proportion of resident domestics among them, the security of the entire community was put in jeopardy.

The Department of Employment stipulated that resident domestic permits would be granted only to single people or to married couples coming to work together in a joint post. Workers with children under 16 were ineligible for such permits. The official explanation for this was that employers would not have to provide family accommodation and that children should not be kept separated from their parents. The unstated advantage of this regulation was that there would be no further immigration commitment and no educational or other social cost to Britain in respect of the workers' children.

These regulations were explained in the Department of Employment's information leaflets sent to employers in Britain. They were not, however, widely known to the women and men needing to migrate in search of work. Papers were filled in by employers, who had no personal knowledge of the woman they wished to employ; she in turn would have no idea of what they had written. In the sending countries, particularly the Philippines, many small employment agencies had sprung up to service the export of labour and to deal with the paperwork, exploiting the vulnerability of the people and charging inflated fees for their services. Some Filipino women, for example, were told that the particular employer with whom they might be placed did not like children, so they should not mention them; one woman who filled in all her application forms as Mrs

Emilia Mendosa had all her documents sent back to her as Miss Mendosa with no explanation for this 'mistake'. It became well known that some domestic workers did have children[12] but no action was taken against them until they were caught within the ever-increasing category of 'illegal entrant'.

Until 1975, this term had been applied only to people entering the UK without passing through immigration control at all, usually by landing on a deserted beach at night. In 1975 the Home Office first expanded the term to include someone who had passed through immigration control but had obtained entry by lying, and the courts upheld this definition. By 1980, a person who obtained entry when the immigration officer was not aware of all the relevant facts had become an illegal entrant. No deceit was necessary; it was enough not to have volunteered unasked-for information even if the person had no idea that this information might be relevant.[13]

Hundreds of resident domestic workers found themselves under threat of removal by the Home Office after Florida Claveria[14] was told that she was an illegal entrant in March 1978. The reason given was that she had had children before coming here as a resident domestic worker; the courts upheld this decision in November 1979. This meant that many women who were unaware of having breached any regulations were suddenly threatened with expulsion from the country. Virginia Santiago, for example, widowed when her husband died in an accident, left her five children with her parents and went to find work in Manila to support them all. She worked in a hotel for several years but found that the money she earned was not enough to support her family. So when she found out that British hotels were looking for Filipino workers she went straight to an employment agency that was advertising jobs in Britain. She paid their fees and was found a resident chambermaid's job in a London hotel; nobody asked her if she was married or had children and she came here in 1973. When she was allowed to settle after four years she wanted to bring her children to join her as her parents had died and the children were being cared for by a neighbour. She was told she did not have enough accommodation for them; with great difficulty, working hours of over-time, she managed to raise the money for a mortgage; her children again applied to come. This was in 1979 and Virginia was told that she was an illegal entrant who would be removed to the Philippines. It was not until September 1980, after a hard and sustained fight with the Home Office, that this threat was lifted and Virginia was told that she could stay here, and be joined by her children.

Shock waves went through the Filipino community as the Home Office threatened over 400 people, mainly women, with removal as illegal entrants. The legal challenge to Florida Claveria's removal had failed, so the Migrants Action Group (MAG) began its Resident Domestics Campaign for justice for these women.

MAG, an umbrella organisation founded by migrant workers and other groups in 1978 to campaign for improved living and working conditions for migrant workers, was in contact with many individuals under threat and with organisations working with them, such as the Filipino Chaplaincy and the Joint Council for the Welfare of Immigrants. The people directly threatened with removal were the most central part of the campaign; they were supported by representatives from several trade unions, church bodies, advice agencies and others campaigning against racism. A new organisation, Pagkakaisa ng Samahang Pilipino, was formed within the Filipino community, to warn people about possible problems and to spearhead the community's resistance.

The campaign first tried to inform as many people as possible, by producing leaflets and organising meetings, about the threat from the Home Office. It operated both within the migrant communities (so that people would not innocently put themselves at risk) and throughout the country (so that more pressure would be put on the government). A pamphlet was published at the end of March 1980[15] and on television *The London Programme* focused on two women told they would have to leave. The campaign thus attracted favourable publicity and support from other individuals and organisations against the Home Office witchhunt.

Two demonstrations were organised in 1980. Public statements and petitions were sent to the Home Secretary. The trade union officials involved in the campaign raised the matter at the 1981 TUC Conference, and the Labour Party Conference of that year passed a resolution committing the next Labour government to stop the expulsions and to allow back anyone forced out of the country for this reason. Leafleting the Tory Party Conference did not bring such a concrete result!

In the same year, the Home Office's offensive widened, to include people who had come to work in hotel and catering jobs under the special quotas of permits issued to the industry. The Home Office alleged that many of them had not obtained the required number of years' prior work experience abroad and therefore that they had entered illegally. The campaign published a second pamphlet[16] on this issue in March 1981. But it took the Home Office another year, until March 1982, to announce that all but 20 of the people under threat of removal would be allowed to stay. These 20 people had to wait until November 1983 before at last being told they could remain. The House of Lords had decided[17] that it was necessary for a person to be *aware* that deception had been practised and for that deception to be material to the entry before he or she could be treated as an illegal entrant; as a result of this decision and the success of the campaign, over three-quarters of the people under threat were allowed to remain.

During its last months, the campaign had plenty of time to assess its effectiveness. The Filipino community had become more aware not only of its vulnerability, but also of its power: several community organisations were established during this time and the campaign also had a positive impact on the wider community.

The Home Office's attack on these women's right to stay in Britain was strongly resisted and they gained widespread popular support. Never before had the Home Office's attempts to expel a group of immigrant women been so visible. The way in which women from the Indian subcontinent had been delayed and denied entry had been largely hidden from public view. Groups not previously well known for their concern for migrant workers — the trade unions in the hotel industry, for instance — expressed their support and urged the Home Office to act with compassion. In 1982 the Home Office took a policy decision no longer to penalise this group of workers by looking back into their original work permit applications, but to accept them as legally settled people. Their children's applications for entry would be considered in the normal way. However this did not guarantee success, as the 'sole responsibility' rule often presented an insurmountable hurdle. And the policy was not extended to women who were not yet settled; Aura Lim, who had come as a resident domestic worker in 1977 and married in 1979, lost her fight with the Home Office and the Department of Employment to allow her to continue to live and work in Britain after her marriage.

Au pairs

As previously explained, work permits for resident domestic work were abolished by 1980. But one group of women was still allowed to come in for domestic work — au pairs. Until 1993, these were defined as 'girls' between 17 and 27. An au pair is supposed to live as a member of an English-speaking family, to help out with the household chores and children for 'pocket money' of about £50 per week, and to attend English language classes. A limitation to Western Europe was introduced in 1980 and justified by the government on the grounds that, since the ban on resident domestic work permits for non-Europeans in 1977, women who came from outside Europe as au pairs were more likely to be treated as servants, but its basis is clearly racist. After the collapse of Communisim, Eastern European countries were added to the au pair list.

If a non-English-speaking family wants an au pair, this is likely to be impossible. A woman is unlikely to be able to come to stay with relatives as an au pair as this will not be seen as a 'genuine' arrangement. Two years is the maximum time an au pair can remain here and there is no possibility of her settling into longer-term work. Between 1973 and 1991, 128,118 non-EC women have come to the UK as au pairs. The numbers rose slightly in 1978 — from 5,650 the preceding year to 6,290 and again in 1980 to 7,110. This increase indicated that au pairs were being used as substitutes for the resident domestics who could no longer be granted permits.

No justification was ever given as to why a man could not be an au pair. Indeed, the papers on 31 August 1992 were full of the story of Johan Egelstedt, a Swedish man who had come to be an au pair but had been refused entry to Britain on grounds of his sex. The outcry resulted in him being admitted for six months, to live with the family as a 'guest'. The then Home Secretary, Kenneth Clarke, publicly committed the government to altering the rules when the next convenient opportunity arose.[18] This occurred in July, so that from 1 September 1993,[19] young men may also be au pairs. The arrival of the first male au pair, Drazen Vitolovic from Croatia, was reported the next day.

Domestic slavery

There is another group of women who still come to Britain as servants, unofficially, but who are in a much more vulnerable position than au pairs. They are domestic servants in rich households. The Immigration Rules do not provide for servants (except for those of diplomats) to enter the UK. Nevertheless immigration officers often turn a blind eye and allow them to come in, either as part of the household of the employer, or as visitors. The Home Office's position in relation to this practice contradicts its usual strict adherence to the Immigration Rules. As David Waddington, then Minister of State at the Home Office, explained:

> there is no specific provision under the Immigration Rules for the admission of private servants of people who do not enjoy diplomatic status, but they may be admitted without a work permit if they are accompanying or joining an employer whom they have served overseas. Admission in such cases is on the basis that the employee will be expected to leave the country with the employer or on prior termination of the employment.[20]

If they enter Britain as visitors, they are immediately placed in a position of illegality, since the conditions of a visitor's stay prohibit employment. These women are trapped in a situation of extreme exploitation and vulnerability, as none of the laws which apply to British workers, in terms of employment protection, apply to them in practice. If they make any complaint, they will lose their jobs; if they lose their jobs they also lose their claim to remain in Britain and therefore can only survive by working 'illegally'. If they are caught, they are often forced to leave the country.

This practice, which amounts to domestic slavery, is only allowed by governments here because it benefits wealthy people, not the women themselves. It is part of a world-wide phenomenon of exploitation of women through domestic labour. Because of their physical isolation and the terms under which such women enter Britain, organised opposition and resistance is extremely difficult.

Maria Gonzalez's experience was fairly typical. She arrived at Heathrow Airport in January 1982 from Bombay. She was with a married couple who told the immigration officers that she was a member of their family coming to Britain for a visit and that they would take care of her. She was allowed in as a visitor, which entitled her to stay in Britain for six months, but not to work here. The truth was that Maria had been hired by this couple as their domestic servant for their home in North London. Though there was no written contract, they had promised her 800 rupees (£50) per month, plus her board and lodging, in exchange for which she was to do the housework and look after the children of the family.

Once in Britain, Maria was told that they would pay her only £40 per month; however, she did not receive even this. Just before the six months were over, her employers took her to Paris for a few days, then brought her back to Britain and again she received a six months' visitor's visa, without the right to work. This happened on more than one occasion. Having no set hours of work, she was made to labour from morning till night with no fixed time off. Finally, in September 1983, she decided that she had had enough and left. She spoke no English and knew nothing of London. She was found wandering in an Underground station by someone who took her to a Citizens' Advice Bureau who then found her temporary accommodation. Eventually, her employers agreed to pay most of the money they owed her, return her passport (which they had been holding) and give her a ticket to Bombay. Maria was in fact luckier than some. There are women brought to Britain from abroad as servants who are not paid at all, who are confined to the house and, in some cases, beaten and sexually assaulted.[21]

The issue of domestic slavery achieved nationwide publicity in 1989 with the case of Mrs Laxmi Swami, employed by two princesses of the Kuwaiti royal family. As explained by Anti-Slavery International:

> she was eventually brought to London by the princesses and stayed with them in a mansion in Bayswater, one of London's more affluent districts. There, for four years, she lived what has been described as a life of hell. She was deprived of food, frequently had only two hours of sleep a night, and her 'bedroom' was the floor outside the locked kitchen. She was never allowed out, received no wages and was whipped every day. She is scarred for life. On one occasion the two princesses forcibly removed her two gold teeth. Her passport was also taken from her.[22]

After four years, she managed to escape and to get help. While the conditions under which she lived may be extreme, the most unusual aspects of her case are firstly that she was brave enough to go to court, fight for compensation and eventually win £300,000 and secondly that the Home Office allowed her to remain in Britain thereafter.

The Independent newspaper deliberately attempted to increase public knowledge of the position of domestic workers with a series of articles in 1991-92. Typical were the stories of Francisca Ifekaozor and Florence Mokolo, brought successively from Nigeria by Elizabeth Onwualu, in order to look after her elderly mother, with promises of being able to study in the UK but then treated as slaves and beaten with belts and shoes, not allowed out of the house let alone go to college, and not given their wages. Francisca escaped through a bathroom window in February 1991, leaving her passport. Ms Onwualu used it in April to bring in Florence, who managed to escape in November. Because the two women were brave enough to speak out against their employer, Elizabeth Onwualu was convicted of assault and assisting illegal entry in February 1993.[23]

Kalayaan (which means 'freedom' in Tagalog, the main language of the Philippines) was formed in June 1987 as a support group for domestic workers forced to leave their employers due to ill-treatment and with no chance of qualifying to remain in the UK. Many women in this situation are Filipinos; but women from many other countries, including India, Nepal, Nigeria, Ghana, Sierra Leone, Sri Lanka are also in similar situations. Perhaps it was because the Filipino community was more close-knit and the women in general highly educated and fluent in English that they formed a group first.

Kalayaan welcomes women of all nationalities and one of its best-publicised campaigns concerned a woman from Nepal, Mahesh Kumari Rai. She travelled to Britain in 1984 with her Indian employers and worked for them here for more than two years. During that time she received no pay, was forced to work long hours and was psychologically and physically abused. After she escaped, she obtained legal help to claim her wages; she received £1349 by way of out of court settlement — which worked out at £13 a week. She was arrested in 1991 and detained for six months while Kalayaan campaigned on her behalf. She was released, but her campaign failed and she was eventually deported in October 1992.

In 1990 the Home Office responded to criticism of its unregulated practice in respect of domestic workers by announcing official regulations for the unofficial 'concession'. These came into force in May 1991. When domestic workers applied for entry clearance, which became compulsory, leaflets were to be given to the employers and to the workers explaining the nature of the concession (so far available only in English and Arabic). Visa officers were to ensure that they interviewed the woman on her own, separately from her employers, to be sure that she understood what she was doing. Only women aged at least 17 who had been employed by the same employers for at least a year would be permitted to accompany them to the UK. This provision was based on the belief that if a woman had been employed so long her conditions could not be that bad and she would not attempt to escape from her employers in the UK. This of course ignores the reality of the situation in many Gulf states.

Women allowed in under this 'concession' are given permission on a yearly basis and the permission is renewed only if the work for the same employer continues. After four years, the woman may qualify for settlement. The Home Office does not keep statistics of women allowed in under this 'concession', but has stated that 8600 entry clearances were issued between January and August 1992 by 'the main posts which issue entry clearance to such workers'.[24] This figure is likely to be an underestimate. But the Home Office has refused to make the only alteration which could significantly empower these domestic workers — giving them the same opportunity as work permit holders to change jobs.

Nurses from abroad

It has already been shown that nurses from the Caribbean were among the first workers to come to Britain from the Commonwealth after the Second World War. To this day women (and to a lesser extent men) are still coming to this country to train as nurses, though in decreasing numbers. Nursing training has had a strange status, between that of a worker and a student. Before 1973, people from non-Commonwealth countries who came to train as nurses were treated as workers and a permit had to be obtained from the Department of Employment for them. By contrast, Commonwealth citizens were treated as students while they were training and needed permission from the Department of Employment only if they decided to work here after qualifying.

The effects of this were felt by the student, not by the employing hospital, as some qualified nurses had to work for longer than others before they could be allowed to settle. Under the 1971 Immigration Act, the situation changed so that all were treated as students — a Filipino pupil nurse who started her training in September 1972 became eligible for settlement after four years, but one who started in March 1973 was not eligible for six years.

Nurses were recruited from abroad because of the needs of the National Health Service, not in order to provide them with training which would be of use in their countries of origin. This is shown both in the courses of training that they followed and in the numbers of trainee nurses accepted. Most nurses from overseas came to follow State Enrolled Nurse (SEN) or Registered Mental Nurse (RMN) courses. The SEN qualification is not recognised anywhere in the world outside Britain and is of inferior status to the State Registered Nurse (SRN) qualification. More and more O-levels or equivalents were required for entry to SRN courses but as the qualifications of overseas candidates were frequently not recognised, these people were channelled into SEN courses where they provided two years' hard work for the NHS and gained little in return. The same applied with RMN courses and the many overseas trainee nurses in hospitals for the mentally handicapped or ill — there were often no equivalent facilities in their home countries and the qualifications they gained would not be of use there.

The number of people accepted for training as nurses has fluctuated with demand in the NHS. In 1973, there were over 20,000 trainee nurses from abroad in Britain; this dropped to 17,000 in 1975, under 12,000 in 1977 and only 4,174 in 1983. Some health authorities attempted to discourage applicants from abroad by implying that they would have to satisfy the criteria of the work permit scheme before they were accepted for training; the vast fall in numbers suggested that this succeeded.[25] It is increasingly difficult for overseas nurses to get a job after qualifying. Women who had assumed that this would be automatic were shocked when permits were not issued and the hospitals that had trained them were not prepared to deal with the bureaucratic problems of getting work permits for them. In fact, the belief that overseas nurses would always be allowed to stay here was so widespread and strong that when a Trinidadian SEN, Merle Ali, was refused a work permit after completing her training in October 1976, the case made front-page headlines in Birmingham.[26]

Health authorities were often confused about the immigration distinctions between trainee and qualified nurses. In February 1983, Newham Health District in east London decided it would be unable to offer any jobs to the overseas nurses qualifying that summer and sent out a letter to them implying that this was because 'the Home Office no longer issues work permits for overseas applicants to Staff Nurse posts.'[27] In fact, the only change in practice was the Department of Employment's increasingly rigid adherence to the work permit regulations; the authority was responding to general pressure to cut down on staff and non-British nurses were the first to suffer. The overseas nurses in Newham, mainly Malaysian women, fought together for the right to have at least the six months' post-qualification experience necessary for them to follow further training courses. This was achieved, but no guarantees of long-term employment were given.

Nurses were particularly affected by the 1990 immigration rule change making it impossible for visa nationals to change their status in the UK to become students. Women who had qualified in Britain and then returned to their countries of origin to work had been able to come back to the UK and take further professional training courses, usually entering as visitors in order to find suitable courses. British High Commissions often do not explain the regulations fully and women have been shocked to find they cannot then enhance their professional qualifications in Britain. Returning to Nigeria or Ghana to obtain a student visa and then coming back for the course is difficult and impractical.

After training for the SEN qualification was phased out during the late 1980s, the numbers of overseas nursing students decreased further. Hospitals trained fewer nurses because of funding cuts, and the possibility of overseas student nurses gaining work permits at the end of their training diminished. By that time, there were no nursing vacancies in London and permits were only issued for jobs in unpopular areas of nursing in remote hospitals. In February 1993 the Department of Employment stopped classifying nursing as a profession with a 'skills shortage' making work permits impossible to obtain for work in the NHS. Private nursing homes might still be able to obtain them; the pay and conditions there are often worse, so they can show no local labour is available. The 1993 draft consolidated immigration rules, published in July 1993, removed the special provisions affording qualified nursing students the possibility of obtaining work permits. If brought into effect, this represents the end of an era and closes an avenue for women coming to work in Britain.

The EC — equality for women?

As already explained, the Immigration Rules about EC citizens are the only ones which have never discriminated against women. The basic tenet of EC law is that there should be no discrimination against EC citizens on the grounds of their nationality and their freedom of movement must not be hindered. Discrimination in such matters as recruitment or pay is ruled out as are restrictions on the person's family members accompanying or joining him or her. EC citizens are entitled under the EC's founding Treaty of Rome to travel to other EC countries to take or to seek work, to run businesses, to be self-employed, to provide or receive services; they may also study or live off their own resources. Freedom of movement rights are widely used; in 1991, for example, 72,000 EC citizens migrated to and from Britain. EC citizens who have travelled for any of these Treaty purposes are entitled to be joined by their family members — their spouse, their children and grandchildren under 21, their children over 21 if still dependent, and their parents or grandparents.[28] These EC family reunion rights have remained constant since Britain joined the EC in 1973, while British immigration rules have changed frequently. However the Home Office has sought to minimise their effects, and has attempted to treat EC citizens as though they were covered by British rules.

EC citizens are entitled to claim social benefits available in the country in which they are living. In Britain, however, the Home Office often pressurises them to leave after periods of claiming and has attempted to prevent them from re-entering the country after an absence if they cannot show other means of support. This in fact affects women more than men as they may be unable to work while pregnant or while looking after small children. For example, Elena Bianchi came from southern Italy to work here in 1975. She planned to marry her British boyfriend but he left her in 1979, when she was pregnant. She felt that she could not return to her family in Italy with an 'illegitimate' baby and she could no longer work while caring for her son. She lived on supplementary benefit and was worried by the letters she received from the Home Office threatening to withdraw her permission to remain here unless she stopped claiming. Though the Home Office could not have deported her for this reason, she was unable to withstand its threats and returned to Italy knowing that her parents had rejected her.

As the internal barriers within the EC come down, the immigration authorities are no longer able to stop people on entry to thc UK. They have therefore stepped up internal methods of surveillance of EC nationals. The European Court of Justice held in the case of *Unger*[29] that pregnancy, maternity leave, and not working because of caring for young children, do not mean that an EC national is not a 'worker'; there should therefore be no question of such a women being requested to leave. Elena's predicament should never have happened.

The government is still attempting to differentiate between EC nationals and others settled in the UK. Changed income support regulations from April 1993 provide that EC nationals looking for work and claiming income support have to show that they have a 'genuine chance of finding work', a higher test than the usual one of 'a reasonable chance or opportunity of finding work'. After EC nationals have been claiming for more than six months, the DSS may make an assessment of their chances of finding work. If the DSS believes that they do not meet this higher test, it is obliged to tell the Home Office. That department may then inform the people concerned that they are 'no longer lawfully present in the UK', though this is doubtful under EC law. Income support regulations state that if an EC national has been 'required to leave the UK' he or she no longer qualifies for income support. Thus the Home Office, in conjunction with the DSS, is pressurising EC nationals to leave, contrary to the spirit of EC law.

Internal immigration controls

It has become increasingly common for authorities other than immigration officers to question the immigration status of black and Third World people living in Britain. This occurs not only in connection with employment, but with access to education, health and welfare benefits. Many black people, even if they have lived in Britain for most of their lives, expect to be asked for passports or to prove their status in many different circumstances — indeed, this has become almost routine.[30]

The immigration service has worked closely with the police in checking immigration status. During 1989 the Metropolitan Police passed details of nearly 7500 people to the immigration service so that their immigration status could be checked; 2632 'immigration offenders' were identified. Thus nearly 5000 people lawfully in the UK were subjected to checks for no reason.[31] People who have been arrested for immigration reasons were often apprehended in connection with quite different inquiries — 'at a family wedding after police were called in to deal with a disturbance, after being stopped driving a car because the indicator did not work, on the Underground for fare dodging'.[32] Although the legal position is that the police should only check if they have reason to believe an offence has been committed, these examples show how this belief may operate in practice.[33]

From October 1982, 'visitors' from overseas have been liable to be charged for NHS treatment. Although the regulations state that only people who are in Britain for a temporary purpose and have been here less than a year should be charged, hospitals have had to set up cumbersome machinery to attempt to check eligibility of patients, and people have been wrongly charged. For example, Pritam Kaur was presented with a bill for £850 after her baby was born by Caesarean section in Britain. Pritam was born in India but came here at the age of 14 with her mother to join her father. She lived in this country for nine years and worked here, only leaving in 1981 when she married and lived in India for a year with her husband. She returned in September 1982, when she was six months pregnant, to be with her mother when she had her baby. She entered hospital without any indication being given that she might be charged. A few days after the operation, when she was still recovering from the effects of her stitches having gone septic, she was questioned about her future intentions and told that she was liable to be charged. A year later, the health authority was still trying to get the money from her, though she should never have been charged at all. Some health authorities do not appear to be clear about the regulations. Cristina and Joao came from Brazil to study English and Cristina became pregnant here. She had her normal ante-natal treatment and Manoel was born in the West London Hospital in July 1991. The day after Cristina returned to her home she received a bill for over £700 for the delivery. When it was pointed out to the hospital that as a full-time student she was entitled to NHS treatment, the bill was withdrawn, but with no explanation or apology.

NHS charges have resulted in people failing to seek treatment because of fear of the costs. Fatima Khezri, an Iranian refugee, believed that the death of her elderly father, Habibollahkhan Khezri, visiting her for the first time in ten years, was partially caused by the bill of £1650 he had received for treatment. He had been admitted to hospital with a heart condition and kept in for six days. When he was again in pain a few days later, he was not admitted, but sent back with tablets for constipation to his daughter's home, where he died the next day.[34]

Staff in the Department of Social Security (DSS), previously Department of Health and Social Security, ask for passports or birth certificates when people first apply for a National Insurance number. Their internal manual of guidance instructs them to ask 'people who appear to have come from abroad' for passports, though it gives no guidance on how to recognise these people. Contradictory statements have been made as to whether or not this is 'purely for identity purposes',[35] but it is clear that information about applicants is passed on to the Home Office. In one instance, a woman applying for a National Insurance number found an immigration officer, who worked on the floor above, being called down to interview her by the DSS official (the woman was in fact an overstayer, although she did not know it). The Home Office stated in explanation:

> the fact that Mrs B. was interviewed by an immigration officer when she went to the social security office is unusual and was brought about by the close proximity of two offices. However, it is true to say that in due course the DHSS would have informed the Home Office of her application under existing arrangements between the two departments.[36]

This shows that any information given to the DSS may routinely, without the person's knowledge, be passed on to another government department. When National Insurance cards were made into plastic ones, with space for machine-readable coded messages, anxieties on this score increased.

The links between the education system and the immigration authorities become closer at the higher education level. Colleges may, without being asked to do so, monitor the progress and attendance of their overseas students, in order to inform the Home Office; some even believe they have a duty to inform on a student's attendance or failure to attend. This information is passed on to the Home Office, often without the student's knowledge, or on the telephone so its source cannot be checked; it may well be inaccurate or incomplete. Yet it is used by the Home Office to refuse extensions of stay on the grounds of irregular attendance at college or lack of progress in studies.

The authorities administering income support also pass on information to the Home Office. Some people — visitors and students, for example — are admitted to Britain on the understanding that they will not have 'recourse to public funds'. 'Public funds' for immigration purposes were not specifically defined before 1985, but the term was usually interpreted to mean most non-contributory benefits. This presented a pretext for disproportionate checks on black and 'foreign-sounding' applicants for supplementary benefit (now called income support). People who were overstayers or illegal entrants had, until the regulations were changed in 1984, 'nil requirements' for supplementary benefit. This meant that no money would be paid and no responsibility taken for them. The consequences could be horrifying: people could be literally starved out of the country — easier and cheaper for the Home Office than deportation. The stories of Parveen Khan and Manjit Kaur show what this means in practice.

Starved out of the country

Parveen Khan and her two young sons had been left by her husband when the Home Office planned to remove him as an illegal entrant. He had come to Britain as a child of 13 to join his uncle, whom the Home Office had thought to be his father. When the facts came to light, he was threatened with removal and Parveen, who knew nothing about this, was told she too had entered illegally when coming to join him. Similarly, Manjit Kaur, who had come to join her husband following their marriage in India, was told that her entry was illegal because her husband was an overstayer; she and her daughter Palbinder had already left him because of his violence. The Home Office tried to remove both Parveen and Manjit and their children. Meanwhile, the then DHSS refused to pay the families supplementary benefit. In April 1982, a DHSS official told Manjit that she should no longer be here because she appeared not to have complied with certain immigration requirements — a value-judgement outside the sphere of competence of the DHSS; Palbinder, although a British citizen, was refused child benefit. Parveen's sons' child benefit was 'suspended for reconsideration' at the same time.

As the legal definition of illegal entry was changed by the courts, so was the financial position of these families. In July 1983 the Home Office decided Parveen had not entered the UK illegally but could not decide what to do about her — the DHSS then paid her urgent needs payments, whilst still refusing her supplementary benefit pending a final immigration decision. The children's child benefit payments were resumed but, for a time, were paid over to their grandfather.

It was only with support from their defence campaign that these families were able to get the limited financial help they did while contesting the Home Office's decisions that they were in Britain illegally. On 30 October 1982, 200 people marched in Manchester to protest against the collaboration between the Home Office and the DHSS. A month later, 30 women occupied the DHSS offices in Manchester to protest at the tactics used against the two families; there was a national day of action on 31 January 1983. Money was collected on an ongoing basis to support the families and the DHSS decisions were contested legally. Only when the Home Office accepted that both women were not illegal entrants did they receive any of the money to which they were entitled. Eventually they were both allowed to stay.

This campaign highlighted the attempt by colluding government departments to prevent people from contesting immigration decisions. The DHSS disregarded the tenuousness of the Home Office's claims that Parveen and Manjit were in Britain illegally and for over a year the women had to survive and to care for their young children without any regular income. It was partly because of this and other campaigns that DHSS regulations were changed in 1984: people contesting a Home Office decision are now entitled to claim income support at the urgent cases rate.

The 1985 immigration rules defined 'public funds' for the first time, as supplementary benefit (now income support), family income supplement (now family credit), housing benefit and being rehoused as homeless persons. Despite this clarification, the harassment of black claimants continues. Women have been refused benefit on the grounds that their husbands (refused permission to join them or waiting in the queue in the subcontinent) should be maintaining them; husbands abroad have received letters from the DSS asking why they are not maintaining their wives. And new income support regulations in August 1993 again restrict eligibility for benefit; the only people who may now claim income support while applying to the Home Office for leave to remain are asylum-seekers. Although women like Parveen and Manjit, contesting Home Office decisions made against them, may still be able to claim, those applying for permission to remain do not qualify for benefit and may therefore face severe hardship, or be forced out of the country like Maria Otomando, whose story is told on page 119.

The Immigration Rules provide for undertakings to be made by people sponsoring relatives abroad that they will support and accommodate them in Britain. A person who has come on this basis may incorrectly be refused benefit on the grounds that she has adequate financial support, or the sponsor may be asked by the DSS to repay the money. For example, Usha Patel, who stated that she was able to support her niece and nephew — British Overseas citizens who had been given special quota vouchers to come here — was asked to pay back the supplementary benefit that they later claimed, even though there is no legal requirement that voucher holders be supported.

The DSS uses the fact that undertakings have been signed to harass claimants and their families, putting pressure on the signers of undertakings to maintain their relatives, and has even taken a family to court. Harish Patel signed an undertaking when his mother, Manjula Patel, applied to join him in Britain. Mrs Patel was allowed in for settlement and lived with her son and grandchildren. When financial difficulties arose, as the children grew up, Mrs Patel, as she was entitled to do, claimed and was granted income support in her own right. But the DSS pursued Harish, reminding him of his undertaking to support his mother. Harish believed that on principle his mother should be entitled to this money, on the same basis as a British citizen living with her family. The DSS took the case to court and Harish was ordered to pay back the income support his mother had claimed. The undertaking was enforced until Mrs Patel became a British citizen.

All officials are immigration officers

The connections between immigration status and other rights have become increasingly formalised and therefore other officials have more routinely made immigration checks over the years. Dora Amoako applied to the Homeless Persons Unit in Wandsworth, south London, for rehousing in 1984. She was threatened with deportation because the Homeless Persons Unit asked the Home Office to check on her immigration status. This revealed that, unknown to her, she was an overstayer. She was able to remain in Britain with her children only after a successful campaign.

Campaigners argued in this and other groups,[37] that immigration matters should be the responsibility only of immigration officials, not of housing officials, or schools, or hospitals, which should deal with their specialist areas. Housing officials have countered this argument. In a case brought by Tower Hamlets council,[38] the Court of Appeal decided in 1993 that housing officials had not only the right but also the duty to investigate immigration status.

Tower Hamlets, still continuing its attempts to deny housing to people entitled to it, as discussed on pages 140-1, had contested the guidance given by the Department of the Environment to officials responsible for dealing with applications from homeless persons. This guidance stated that any information on immigration matters gained in the course of housing inquiries was confidential and should not be revealed to other departments without consent. Tower Hamlets argued that it had no duty to house people who were 'illegally' in the UK and also that it should pass any information about immigration illegality on to the Home Office. The local authority lost in the Divisional Court but the Court of Appeal ruled in its favour. Housing officials were to make decisions about immigration status, in spite of having no training in the complex laws involved. Many people will thus risk being wrongly refused housing, and being investigated by the Home Office, when there is no irregularity in their immigration status.

A further attack on housing rights followed three months later. The Asylum and Immigration Appeals Act 1993 reduced housing authorities' duties towards asylum-seekers. It provided that if asylum-seekers and their dependants had any accommodation available to them, however temporary, they should not be classified as homeless. And if they are accepted as homeless, the local authority can provide only temporary accommodation for them until they have been granted leave to remain.

These two changes give a legal justification for asking immigration questions of applicants for housing. Families are forced to remain in inadequate, unhealthy and dangerous housing because of fears about the immigration consequences of trying to improve it. The implications could develop more widely; if access to welfare benefits, education, health treatment and other essentials of life are to become conditional on the outcome of immigration checks, people with irregular status will be discouraged from claiming. Even more importantly, people who are unsure or worried about their status, often without cause, will be deterred from making any contact with officialdom and from claiming their entitlements.

Increased official liaison between different government departments was highlighted in a press release put out by Michael Howard, the Home Secretary, in October 1993 in the context of 'tackling illegal immigration'. He announced a study of 'the efficiency of existing arrangements for co-operation' between the Home Office and other government departments, to 'ensure that all of us are making the most efficient use of the information available to us...we should look afresh at ways in which Government as a whole — central and local — could co-operate more effectively to prevent abuse of the immigration laws and the drain on public funds which it often represents.'[39] These developments, intended to reduce people's rights to benefits and services, will make life even harder for black and migrant women and their families.

'Unauthorised' workers

As has been shown, the British Immigration Rules and the work permit system make it extremely difficult for women to come to the UK to work legally. Those who have come legally may be end up staying on illegally, thus placing themselves in an extremely vulnerable position. Any contact with authority may result in questions about immigration status and discovery, arrest and deportation. Yet the British economy depends on many such women, working in cafés, restaurants, factories, homeworking or employed as contract cleaners. Employers are often aware of the immigration difficulties of such employees and exploit the situation, by paying low wages and providing bad working conditions, while giving the impression to the workers that they are doing them a favour. Immigration officials recognise that a blind eye is turned to much illegal working; 'if we had enough staff, we could bring the whole restaurant trade in London to a halt'.[40]

At different times different groups have been alternately ignored or targeted by the immigration service. This may depend on the economic situation or the prominence given to a particular community at a specific time. The immigration service and the police may work together in order to arrest people. Gunul, a Turkish worker, describes a raid on a textile factory in Hackney, east London, in 1984:[41]

> 'The boss came in and he said, 'Be careful, the police are coming. Illegals, quick, outside!' I don't know how this happened; it was very quick, all this...But some people went out and some people couldn't, because the police came in quickly into our factory. And they asked questions quickly, 'All people this way' — you know. I went in first because I thought, maybe they are not legal people; I am legal...so it would give them some time...They came looking for Halil. First they looked downstairs, but Halil was not downstairs so they came up to our factory. The police said, 'We know in this country who is legal and who is not legal'...they asked people to be questioned in separate rooms. The one I was questioned by, he said, 'Why did you come to this country? Are you political?' I said, 'Before I came in as a visitor but now I am married and I can stay in this country. My husband is British.' 'All right,' he said, 'you go away'.'

This account illustrates several points; the immigration service and the police working together in a raid spearheaded by the police, the ostensible reason being to find a named individual, but using this to check others; and the solidarity of the workers, attempting to shield those who might be illegal.

There have been many other raids; for example, a raid at Liberty's department store on 30 January 1986, when police were ostensibly investigating a suspected theft, as a result of which 19 people were arrested, five charged with working illegally, three treated as illegal entrants and one charged with overstaying. Nobody was charged with theft.[42]

Other well-publicised raids have targeted workers employed as contract cleaners, often for large companies or government departments in central London. As much of the work of government departments has been privatised, cleaning services have been contracted out to commercial companies, who take on employees directly, often with minimal employment checks. There have been joint police/immigration service raids at BP's London headquarters, the Ministry of Defence and the Department for Education. On 12 December 1986 raids on the Prison Department and the Parole Board, carried out by 16 police and 15 immigration officers, resulted in the arrest of 25 Ghanaians and one Nigerian, who were earning £17.50 per week as early-morning cleaners.[43] The harsh conditions endured by such workers were well illustrated in a Channel 4 television programme where west African asylum-seekers or visitors were interviewed.[44]

During the early 1990s other targets of raids were eastern Europeans, able to travel more freely as a result of political changes in their countries of origin, who have entered as visitors and then worked. There have been reports of dozens of seasonal harvesters arrested while working in south-eastern England. In May 1992 100 agricultural workers at a farm near Byfleet, Surrey, were interviewed by immigration and DSS officers in 'Operation Penelope'; 69 people were detained for further questioning and 11 treated as illegal entrants; they were paid between 60p and £1.20 per hour.[45] On 21 July 1993, in 'Operation Electra', a 'surveillance operation lasting several weeks', 81 people, 55 Czechs, 21 Poles, two Georgians, two Bolivians and a Peruvian, including women with children, were arrested raspberry picking near Ashford, Kent. A Home Office spokesperson was quoted as saying 'we had expected to find about 30 people but they just kept coming out of the woodwork'.[46]

Large and publicised raids are only the tip of the iceberg. Many women working illegally live in daily fear of questioning by officials that might result in their immigration status coming to light. Such women are particularly vulnerable to exploitation and may even be tricked into prostitution. There are also reports of women lured from Far Eastern and east European countries by promises of work as waitresses or musicians, who find themselves forced into prostitution on arrival. This is not confined to Britain; Belgium, for example, introduced new measures against the exploitation of women and forced prostitution in January 1993,[47] which enforce the signing of a work contract and make working without a permit more difficult. But it was not effective against those carrying out the trade, as women were often not given temporary permits to remain in Belgium to testify against them. In June and August two groups of Filipino women were freed from forced prostitution in Antwerp.[48]

Conclusion

The facts show that thousands of women have come to Britain as independent workers. This is in addition to the women who have come to work but are not counted as such in government statistics — women who have come to join settled husbands, women who have come because their husbands are studying in Britain and who are working in order to support them through college. They all face similar problems of low pay, insecurity and harassment at work. But their independent position has often not been recognised by the government. The myth that immigrant women were dependants was used for many years to justify sex discriminatory Immigration Rules which prevented women workers from bringing their husbands to join them. With the long-term western recession and cuts in service provision, jobs have dried up; increased internal immigration checks have made work still more difficult. As the economic and political importance of continental Europe and the freedom of movement afforded to EC workers has grown, workers without that mobility are at an increasing disadvantage. The position of EC workers and the growing gap between their rights and those of non-EC citizens living and working in Europe is the subject of the next chapter.

Chapter 7

Sex equality and race division: migration and Fortress Europe

Until the late 1980s, recognition of the importance of Britain's membership of the European Community[1] was mainly restricted to the world of business and trade. Its effect on British immigration law was not widely appreciated, either by those concerned with immigrants' rights or indeed by the government. The Home Office's evidence to the 1978 parliamentary Select Committee on Race Relations and Immigration investigation into the effect of the UK's membership of the EC on race relations and immigration stated 'The available data suggests that UK accession has not led to increased migration of labour from other member states...', its main area of concern.[2] Today the importance of 'Europe', both as a legal and a political force, cannot be overlooked. There is a dual effect at work here. On the one hand the division between EC and all other nationals is central to immigration law in Britain — it has replaced the distinction between Commonwealth and non-Commonwealth, so crucial in former times. Only EC nationals and their families have freedom of movement between EC countries. On the other hand, as a political entity, it is Europe, ministers of the EC working together, rather than the British government alone, that is increasingly formulating immigration policy.

Sex discrimination has never been a feature of European Community law. On the contrary, EC law has prohibited such discrimination, and Community institutions have played a crucial role in the fight against it. As a result this chapter cannot focus on the discriminatory aspects of law and practice in the way previous chapters have done. It is not specifically *about women*. But European developments are considered in some detail because they are of crucial importance to women (as indeed to all concerned with immigration and nationality in Britain).

Britain joined the European Economic Community, as it then was, in 1973[3]. The European Communities Act 1972, which incorporated the EEC's[4] founding Treaty of Rome into UK law, came into force on 1 January 1973, the same day as the 1971 Immigration Act. The Immigration Act, however, contained no reference whatsoever to Community nationals or to Britain's obligations under the EEC Treaty. Nevertheless, from that date onwards not only did European law become part of UK law, but wherever there was a conflict between the two, European law prevailed. The political debate about sovereignty and subsidiarity which occurred during the ratification of the Maastricht Treaty was two decades too late.

However the implications of these far-reaching measures took some time to filter through in Britain. At the political level, it was the negative aspects of European Community membership that first came to the fore. There was a gradual recognition that Europe, rather than the ex-colonies and the Commonwealth, was the focus of future political and economic developments; that from a terminally declining ex-imperial power, Britain had become — albeit reluctantly and ambivalently — a member of the new European economic order.

British nationals for EC purposes

This change was reflected in the government's definition of British nationals for EC purposes. British citizens and the numerically insignificant category of British subjects with the right of abode[5] were included in the definition; so were British Dependent Territories[6] citizens from Gibraltar but from no other existing colonies (e.g. Hong Kong). This was a conscious political choice on the part of the British government to exclude all the non-'European' colonials. It was not inevitable, as the decisions made by other countries illustrate. France, for example, treated its overseas 'departements' of Guadeloupe and Martinique quite differently, including them within the 'mother' nation for EC purposes. Portugal chose to include as Community nationals Portuguese citizens of Chinese ethnic origin in Macao.

From an immigration perspective this meant that the erosion of Commonwealth citizens' rights (to the point where their former privileged status had become almost insignificant) was in direct and stark contrast to the dramatic benefits gained by EC citizens. Far from Britain being so overcrowded that no new sources of immigration could be countenanced, it became clear that the origin, and most crucially the race, of potential immigrants was the decisive issue. The immigration consequences of European Community membership had not caused any noticeable political concern. The lack of debate, in 1973, about the millions of potential new European migrants was in stark contrast to the previous year's political hysteria about the possible arrival of a few thousand UK passport holders of Asian origin expelled from Uganda by Idi Amin.

Hostility from sections of the British left to this racist Eurocentrism in government policy, together with labour movement opposition to the strengthened might of trans-national capital, resulted in anti-racist and civil libertarian organisations initially avoiding involvement in Europe. Moreover, at this stage, during the 1970s and early 1980s, few practical effects of UK Community membership were discernible. However, gradually a change in direction became evident. The positive aspects of EC membership, including the progressive, non-discriminatory social provisions and the generous rules about free movement, encouraged those concerned with individual human rights and social justice to work with the new legal and social order.

EC nationals — freedom of movement within the Community

A single market without internal frontiers

Fundamental to the concept of the European Community is the creation of a common or single market, 'an area *without internal frontiers* in which the free movement of goods, persons, services and capital is ensured'.[7] The unhindered, free movement of persons is therefore central to this scheme. The persons concerned are Community nationals and their families.

Britain's definition of a Community national is set out above. While in theory, under Community law, the agreement of all member states is required to define who counts as a Community national, in practice there has been no limitation on states' own definitions, which are binding on other states. So Britain must treat as Community nationals French citizens from Martinique as much as from Lyon; British Dependent Territories citizens from Hong Kong are not Community nationals throughout the Community.

The basic idea is that, within the Community, nationals of member states must enjoy complete freedom of movement to enter or take up residence in a member state other than their own, so that they are not at a disadvantage if they choose to work, study or simply live off their savings there. The easy movement of nationals from one member state to another facilitates the creation of a single market, indeed more than that, a single 'community' as cultural and national barriers are progressively eliminated.

This approach is in stark contrast to the attitude to non-EC nationals, in Britain and, to an increasing extent, in all other EC countries. Domestic immigration law for non-EC nationals is based on the fundamental objective of restricting entry, particularly the entry of black and non-Western people. European Community law, by contrast, is framed so as to facilitate movement; removing obstacles to free movement within the Community is a priority. For this to occur, all EC nationals must be treated equally; and indeed the right not to be discriminated against on the grounds of nationality is fundamental to EC law. Article 7 of the EEC Treaty provides that:

> within the scope of application of this Treaty, and without prejudice to any special provisions contained therein, any discrimination on grounds of nationality shall be prohibited.

EC nationals must be put on the same footing as nationals of the host member state, not only with regards to all employment-related opportunities and benefits, but also all tax and social advantages. Otherwise, as barriers to free movement, these would be incompatible with the basic objectives of the internal market. Thus, for example, Community nationals have the same rights to local authority housing as people resident in Britain, 'true-born Englishmen' as Lord Denning put it in the case confirming this right.[8] They are entitled to education grants on the same basis as 'home' students, and to claim benefits. However the Home Office has attempted to discourage this; its tactics are discussed further on pages 187-8.

Sex discrimination is also completely ruled out under EC law. One of the original reasons for this was to ensure that free competition within the internal market, a fundamental EC goal, was not distorted; this would have occurred if employers could produce goods more cheaply than their competitors by employing women to do the same work as men at lower wages. Article 119 of the Treaty laid down the principle that men and women should receive equal pay for equal work. This has subsequently been amplified so that EC law now prohibits all discrimination on the grounds of sex, whether direct or indirect, and whether by reference to marital or family status.[9]

No such general prohibition on race discrimination exists at present within the EC.[10] This reflects the low political priority accorded to this area from the outset in Community policy making. Several proposals and political moves to remedy this situation are being canvassed, their urgency highlighted by the rapid escalation in racist activity within the Community since the late 1980s.

The scope of free movement provisions — Treaty rights

Initially the scope of the freedom of movement provisions, 'Treaty rights' as they are commonly called for short, reflected the emphasis on creating a single *market*, an area where economic activity could take place without restrictive national barriers. Accordingly, workers and those seeking work were covered from the outset, as were business people, the self-employed and providers and receivers of services. All these categories of EC nationals have always been entitled to move freely and to bring their families with them, whether the family members are EC nationals themselves or not.

Workers includes both full-time and part-time workers, however minimal the income and whatever the motive for taking the job. For example, Ms Levin, a British citizen, went to the Netherlands with her South African husband. She took a job as a part-time chambermaid expecting to be supported largely by her husband's income. Despite the fact that her income was less than the official minimum subsistence level and that it had to be supplemented, the European Court held that she counted as a worker; it also decided that, provided the job was a genuine and effective one, the motives for taking it were irrelevant. She was covered even if she had taken the job simply to enable her husband to work within the EC.[11]

Unemployed workers are entitled to stay if their unemployment is 'involuntary', for example as a result of illness or if they are actively seeking another job. Women who give up work, are capable of returning but have not because of pregnancy or maternity leave, do not count as 'voluntarily' unemployed; they are still exercising Treaty rights.[12]

Those who wish to set themselves up in business or to become self-employed, and providers and receivers of services are also covered by the free movement provisions. There are no minimum income requirements as under British immigration law for non-EC nationals. Since July 1992[13] freedom of movement rights have been extended to a far wider group: Community nationals and their families enjoy these rights even if they are not directly connected to the world of work, but are students, persons of independent means[14] or retired, so long as they do not become a burden on the social security system of the host state. In other words the scheme of free movement covers Community nationals virtually from the cradle to the grave.

EC nationals carrying out any of the activities just mentioned are entitled to *enter* a member state other than their own without obtaining prior leave. This is in stark contrast to the stringent rules for non-EC nationals wishing to enter the UK. So no entry clearance or visa is required. But at present EC nationals still need to produce a valid passport or identity document. This manifestly contradicts the aim of a single internal market without frontiers, planned to start on 1 January 1993. But the British government, among others, still insists on passport checks for all at the borders.[15]

The legality of these checks is currently being challenged by a test case going through the courts, discussed on page 224. The European Commission, encouraged by the European Parliament, is also considering challenging these border controls by taking governments who persist with passport checks before the European Court of Justice.

Since EC nationals are entitled to seek and take work on the same terms as own country nationals, *residence rights* are central. Under the British immigration rules, EC nationals can apply for a residence permit if they wish to stay longer than six months. But, under EC law, no one is *required* to apply for a residence permit; as the European Court of Justice put it:

> the right of nationals of a member state to enter the territory of another member state and reside there for the purposes intended by the Treaty — in particular to look for or pursue an occupation or activities as employed or self-employed persons, or to rejoin their spouse or family — is a right conferred directly by the Treaty... It must therefore be concluded that this right is acquired independently of the issue of a residence permit by the competent authority of a member state. The grant of this permit is therefore to be regarded not as a measure giving rise to rights but as a measure by a member state serving to prove the individual position of a national of another member state with regard to provisions of Community law.[16]

Limitations on free movement rights

Only in very limited circumstances can the free movement rights of EC nationals and their families be curtailed; these occur when public policy, public security and public health so require. The European Court has not permitted governments to broaden these definitions. The mere fact of having criminal convictions is not sufficient, nor is the fact of having entered a member state illegally or having failed to comply with registration requirements. Danielle Roux, a French national, arrived in Belgium at the end of 1988 and applied to the Belgian authorities for a residence permit on the basis that she was a self-employed waitress. The authorities turned down her request because they decided she was not self-employed at all and should have registered as a worker; they therefore ordered her to leave the country. The European Court held that she should have been granted a residence permit, and that this could not be made conditional on complying with local registration requirements (as a worker rather than a self-employed person in this case).[17]

However, despite the provisions of EC law, there has been an increase in disturbing reports of black EC nationals receiving discriminatory treatment at the hands of Member States other than their own. A vivid example is provided by the case of Natasha Oldham. She was born in

Jamaica but lived in Britain since she was 18, and became a British citizen. As an EC citizen she had freedom of movement rights and used these to make frequent visits to Denmark. She first had a holiday there in 1980, when she made many friends, and she returned for several other visits. In 1991 she hoped to marry a Danish friend, once they were both free to do so, and wanted to spend more time in Denmark. She therefore rented a flat in Copenhagen and began to look for work. While clearing up the flat preparatory to moving in, she was arrested by police, taken to the police station, and told that she was illegally in Denmark because British passports were 'only for Europeans'; the police accused her of being a prostitute, detained her for three days and deported her to Britain. As she still hoped to marry and settle in Denmark, and had the lease to the flat, she returned there three months later. After three weeks, she was once more arrested at the flat, detained and deported, again unfounded allegations of prostitution being made.

This treatment is reminiscent of an age-old attitude to alien women, captured in the statement by a British MP during the 1948 British Nationality Act debate, and already quoted on page 26.

Whether or not Natasha Oldham had been a prostitute, her deportation would have been unlawful; an EC national (including a prostitute) cannot be expelled when no comparable penalty exists for nationals of the country.[18] In this case racial discrimination was the reason for her treatment; she was not a prostitute. But had she been a prostitute, even a white prostitute, she may well have encountered similar difficulties. Several cases of prostitutes have come before national courts in various European countries; despite apparently quite legitimate claims to be 'workers' within the meaning of Article 48 of the Treaty of Rome, they have uniformly been held not to be workers. Prejudice and discriminatory treatment against this group of women workers appear as firmly entrenched in European as in many other areas of law. Even an eminent and otherwise liberal scholar describes the case-law in this area with palpable sarcasm:

> In several cases national courts have been urged, in all seriousness, to hold that persons engaged in prostitution and similar activities were 'workers' within the meaning of Article 48. The uniformity of the court's answer to this question is, perhaps, less surprising than the elaborate and scholarly attention given to it.[19]

Enhanced family reunion rights for EC nationals

European Community law recognised from the outset that family reunion rights were an integral part of the free movement rights accorded to workers and other EC nationals covered by the Treaty. If people could not take their families to live with them this would constitute a major obstacle to moving. The family reunion rights derived from EC law are generous when compared with those that exist for non-EC nationals. They apply irrespective of the gender of the EC national, and irrespective of the nationality of the family member. For example, a Spanish woman coming to study in Britain is entitled, just like a Spanish man, to bring her Moroccan spouse with her. By contrast, a non-EC woman coming to the UK to study still cannot bring her spouse, whereas a non-EC man in the same situation can.[20] By comparison with the complications and restrictions of the UK family reunion rules, particularly those regarding spouses discussed at length above, the EC rules appear simple and straightforward.

The spouse of an EC national exercising rights to travel and live in Europe benefits from the family reunion provisions of Community law whatever the motive or intention behind the marriage. Intention is, in fact, irrelevant in this context; Community law is designed to facilitate free movement, not to enquire into the motives behind it (as shown in the *Levin* case, quoted earlier). Other relatively liberal provisions also flow from this basic premise: the couple do not need to cohabit, they can live in separate accommodation and indeed in different parts of the member state; they can be legally separated and not intending to cohabit in the future as long as the marriage has not been finally dissolved.[21]

For example, Sabina, a German woman, came to work in Britain with her Barbadian husband, Martin. When applying for her residence permit and that of her husband Sabina had quite candidly told the British immigration authorities that they were not cohabiting as they were going through a bad patch. The Home Office gave them wrong information, as if non-EC immigration law applied; the couple were told that unless they got back together and produced a letter from their landlord confirming cohabitation Martin would not be allowed to stay. Only after representations on their behalf and a formal complaint did the Home Office apologise for failing to apply EC law correctly and issue Martin with a residence permit in line with Sabina's.

The British government's hostility to the generous EC scheme of family reunion is evident not only in incidents of this sort, feared to be far more common than Home Office officials admit. It is also evidenced by the persistent failure to implement the freedom of movement provisions fully and clearly in the immigration rules.[22] What is more, recently revealed secret internal instructions to immigration officials on marriages with EC citizens state, quite contrary to European law, that because 'immigration offenders can exploit [the EC] approach by entering into marriages of convenience with EC nationals' their removal may be justified.[23] It has recently come to light that the Home Office, presumably with these suspicions, subjects some couples, where there is an EC partner, to detailed questioning. These procedures are being challenged and it will be interesting to see whether the courts will allow the government to undermine the broad intentions of EC law in this way.

Under Community law, marriage is not always essential for family reunion for couples. Thus, Dutch law allows cohabitees and same sex couples to join their Dutch or permanently settled partners in the Netherlands. Denmark also allows family reunion for cohabiting or same sex couples.[24] By virtue of the non-discrimination provisions of EC law, EC nationals exercising their Treaty rights in those countries can also benefit from the same family reunion provisions.[25] The contrast with domestic UK immigration law is very pronounced, and several lesbian and gay couples have been forced to consider uprooting themselves for this reason.

The family reunion rights for other relatives of EC nationals are also more generous under EC law than under the British immigration rules for non-EC nationals. All children under 21,[26] and those over 21 who are still dependent on their parents, benefit from the regulations. This covers[27] adopted as well as natural children, and the children of either spouse, (including the non-EC spouse), as shown by Erlinda's story.

Erlinda, a Filipino nurse, came to the UK in 1980 to work in the National Health Service. Her marriage in the Philippines had broken down and she left her three year old daughter in the care of her mother. Some time after coming to the UK she got married to an Italian waiter. In 1993 her mother's health deteriorated and Erlinda decided to bring her daughter to the UK to live with her and her husband. As a lone parent applying to bring a child over 12 she would, if considered under domestic law, have had to embark on the lengthy and perilous course of proving that she had

had sole responsibility for the child. However, as the spouse of an EC national exercising his Treaty rights in the UK, she was covered by EC family reunion law; all she had to prove was that she was married to such an EC national, was the mother of the child in question and could accommodate her. The question of her involvement in the child's upbringing, of financial support over the years, of the whereabouts and actions of the child's father, of the ability of the elderly mother to carry on caring for the child — none of this was relevant. Within three months of the initial application, Erlinda's daughter had obtained her visa and joined her mother in the UK.

No concept of 'sole responsibility' or 'adoption of convenience' exists in Community law. Nor does the disgraceful notion of excluding children other than in 'exceptional compassionate circumstances', an important provision of UK immigration law, as discussed in Chapter 5.

Though the rights derived from EC law are clear, it has not always been easy for families to enforce them. This is partly because, as the government is well aware, UK law does not adequately reflect the Community law rights of EC nationals; but no steps are being taken to remedy the long-standing and substantial incompatibility between the two legal systems. The official attitude is at best complacent; according to the Assistant Director of the Immigration Service, 'the Immigration Rules... no longer accurately reflect current interpretation of Community law, and are therefore not relied upon by immigration officers.'[28]

In fact, quite contrary to this assertion, court action has on occasion been necessary to compel the Home Office to recognise its EC obligations. Carolina Gomes left four children in Colombia when she travelled to Britain in 1985. There she met Henry Connolly, an Irishman, who had travelled to Britain several years earlier; they married, had a daughter and Carolina was allowed to settle. The following year she went to Colombia and brought back her three younger children; although they were allowed in at the airport, she was warned that she should have obtained entry clearance for them. So when Diego, her eldest son, finished his schooling the next year, he applied for entry clearance at the British embassy, just before he was 18. There was no response to the application for months, so as Diego needed medical treatment, the family decided he should come to Britain and explain at the airport, as his sisters had done. He was refused entry; the Home Office argued that because Henry had registered as a

British citizen in 1989, he had forfeited his EC rights and his family should be treated under the general, non-EC immigration rules. The Home Office also alleged that Diego was not really Carolina's son, as she had left him behind when she brought the other children. It took a DNA test and an application for judicial review before the Home Office allowed Diego to stay, over a year after his arrival.

Access to a competent lawyer should not be a prerequisite for obtaining legal rights. Whether through ignorance (reflecting reluctance) or by design, it is clear that the British government is often not applying EC law unless this is specifically drawn to its attention.

Other relatives covered by EC law include grandchildren and dependent relatives in the ascending line, such as parents, grandparents, and in some cases even uncles and aunts where they are dependent on the person they are coming to join. The regulations specifically encourage member states to facilitate the admission of family members who do not fall into the above categories if they were dependent and living together before the move. Maria Dias and her three children fled from Angola to Portugal after her husband was killed and they continued to face danger there. They hoped to be able to manage in Portugal because they spoke Portuguese and other Angolans lived there. But with no jobs available the family only managed to survive because of the money sent to them by Maria's sister-in-law Luciana, a self-employed childminder in Britain. Luciana had acquired Portuguese nationality when living in Portugal at an earlier stage. As an EC citizen her family reunion rights extended to her Angolan in-laws in Portugal; so Maria and the children were able to enter and stay in Britain as EC dependants.

Who are EC nationals exercising Treaty rights?

Given the immigration advantages conferred by Community law, it is of considerable importance to know who is covered. The definition of a British national for EC purposes has already been set out above. Each state has evolved its own definition. But not all EC nationals benefit.

Firstly, the EC national must have moved from one member state to another.[29] Secondly, this move must have been in exercise of a Treaty right, as discussed above. But, thirdly, EC rights can benefit Community nationals returning to their own country after having exercised Treaty rights in another EC country.

This was established by the case of *R v Immigration Appeal Tribunal ex parte Surinder Singh* which came before the European Court of Justice in Luxembourg in 1992. This case[30] ruled that, because Rashpal Purewal, a British citizen, had lived and worked in Germany, she had gained Treaty rights which should benefit her husband, Surinder Singh, on their return to Britain. Instead of the one year's initial leave to remain that he was granted according to British immigration law, he should have been allowed to stay permanently.

This has important implications for family reunion rights within the EC. The British women separated from their Asian husbands by the primary purpose rule, or the lone parents of Caribbean children separated by the sole responsibility rule can now benefit from the *Surinder Singh* decision provided they can bring themselves within EC law. But there must be a 'Community nexus', a real link to one of the situations envisaged by Community law. So EC nationals and their families who travel to one member state to look for work are not entitled to assert free movement rights if, for example, after a short unsuccessful search, they return to work in their own member state.[31] But if they travel to another member state, and live there with the family member while working, setting up a business or studying, the concepts of primary purpose and sole responsibility will not apply to the family member if they decide to return to Britain.

This may be the only strategy for family reunion open to British citizens who have been separated from their families by the sole responsibility or primary purpose rules. But it is a very cumbersome way of achieving family unity. To compel people to uproot themselves and live in another country for a period of months or years in order to be reunited with a spouse or minor child is, arguably, unacceptable. It may also be a violation of the right to family life, protected by Article 8 of the European Convention of Human Rights, to which the UK is a signatory. That article states: 'Everyone has the right to respect for his [sic] private and family life, his home and correspondence'. Whether a challenge to UK immigration rules along these lines will be successful remains to be seen.

The EC and third country nationals

Anti-racist and human rights groups concerned with immigration view Europe in a dual light. On the one hand the moves towards a single market and the free movement provisions for EC nationals discussed above represent a welcome improvement on the increasingly restrictive approach of British immigration legislation. But, on the other hand, discrimination on grounds of nationality is fundamental to EC law (at least as currently implemented). Non-EC nationals, third country nationals [TCNs] as they are often called, are excluded.[32] Yet over eight million legally resident TCNs within the Community are thus relegated to an inferior legal status.[33] Worse, the rules regarding their immigration into and stay within the Community are being harmonised across the EC in an increasingly restrictive, oppressive direction. Far from gaining rights and freedoms, they are becoming the objects of growing internal controls, restrictive rules for family reunion, limited travel rights, all manifestations of ever-increasing official hostility and repression. In direct conflict with the government contention that race relations within a country or area are improved by strict immigration controls, it is evident that racism and ethnic chauvinism at the borders and within the territory of the EC have developed in tandem, the one feeding off the deceits and distortions produced in the other.

At about the same time as the positive benefits of EC membership for member state nationals began to be appreciated, news of far-reaching policy decisions about non-EC immigration into the Community started filtering through. It emerged that these decisions were being arrived at by European governments, represented by Ministers and high-ranking civil servants meeting in secret, outside any of the democratically accountable EC institutions, and that they were developing joint policies and agreements designed to restrict and control third country, particularly black, immigration into Europe. Anti-racist and civil rights organisations in the various EC states responded by forging links with each other and formulating common concerns and strategies.

How the EC works

Policy formulation within the EC is the responsibility of the European Commission, which has 17 Commissioners among whom all 12 member states are represented. Its members are appointed by governments, not elected; this is the body that drafts legislation. The legislative body that takes most of the final decisions is the EC's Council of Ministers, consisting of Ministers from each of the twelve member governments. The European Parliament, the only directly elected EC body, has a small but increasing legislative role. The European Court of Justice, based in Luxembourg (and not to be confused with the European Court of Human Rights in Strasbourg) decides on disputes and questions of interpretation arising out of Community law.

Immigration policy development on TCNs within EC institutions

As discussed above, the European Community is based on the idea of a single market without internal frontiers. But if there are to be no internal frontiers it follows that TCNs should not, any more than EC nationals, be subjected to checks when they move from one Community country to another. EC countries have not so far accepted this logical consequence of the moves to create a single market. They have, however, been compelled to develop a common policy towards third country nationals. But it was not until 1985, 17 years after the EC Council had issued the rules regarding free movement for EC workers, that the EC started considering joint policies in this area. Before that EC policy makers had failed to effect any policies for third country nationals, an indication of the indifference and blindness captured by John Berger in his graphic portrayal of the experience of migration in *A Seventh Man.*

In 1985, the European Commission attempted to ensure that governments would communicate with and consult the Commission on any proposals for changes in their migration policies for TCNs. The aim was to ensure coordination in this area between the various member states. But the EC governments called into question the Commission's role and refused to allow it to intervene in policy formulation in this area.[35] They challenged the Commission in the European Court of Justice. The Court eventually annulled the Commission's proposals on the basis that the

Commission lacked 'competence' to ensure conformity between draft national legislation concerning TCNs and Community policies.[36] As a result the Commission has not been allowed to take the lead in the process of harmonising Community policies on TCN migration; it has been relegated to the position of an observer. And instead of Community institutions, governments themselves have kept firm control of policy, as is shown below. This has had a significant effect not only on the form of the decision-making but on the content of the decisions. For whereas the Community institutions had directed their attention to formulating a common immigration policy for the Community, EC governments have been concerned to promote their own separate (and exclusionary) interests through the harmonisation process.

The lack of political will to improve the position of TCNs is also evidenced by the absence of a concerted political attack on the widespread and widely acknowledged discrimination and racism within the EC. In 1986 the Council of Ministers, the Commission and the European Parliament published a Joint Declaration against Racism and Xenophobia. But a May 1990 Resolution by the Council on the fight against racism and xenophobia did not give the Commission scope to become active in this field by undertaking new initiatives; it merely called on member states to sign and ratify existing international instruments and apply national laws against racial discrimination. The European Parliament has adopted various resolutions and reports attacking racism and xenophobia but lack of political muscle has rendered these ineffective.

Immigration policy development by groups of EC governments

It has been governments, therefore, not EC institutions, that have formulated Community policy in respect of TCNs. Within the EC, several smaller groupings of countries have developed common policies on immigration or immigration-related matters.[37] The first such grouping was the Benelux Economic Union[38] of 1960; Belgium, the Netherlands and Luxembourg abolished controls on people crossing their common (internal) borders and transferred all checks to their external borders. This model was followed in the early 1980s by the Schengen agreement, signed by France and Germany, together with the Benelux countries, in 1985.

But whereas the Benelux Economic Union had been negotiated openly and had provided for an international court to arbitrate on disagreements and ensure uniformity in implementation, the policies being evolved within the Schengen process provided for no such judicial control. In fact it was clear from the forum in which the discussions took place and the procedures adopted that democratic accountability and control were to be excluded from the outset in the interests of political expediency. In only one of the five signatory states, the Netherlands, was the agreement subjected to parliamentary scrutiny before it was to enter into force. In France, 'le secret Schengen' came to public attention through newspaper revelations; it emerged that even the Ministry of Justice had been kept in the dark.

As information about the agreement gradually emerged, the reasons for the ominous secrecy became apparent. For though the prime motive for the negotiations had been economic, namely to remove cumbersome and costly barriers to free trade, a substantial inroad into individual civil liberties, particularly those of would-be immigrants, was at the heart of the proposals. Checks at internal borders on both goods and people were to be eliminated and replaced by common visa policies and more stringent checks at the external borders. Internal controls would be stepped up and a common information system established to improve police cooperation. Information about 'undesirable aliens' would be exchanged freely between immigration and police forces in the different countries, with safeguards about accuracy (and protection of refugees) clearly overshadowed in the process. The EC Commission from the outset only participated in the Schengen meetings as an observer. It became increasingly clear that non-European immigration into Europe was being classed as something akin to a criminal activity. The 'Fortress Europe' approach had been forged.[39]

The 1985 agreement provided for an Implementing Convention and this was signed on 19 June 1990. The Schengen policies now include a common visa policy throughout the Schengen territory, with a three month uniform leave to enter for non-EC nationals admitted, and the right to move freely for three months without entry visas for third country nationals living within the EC. The final agreement is expected to come into force in the near future, though some signatory states, France for example, may continue with internal border checks thereafter.[40]

Immigration policy development by all EC governments outside EC institutions

As far as the EC as a whole was concerned, the forum within which immigration policy was first discussed was the so-called 'Trevi Group', comprising all EC Interior Ministers. This was a structure for national politicians established in 1976, which excluded the policy making institutions of the EC, namely the European Commission and the Council of Ministers. The point of this structure was to discuss questions on individual countries' agendas, rather than to formulate a coherent and fair policy for the EC as a whole. The focus was on border security and crime prevention; the discussions about immigration were on the same agenda as issues of state security and law and order such as drug-trafficking, international terrorism and tax evasion. Instead of a common policy on harmonised border controls being evolved from within the EC institutions, questions of third country immigration were hived off the Community agenda and into the intergovernmental process, reflecting the restrictionist interests of individual governments. The tension between Community and national interests is illustrated by the fact, already discussed on page 204, that some member states including Britain have continued openly to violate Article 8a of the EC Treaty (now Article 7 of Maastricht) by checking everyone entering the country, Community national or not.

The first Schengen agreement set the terms for what followed. Discussions on immigration and asylum issues at a European level continued to take place outside the ambit of parliamentary scrutiny or public discussion. In 1986, while the Trevi Group concerned itself with international crime, drug trafficking and related police concerns, the 'Ad Hoc Group: Immigration' was set up as the intergovernmental body primarily concerned with immigration and asylum matters. The name is misleading; the group has met consistently and with increased frequency over the past seven years and now consists of six long-standing subgroups. Nor did the separation of responsibility result in a different perspective: the ministers responsible for supervising the Ad Hoc Group are the same as those involved in the Trevi discussions. Secrecy and an overriding concern to restrict access to Community territory has continued to dominate the discussions on immigration and asylum.

Working groups on immigration and asylum matters have proliferated and in 1988 a Group of Co-ordinators on the Free Movement of Persons, also known as the 'Rhodes Group' was set up by the EC Council of Ministers to co-ordinate the activities of all the various intergovernmental bodies and to try to eliminate delays on the part of member states. It consists of high-ranking civil servants from the 12 EC states; its first task was to report on two categories of measures, those *indispensable* for the suppression of internal borders, and those not indispensable but *desirable.* The report, which was adopted in June 1989, is known as the Palma Document.

But at the Maastricht summit in December 1991, the EC heads of state refused to bring the fields of justice and home affairs, including most of the areas of common interest in the field of asylum and immigration, within Community competence. The Treaty on European Union (known as the Maastricht treaty or simply 'Maastricht') singles out immigration for a twin-track procedure; the list of non-EC countries whose nationals will require visas to enter into the EC territory is to be proposed by the European Commission, and a common visa format is therefore to be formulated within EC competence. On the other hand all other matters of common concern, such as asylum policy, external border controls, and immigration policy for third country nationals, legally and illegally within Community territory, are to be dealt with by means of inter-governmental cooperation, outside the ambit of parliamentary scrutiny or control, or judicial supervision. Member states have shown their determination to retain absolute control over these areas of policy. The political will to allow oversight by Community institutions is clearly lacking and most likely will be for some considerable time to come.[41]

The Ad Hoc Group has been responsible for the formulation of two major immigration conventions. Though neither is yet in force, Britain and several other EC countries have already implemented most of the terms of both conventions.

The External Borders Convention

Mention has already been made of the EC's 'Fortress Europe' strategy. A central plank in this approach is the Ad Hoc Group's draft External Borders Convention.[42] Its clauses are practically indistinguishable from those of the Schengen Convention of 1990, passed in order to implement the 1985 Schengen agreement mentioned earlier. But the Schengen agreements will only apply, once ratified, to the signatory states while the External Borders Convention, once brought into force, will apply to all EC member states. It provides for stringent controls on the entry of TCNs and for sanctions for unlawful crossing of borders. It is the legal underpinning of the external fence.

The nationals of all but a handful of rich, white countries will be required to obtain a common European visa before entering the European fortress. The list of countries for which visas will be required is being formulated on a lowest common denominator basis,[43] the siege mentality having taken a firm hold. Race and wealth are the defining criteria for exclusion from the visa list, not historical ties, or humanitarian desperation. Examples are the USA, Australia and Japan, whereas visa countries include India, Iraq, Somalia and most of the Balkan republics. Preserving European self-interest is the current policy yardstick.

Of course, member states already have visa requirements for increasing numbers of nationalities as the harmonisation process gathers steam and obliterates the past. In the UK, for example, Tunisia, Algeria and Morocco were added in 1990 to meet the requirements of France; in Portugal, Mozambique was added to match practice in other member states. But the lists are not yet entirely uniform.

The human consequences of these policies are kept firmly out of European view by ensuring that those who do not qualify for entry are kept away from the portals of Europe in the first place. Thus the Convention stipulates that fines should be imposed on all airlines and shipping companies who transport undocumented or inadequately documented passengers. Unqualified airline staff are being turned into immigration officers, primarily charged with safeguarding their employers' financial liabilities rather than applying complex immigration or human rights legislation. The mechanism for doing this is already clear; Britain has enforced just such punitive measures against airlines and ferries since the Immigration (Carriers' Liability) Act 1987. Carriers now have to pay a fine of £2000 for each passenger brought to Britain without the correct passport or visa. Between March 1987, when the law was first introduced, and May 1993, the total amount of fines imposed on carriers exceeded £55 million.[44]

What therefore makes good commercial sense is 'When in doubt, keep them out'. Wrongful exclusion has no price tag, erroneous inclusion does.

Yasmin, a young Somali woman, was granted full refugee status in the UK in 1990. When she fled to Britain, she was forced to leave her elderly mother, a widowed sister and her three young children in a refugee camp in Kenya. For over a year and a half she has been trying to bring them into the UK. They require visas to be admitted and delays in dealing with such cases currently stretch to over two years. Without a visa no airline will issue them a ticket. Yet if the relatives were able to get on a plane and present themselves at a UK port they would in practice be allowed to stay, as refugees in their own right.

Meanwhile, far away from 'Fortress Europe', their situation in Kenya is nothing short of tragic. The refugee camp where they live was visited in January 1993 by two London immigration specialists. Their report on conditions in the refugee camp states:

> 'Conditions in Thika [Refugee Camp] are disgraceful. Hygiene is appalling. The refugees are filthy and malnourished. There [are] wholly inadequate medical supplies; malaria is rampant. The refugees are completely uninformed as to what their fate will be...We met refugees who had UNHCR [United Nations High Commission for Refugees] ration books which were issued in May 1992 but no UNHCR rations had been received...There was a tremendous sense of fear hanging over the camp...There was a very real fear of repatriation as a result of announcements in the Kenyan media.'[45]

The female relatives are at particular risk. According to a report published by *Africa Watch Women's Rights Project* in October 1993, 'hundreds of women in the refugee camps in Kenya's North Eastern Province have been raped in the past year and a half'.[46] But children have also been victims of the generalised breakdown of civil society: the report documents, for example, the rape of a four-year-old girl and a seven-year-old boy, by another, 50-year-old Somali refugee. The incident relating to the girl is described thus:

> '[The mother] heard her daughter screaming one night and when she went to investigate she found Mr Mohammed holding her daughter. He handed the girl to the mother and told her that her daughter did not want to sleep. The mother thought nothing more of it, until she discovered that her daughter was unable to urinate. When the mother examined the girl, who had undergone genital mutilation, she discovered a tear in the little girl's vagina. She had wanted to take her

daughter to the medical centre for treatment, but Mr Mohammed threatened to beat her if she did. Later, a nurse examined the little girl and confirmed that she had been raped.'[47]

UNHCR has also condemned the Kenyan refugee camps. Yet they continue, year after year, filled with people entitled by international law to enter Europe but conveniently hidden from public view apart from the occasional journalistic exposé.

The External Borders Convention also provides for the compilation of a secret list of inadmissible aliens, accessible only to governments through the computerized European Information System. The criteria for inclusion in the list raise grave civil liberties concerns.[48] Inclusion will have dramatic consequences, as it will exclude the person from Europe (and most likely from other Western countries) indefinitely. Yet it is not clear how, if at all, the decision will be challengeable since the European Court of Justice is specifically excluded by the Convention. If, for example, a Moroccan woman is excluded from France because of an undesirable classification by Spain, will the decision be challengeable in Spain or France, or in some third, as yet non-existent, intergovernmental forum? It is also not clear whether having one's name on the list will override other rights, such as the right to family reunion.

The Dublin Convention

The second major convention formulated by the Ad Hoc Group is the Dublin Convention on Asylum, signed by the 12 EC Member States in June 1990.[49] Like the External Borders Convention, its terms were taken from the Schengen Agreement, and it is not yet in force. The thrust of this convention is to restrict asylum applicants to one application only within the EC and to limit responsibility for considering the application to only one state. Its implications for refugees are discussed in the following chapter. Like the External Borders Convention, this convention is already applied in practice.

Refugees fleeing the war in the Balkans, in the absence of a direct route to Britain from much of former Yugoslavia, were presented with a Catch-22 situation: to get to Britain they had to transit through another EC state, but on arrival the government sent them back to the transit country to have their claim considered there. Ljubitza Kendall offered her sister and nephew refuge from the war in Bosnia, but when they arrived from Germany they were sent back. Voicing a widespread view, she commented: 'I truly cannot believe that people would not accept her and her son even though she had relatives who could look after her financially. She would not have been a burden to the Government at all.'[50] The application of this policy to refugees from the Balkans, some of whom had only spent as little as half an hour in the 'first country', was only suspended as a result of widespread media criticism embarrassing to the government.[51]

Stays of as little as a couple of hours, for whatever reason, have been held to justify returning asylum applicants to 'third countries' through which they have passed en route to the UK. In April 1993, a Colombian asylum-seeker travelled to London on a flight which was forced to make an unscheduled overnight stopover in the Azores following a fire scare on board the plane. Passengers were accommodated by the airline in a hotel on the island for the night before continuing their journey to London. The Home Office insisted on sending the asylum seeker back to Portugal even though he had a sister in London and knew no-one in Portugal.[52] His sister followed him to Portugal and found that he had suffered a nervous breakdown due to his experiences. She campaigned vigorously on his behalf and eventually he was returned to Britain for his asylum application to be considered.

A convention parallel to the Dublin Convention is being agreed by member states with Austria, Finland, Norway, Sweden, Switzerland and Canada.[53]

Harmonisation of immigration law across the EC

Member states have been reluctant to ratify the conventions and the process has proved far more time consuming than anticipated or desired by policy makers. As a result EC governments have recently adopted a more informal mechanism for formulating policy. At their six-monthly meetings, EC immigration ministers approve policy recommendations formulated by the Ad hoc group with agreed implementation dates for member states. No parliamentary ratification is required and the European Court of Justice is, as with the Conventions, excluded from any regulatory role. Though the recommendations are not legally binding 'they are not without importance or effect as they have a political and moral weight which member states will always be slow to ignore'.[54] They set the framework for harmonisation of immigration control across the Community. As in the case of the visa lists, the most restrictive policies in any member state are enshrined as a possible approach for all.

One of the proposals agreed so far, a recommendation on expulsion of people unlawfully present in a member state, is a good example of the 'Fortress Europe' approach in practice. For what it states is that expulsion should be to a territory outside the Community, and that readmission agreements should be concluded with third countries to facilitate this process. Europe's rejects will be dumped on poorer east European or developing countries, who will be forced to agree in return for desired trade or economic benefits.[55] Intrusive checks on non-EC nationals living within member states are encouraged, to detect people without legal immigration status. Women fleeing violent husbands from whom they derived their right to remain may, under these proposals, face increased risks of detection and therefore expulsion.

The expulsion provisions include a radically new and potentially drastic clause: member states can 'expel those people who are subject to immigration/aliens provisions who have been involved in the facilitation, harbouring or *employment* of illegal immigrants'.[56] [emphasis added]. To illustrate, a Jamaican hairdresser, living and working in the UK since 1975, might fall foul of this provision if she employed, as an assistant, a Trinidadian student needing extra funds to complete her studies, working without the required authorisation; this would be the case even if the hairdresser had no knowledge of the requirement, and no reason to believe the student was working illegally. It remains to be seen how this provision will be implemented, given that it contradicts a long line of cases developed by the European Court and Commission of Human Rights, on the residence rights of settled immigrants in the face of deportation threats.[57]

The proposals on family reunion illustrate the ever-increasing gap between the protected first class human rights of Community nationals and the third class rights of non-nationals; member states can introduce into their domestic legislation all the most restrictive aspects of current national policy. States are free to limit to 16 the age by which dependent children must apply to join their parents; only Germany operates such a low limit at present. This is despite the fact that the 1961 European Social Charter to which all EC states are signatories and which enshrines a number of social rights (just as the European Convention on Human Rights enshrines civil and political rights), defines as dependants children under the age of 21.[58] Once admitted, family members may be refused permission to work, as is the case in Ireland; minimum residence periods can be imposed before family reunion is allowed, following the practice in many states, though not the UK. The resolution makes no mention whatsoever of the rights of elderly parents to join their grown up children. Despite earlier ministerial statements to the contrary, it is clear that such policy is being formulated with human rights considerations firmly in the background.

Britain's contribution to this restrictive menu is the infamous primary purpose rule, discussed in detail in Chapter 3. It is applied not only to spouses but also to adopted children. The parties to the adoption will have to prove that the main purpose of the adoption was *not* to enable the child to enter the receiving member state. De facto adoptions (with no recognised adoption order) are also excluded. To many other EC countries, the concept of an 'adoption of convenience' is quite shocking; children's interests are paramount within relevant international law and in many areas of domestic law too.[59] Yet the wording of the draft resolution regarding adopted children is even more restrictive than the current UK rules. It provides for member states 'normally' to grant permission to 'children adopted by both the resident and his or her spouse while they were resident together in a third country...and where the adopted children have the same rights and obligations as the other children and there has been a *definitive break* with the family of origin.' [emphasis added].

The fightback

The secret and undemocratic process by which these policies are formulated and eventually agreed has already been described. The scope for intervention and modification, let alone challenge, seems non-existent. Nevertheless there are signs of a growing public awareness of the implications of these machinations; community groups, human rights organisations, concerned lawyers and academics are now pressing for more information and attempting to publicise developments as they occur. European meetings and conferences on these topics are multiplying, as are newspaper and journal articles exposing them.

In Britain several major conferences on these topics have been organised in the last two years, with delegates attending from all over Europe; publications such as the *JCWI Bulletin, Statewatch, Migration News Sheet*, and the journals *Immigration and Nationality Law and Practice* and *Race and Class*, carry regular articles. Organisations that are developing European links and coordinating political action include the Migrants Forum, the Black Women and Europe Network and the Standing Conference on Racial Equality in Europe (SCORE). The latter organisation recently initiated a challenge to the British government's continued policy of border checks: on return to the UK after a day trip to Calais, a group of 12 people refused to comply with the immigration officer's demand to see their passports. The contention that this demand contravenes Article 8a of the EC Treaty as amended by the Single European Act (now Article 7 of the Maastricht treaty) is currently the subject of a legal test case. This is a far cry from the demonstrations, pickets and mass lobbies of the 1970s and 1980s; but given the difficulties and the challenges presented by organising at a European rather than purely national level, the signs of increased cooperation and coordination are encouraging.

A hierarchy of rights

As far as free movement within the EC is concerned the difference between the rights of EC nationals and their families on the one hand and non-EC nationals on the other covers all areas of immigration law, from entry formalities to family reunion rights. These differences apply whether the non-EC nationals live outside or within the EC. An Indian worker who has lived in Britain for 20 years is in the same position as a newly arrived Colombian visitor. This exclusion of resident third country nationals from the benefits of European free movement has no basis in logic or justice; the European Commission supports abolition of the distinction as do other concerned bodies.[60]

The distinction has several far-reaching consequences. It has institutionalised discrimination on the basis of nationality across the Community, fuelling political controversy over access to citizenship rights. In addition, nationality and race are closely connected: most of the 8.3 million resident third country nationals excluded from free movement rights are non-white, a substantial proportion nationals of Europe's ex-colonies. Britain's unceremonious discard of the colonised and ex-colonised is clearly exemplified by the 1981 British Nationality Act, discussed in detail in Chapter 2; France passed legislation reducing access to citizenship in 1993.

This process has been a general one; now that the material interests of Europe have shifted from close ties with the colonies to cooperation within Europe and the surrounding area, so too has the preferential treatment. Two developments arise out of this. First, while the EC fortifies itself against immigration from outside Europe, a substantial group of non-EC non-resident nationals, all white, have had EC free movement rights extended to them. This is a consequence of the agreement signed between the EC and the signatory countries of the European Free Trade Association (EFTA).[61] In force from 1 January 1994, it ensures free movement rights for nationals of all EFTA countries except Switzerland (because the Swiss voted against this in a referendum) and Liechtenstein on a par with those of EC nationals, throughout the common area, known as the European Economic Area.

The fact that the beneficiaries of this agreement, in contrast to most settled non-EC residents within the Community, are white and affluent explains the almost total lack of public discussion or awareness of the immigration implications of the agreement. The EC's differential treatment of these two groups could not be more stark. Discrimination on the basis of nationality slides imperceptibly into racial discrimination. It is hardly surprising then that, in the official eye, white has often become synonymous with EC national, non-white with non-EC national. The unjustified suspicions and discriminatory treatment, illustrated by the story of Natasha Oldham, seem bound to increase.

There is a second rung in the hierarchy of European immigration rights. The European Community has entered into 'association' and 'cooperation' agreements with many of the surrounding states.[62] They reflect the importance to the EC of workers from those countries and cover anti-discrimination in the field of employment and social security rights. Workers from some of the countries covered also have residence rights within the EC once they have gained lawful access to the labour market. In the case of *Kus*, the European Court of Justice ruled that a Turkish worker's right to have his work permit renewed was not invalidated by dissolution of the marriage that had secured the worker's entry into the member state in the first place. Moreover the court ruled that a worker who meets the requirement for having a work permit renewed must also necessarily have the right to renew his or her residence permit.

These agreements do not give people rights of access to seek employment; so they will not bring to an end the raids, publicised during the summer of 1993, against Polish or Czech workers illegally employed on farms in southern England discussed on page 197.[63] Nor will they protect young Russian and Serbian women, lured from poverty by false promises of good employment, and then forced into prostitution under slave conditions by the growing number of vice racketeers operating in several EC cities.[64] However they do offer some protection against enforced departure to workers already lawfully employed within the member states.

The agreements also mean that nationals of some of the countries may have rights of residence and family reunion within the EC which put them in a far better position than other third-country nationals. For example, Fatima, a young Turkish woman, worked as a shop assistant while her Pakistani husband Mustafa studied engineering for four years. At the end of his studies Mustafa has no independent right to remain in Britain; but, because of the EC agreement with Turkey, Fatima is entitled to carry on with her job, and therefore to reside with her husband in Britain. Had she been Pakistani too, the couple would have been forced to leave the UK.

Conclusion

There is a stark and growing contrast between domestic and European Community law in the field of immigration. British immigration law for non-EC nationals is becoming ever more restrictive, the process exacerbated by the European harmonisation process which imports into national legislation many of the most stringent measures in existence in other European countries. Community law, on the other hand, provides a model for a relatively humane legal framework for migration; furthermore the scope of Community law is being progressively enlarged through the European Economic Area, the association agreements with surrounding states, and successful legal challenges to governments' restrictions of the free movement ideal (see the effect of the *Surinder Singh* case discussed on pages 86 and 211, for example).

Most EC nationals exercising Treaty rights are doing so out of choice; they move for a change of scene or to better their life chances, economic migrants par excellence! Many non-EC migrants, by contrast, embark on the perilous journey into the European fortress to seek basic human rights; to stake their claim to family life, to obtain an educational qualification which will enable them to earn a living back home, or simply to pull themselves and their families up to a subsistence standard of living. Witness the intrepid Moroccans risking death on the flimsy 'pateras' or boats to the Spanish coast, the Angolan students selling trinkets at Italian tourist attractions and the Caribbean children seeking to be reunited with their parents by answering perplexing questions at European embassies abroad. The ease of access into and within the EC seems inversely proportional to the humanitarian need for it.

The picture that emerges is of a division, according to European self-interest and political expediency, between states whose nationals have access to full rights of free movement with generous family reunion rights attached, and states whose nationals have access, by varying degrees, to much lesser rights. In this scenario, sex discrimination also applies unevenly. Insofar as they are covered by EC law, nationals of EC countries and their families are not affected. Third country nationals, however, and EC nationals covered only by their own country's immigration laws may still be.

Chapter 8

A well-founded fear of exclusion: the legal problems of women refugees

One of the most dramatic developments in the migration field over the past decade has been the growth in the numbers of people seeking asylum. There are estimated to be 17.5 million refugees worldwide; two thirds are female[1] and women refugees face particular difficulties at all stages of the asylum-seeking process. This chapter will focus on the legal problems of refugees seeking asylum in Europe, particularly Britain, and highlight some of the special difficulties encountered by women refugees.

Apart from a brief fall in 1987, the numbers of people seeking asylum in European Community countries rose steadily from 1983 reaching an all time high of over half a million in 1992.[2] The most stark illustration of this phenomenon has occurred in Germany, which has received by far the largest number of asylum seekers,[3] but the picture is mirrored in Britain, where there was a tenfold increase in asylum applications between 1985 and 1991.[4]

The reasons for the refugee increase are varied. A look at the countries of origin of the leading groups of asylum applicants reveals that war, human rights abuses, the rise of fundamentalism and dictatorial regimes intolerant of minorities are the prime factors: between January and August 1992, the Balkans, Sri Lanka, Turkey, Somalia and Iraq were among the 10 leading countries of origin of UK asylum seekers. Western economic and political policies, which have progressively impoverished the third world, propping up authoritarian regimes serving Western interests, have had a large role in this process of refugee creation. The dramatic developments in eastern Europe have been another central factor.

Within the overall trend, the numbers of applicants for asylum have been unevenly distributed, reflecting the different policies of the receiving governments. Germany, as already indicated, has been the main receiver, because of its relatively liberal asylum law, formulated in order to expiate the guilt of past Nazi atrocities. Britain, by contrast, has received relatively few refugees. In 1991, for example, a year in which the number of applications for asylum in the UK was higher than ever before or since, fewer applications in relation to population size were received in Britain than in any comparable European country, one for every 1,277 head of population compared to one for every 158 in Switzerland, and one for every 303 in Germany.[5] This is explained partly by the tactical 'advantage', from an exclusionary point of view, of being an island, and partly by the lack of political will to assist refugees.

The British response to the civil war in Bosnia illustrates this starkly: Germany has received 230,000 asylum-seekers from the former Yugoslavia whereas Britain promised to accept a mere 5000 from the refugee camps and by August 1993 had admitted only 700 people, despite raging civil war and widespread atrocities and casualties. Instead of taking steps to identify refugees eligible for the remaining places the British government has cut funds promised for Bosnian refugee centres.[6] The evacuation of Irma Hadzimuratovic, a wounded five-year-old Sarajevo girl, mounted as a publicity exercise following months of wilful neglect of known emergency situations in Bosnian hospitals, and the subsequent insistence on strict qualifying criteria for evacuation has led to widespread condemnation of the British government's 'meat market' attitude.[7] Hamdija Suhonjic, a Bosnian Muslim, came to Britain after being rescued from a detention camp. The Home Office told him that his wife, Safija, could join him but that his two adult daughters — Azra and Mirzeta — could not. Safija refused to leave Bosnia without her daughters and in May 1993 she and Mirzeta were captured by Serbs, raped and murdered.[8]

Given the scale of the problem world-wide, and the relative wealth of Europe, its contribution has been most limited. The main host countries for refugees are all in the third world. By 1992 there were about 1.3 million refugees and asylum-seekers living in Europe; by contrast Sudan, one of the poorest countries in the world, has an estimated 2 million refugees.[9] Nevertheless the reaction of western governments to the arrival of asylum seekers has been increasingly harsh, not to say hysterical. Following a generally poor record towards refugees in the 1930s (the Home Office, for example, imposed visas on Austrians and Germans in May 1938 to block the entry of Jewish refugees),[10] Britain, along with other EC countries, has adopted increasingly restrictive measures. A chain reaction has ensued with governments emulating each other to deflect potential refugees from their borders.

British government policy and ministerial pronouncements in recent years do not acknowledge its mean-minded, minimal contribution. The image presented is the familiar one of swamping and overcrowding; to this is added a new twist, the ubiquitous accusation that refugees are 'really' only economic migrants, not persecuted individuals fleeing for their lives.

There are clear signs that the restrictive policies being pursued by western governments are achieving the desired reduction in the number of arriving asylum seekers. In Britain there has been a decline from 1992 onwards.[11] A similar trend is evident in Germany. In response to the controversy surrounding ever-increasing refugee admissions and the dramatic escalation in xenophobia and racist violence over the preceding 18 months,[12] the German Parliament voted on 26 May 1993 to amend the constitution and revoke the guarantee of asylum. As of 1 July 1993, the new, restrictive policy has been operated, changing Germany overnight from one of the most to one of the least liberal countries for asylum-seekers in Europe. There are news reports of hostels for refugees being closed as the numbers of asylum applicants fall rapidly.[13] The post-war commitment to human rights has been betrayed in deference to the militancy of the far right. As the examples of Britain and Germany illustrate, current government attitudes are a far cry from the political consensus which generated the modern concept of 'refugee' in international law.

The legal position of refugees

Though refugees and mass movements of displaced peoples have existed since time immemorial, the modern definition of a refugee was formulated as a response to a specifically European problem, the widespread devastation and human displacement caused by the Second World War. The Universal Declaration of Human Rights, the international community's response to the tragic human consequences of the war, stated, at Article 14: 'Everyone has the right to seek and enjoy in other countries asylum from persecution'.

However, this Declaration has no binding force; in other words, signatory countries are not compelled to implement it. As a result, most of the rights it sets out have been incorporated into subsequent, binding instruments. Not so the right to asylum, as all efforts to include a binding right to this effect in later international conventions have failed, having been strongly resisted by individual governments anxious to preserve their sovereignty on the question of who has a right to live within the national territory.

The 1951 Geneva Convention on Refugees

The main international instrument governing refugee protection is the 1951 Geneva Convention relating to the Status of Refugees. As a measure specifically arising out of the aftermath of the Second World War, it was initially limited to events which had occurred before 1st January 1951 and was formulated largely in response to European refugee flows. It was subsequently extended beyond any geographic or time limitation by the 1967 New York Protocol. However its structure reflects the concerns of the period when it was drafted, which were to clarify the legal status of known, European displaced populations whose presence in the receiving countries was already tolerated if not lawful. The Convention's appropriateness for current realities which concern regulating the admission or resettlement of primarily third world refugees has therefore been questioned.

The term 'refugees' refers to people who have fled their country to avoid persecution. 'Asylum' refers to the legal status which may be granted to an individual refugee by a host country. An 'asylum applicant' or 'asylum-seeker' is someone who applies for asylum. Though normally co-extensive, the terms 'refugee' and 'asylum applicant/seeker' are not synonyms. A person may not fear *persecution* but nevertheless apply for asylum because he or she does not wish to return to the country of origin, for example because it would be impossible to get a job there. Such a person would be an asylum applicant but not a refugee. A more valid claim would arise in the situation where the person faced the death penalty for avoiding the army. Prosecution for a criminal offence does not generally count as persecution; nor does punishment for avoiding conscription into the army. The claim for asylum could be based on Article 3 of the European Convention on Human Rights according to which 'No one shall be subjected to torture or to inhuman or degrading treatment or punishment'. Conversely a person who feared persecution but had a satisfactory immigration status in the host country might not apply for asylum despite being a refugee. For example, a Bosnian refugee worker with indefinite leave to remain or a Somali refugee married to an EC national would not need to apply for asylum in order to secure a safe refuge.

The Convention does not grant a *right to asylum*; it merely regulates the status of those who have been accepted as refugees by a national authority. Thus the decision about who to accept and who not to accept as a refugee is left entirely to national governments. It is important to bear this in mind because much government rhetoric in Britain and elsewhere in Europe attempts to conceal the ever deteriorating human rights record as regards refugees by claiming to uphold international obligations as if these set out a clear mandate for states. This is not the case. There is no international forum, such as a court or tribunal, which can provide, let alone enforce, a consistent interpretation of the definition itself or to which wrongly excluded refugees can appeal. The only *requirement* imposed on signatory states by the Convention is that they shall not return ('refoule') people to the frontiers of a country where their life or freedom would be threatened. Article 33, the 'non-refoulement' clause, has become an important international tool safeguarding asylum-seekers' interests, though its precise scope is unclear because of the absence of authoritative judicial interpretation.[14]

The definition of a refugee

Article 1 A(2) of the 1951 Geneva Convention relating to the Status of Refugees defines a refugee as a person who 'owing to a well-founded fear of being persecuted for reasons of race, religion, nationality, membership of a particular social group or political opinion, is outside the country of his [sic] nationality and is unable or unwilling to avail himself of the protection of that country...'.

The Convention is the main international instrument governing the treatment of refugees and European governments have tended to incorporate the Convention definition of a refugee into their domestic legislation (even if, as shown below, they are placing increasingly restrictive interpretations on it). This definition therefore, though formulated over 40 years ago, is still of central importance. It provides the parameters within which decisions about who qualifies for refugee status, and legal challenges to those decisions, take place.

The Geneva Convention is inadequate for modern realities. It excludes people fleeing from war or natural disaster, in contrast to the broader refugee definition adopted by African and Central American states. The Organisation of African Unity, for example, extends the definition of a refugee to every person who 'owing to external aggression, occupation, foreign domination or events seriously disturbing public order in either part or the whole of his country of origin or nationality is compelled to leave his place of habitual residence in order to seek refuge in another place outside his country of origin or nationality.'[15] There may therefore be *non-Convention refugees* who nevertheless qualify for asylum. But asylum applicants excluded from the definition are much less likely to be granted refugee status and therefore to receive protection than those included in the definition.

Discouragement of asylum-seekers: imposition of visas

Along with other EC countries, the UK has been assiduously seeking to restrict the entry of asylum-seekers. One strategy has been the imposition of visas on nationals of refugee-generating countries, to prevent the 'problem' from even reaching British shores. This strategy was first deployed against Iranians in 1980 and then against Tamils fleeing from Sri Lanka. The extent of persecution and threats to life and freedom in Sri

Lanka were well known internationally, so much so that in April 1984 the British government was compelled to announce a 'no return' policy for Tamils reaching Britain. However as the violence in Sri Lanka escalated and the numbers of fleeing Tamils grew, press reports linking the exodus to 'economic migration' increased. The government took advantage; on 29 May 1985 visas were imposed on Sri Lankans, the first time these had been required of Commonwealth citizens.

This official hostility to Tamils was also evidenced by the increasing use of detention on arrival and widespread reports of maltreatment. Some Tamils were taken into detention handcuffed; three women detained at the overcrowded Harmondsworth detention centre near Heathrow airport had to sleep in the telephone room, one just with a mattress on the floor.[16] Up to 100 Tamils were detained in appalling conditions on board a disused Channel car ferry, the *Earl William*. Four Tamil women detained on the ferry complained of being denied sanitary towels for two months.[17] The detainees were only released after a ferocious gale in October 1987 made the ship slip her moorings and drift out to sea until grounded by a sandbank. The increased use of detention as a deterrent to potential asylum-seekers is a feature of government policy throughout the EC. In one reported case, a seven-month pregnant asylum-seeker, Jacqueline Mulata, died in prison in Holland.[18]

The majority of Tamils granted permission to stay were denied full refugee status,[19] despite medical evidence of torture in many cases and widespread publicity about continuing atrocities in Sri Lanka. They were instead granted exceptional leave to remain (ELR), a status which has to be renewed every year and affords no immediate family reunion rights. Home Office policy is normally not to make any further exception to allow any family members to come until people have had exceptional leave for four years; and then only to consider spouses and children.

The effect of this policy is shown by the situation of Nirmala, an 18 year old Sri Lankan Tamil, who arrived in Britain alone in April 1985, having managed to escape a raid on her house by the army who arrested her two brothers. Though relieved to have survived, her prime concern was with the safety of her family back home, particularly her elderly parents, left to fend entirely for themselves in what had effectively become a war zone. Nirmala's family had well-known links with the 'Tiger' guerrilla movement; she had been arrested on several occasions before fleeing. Yet her application for refugee status was rejected. With no international forum for challenging this, she was left with her ELR status. This gave her no rights to immediate family reunion. The visa requirement prevented her parents from applying for entry directly. Nirmala had withstood the ordeals of the war in Sri Lanka with fortitude. However the prolonged family separation and her isolation in Britain resulted in her becoming clinically depressed and requiring hospitalisation.

Unlike some other western countries, the United States and Canada for example, Britain has no official procedure allowing people fleeing persecution to apply from abroad for refugee status. However when visas were imposed on Sri Lankans the Home Office stated that applications at the British High Commission in Colombo from those suffering 'exceptional hardship' would be considered. Very few such visas have ever been granted, and the 1993 Asylum and Immigration Appeals Act removes this chance altogether. Asylum-seekers must have already fled the country of persecution; however the EC requires visas for nationals of most of the refugee-generating countries. The European fortress has become particularly impenetrable for refugees.

The next group of refugees blocked by the summary imposition of visas were Turkish Kurds, fleeing widely publicised human rights violations. Following a familiar course, immigration officers fed the press with stories about the arrival of increasing numbers of Turkish asylum-seekers, to counter the Foreign Office's reluctance to impose visas on citizens of a NATO country. The same pattern as for Tamils recurred; widespread and prolonged detention, the imposition of visas, the unjustified denial of full refugee status to many.

Hatice, for example, was first arrested in 1978, aged 14, when she and her schoolfriends were organising a left-wing political education programme. She was detained at the police station and beaten with truncheons, for distributing leaflets produced by Dev-Genc, the youth wing of Dev-Yol, a left-wing group in Turkey. Throughout her adolescence, she and her brother were frequently arrested, detained and beaten, but they continued their political activities, recruiting for the organisation, leafleting and attending marches. The family eventually moved from Sivas in south-eastern Turkey to Istanbul, in the hope that they would be safer there, but the harassment and persecution continued. At a May Day rally in 1988, Hatice was arrested, detained for 10 days, and tortured; she was subjected to falaka (beating on the soles of the feet), she was held by her hair and had her head hit against a wall, she was kicked in the stomach and kept in a damp cell. After her release, she fled from home and had to move around, never staying long in one place. Eventually she decided to leave Turkey, as she could no longer take the pressure of living in hiding. She came to Britain on 21 June 1989 and applied for asylum. In February 1990, she was refused full refugee status and only granted exceptional leave to remain. It was not until April 1993, after her representatives had submitted further detailed medical evidence of torture, that her claim to refugee status was finally granted.

These policies have had devastating consequences. Families have suffered prolonged separation, there have been several suicide attempts and two men have burned themselves to death.[20] The arbitrary nature of the decision to grant ELR rather than full refugee status is highlighted by the fact that, in the face of concerted pressure, appeals against the refusal of refugee status or an effective campaign, the Home Office has on occasion reversed its decision.

Sultan, a Turkish Kurd, was forced to flee persecution in Turkey leaving young children behind. Her husband had escaped and been granted ELR after a substantial delay, before her arrival. Sultan waited over a year for her political asylum claim to be determined. Refusing to accept further separation from her children, she went on hunger strike; on the 17th day without food both she and her husband were granted full refugee status. They were then able to bring their children to join them in Britain.

A recent development is the imposition, for nationals of some countries, of a visa requirement simply to transit through Britain. That this is another device to exclude refugees is clear from the list of countries affected: Sri Lanka, Iraq, Lebanon and Somalia were the first; in July 1993 this was extended to nationals of Afghanistan, Iran, Libya, Turkey, Uganda and Zaire.[21]

Carriers' Liability Act

Since the UK and other EC countries have blocked direct access to fleeing refugees by the imposition of visas, many asylum-seekers have had to obtain forged documents in order to seek safety. This may be through political contacts or by using the services of middlemen, who are often unscrupulous and extortionately expensive. Obtaining valid travel documents is, in any event, far harder for refugees than for those not out of favour with their national governments. However the UK, along with other EC governments, has acted to close off this escape route too by imposing heavy penalties on airlines and shipping companies who carry passengers with false or forged passports — or no passports at all.

The British version of this legislation is the 1987 Immigration (Carriers' Liability) Act, which currently imposes a £2000 fine on airlines and shipping companies for each ineligible passenger brought to Britain, even if the passenger is eventually allowed to stay.[22] Additionally, the carriers have the burden of turning staff who lack the appropriate qualifications and training into immigration officers. Since the law was introduced in 1987 the government has imposed £55,557,000 in fines, of which £25,044,000 had been paid by July 1993.[23]

The Dublin Convention

As if these measures were not sufficiently stringent, the UK, along with other EC governments, has entered into a formal agreement to curtail the rights of refugees further. This is the Dublin Convention, signed by the EC states in 1990.[24] Its main provisions are to limit responsibility for each asylum-seeker to only one state, thus exonerating other states from analysing the merits of the application.[25] Unless an asylum-seeker has 'close connections' elsewhere, the country that he or she first entered must process the claim. States can exchange information to help them determine which should be the responsible state. The Dublin Convention has not yet been ratified by all the member states[26] and cannot come into force until this is the case. However, in practice, the UK and other governments, supported by domestic courts, have been rigidly implementing its provisions for some time. These include the bouncing back of 'third country' cases to the state considered responsible.

For example, Martha, a 23 year old Sri Lankan Tamil, arrived at Heathrow airport on her own in August 1993 and requested asylum. The only relatives she had in Europe were several uncles in London. The immigration officer refused to consider the merits of her asylum application because he thought she had travelled through France before arriving in the UK. Martha did not know what countries she had travelled through, but did not think she had been to France. Moreover her lawyers pointed out that France was sending some Tamils back to Sri Lanka and that Martha would be at risk, particularly as a young single woman. Nevertheless she was 'returned' to France. The French authorities denied that she had ever passed through France and sent her back to Britain. She was interviewed at length again, and again told she had travelled through France; her asylum claim was refused on the basis that she should have applied in France.

The Home Office operates a restrictive definition of the refugee family when considering applications for family reunion. Only the spouse or unmarried children under 18 of a refugee are allowed, and in the case of an unmarried minor refugee, the parents; sibling relationships are therefore not recognised, even for very young refugees. This causes particular hardship in cases such as that of Khadra, where, through war or illness, an older sibling has replaced the parents as head of the family.

Khadra, a 16 year old Somali girl, arrived in London in December 1992 with her three younger brothers. They came from Germany where they had been living alone for over a year, following the death of their father. Formerly a high ranking police officer in Somalia, he had been persecuted because of his clan membership by the Siad Barre regime and forced to flee. Having claimed asylum for himself and the four children, he died two months after arriving in Germany. Khadra had to fend for herself and her younger brothers, lying about her age to prevent the German authorities from taking the boys into care. After two racist attacks on their home she decided she could cope no longer and fled to the UK where her older brother, with whom she had lived prior to leaving Somalia, had full refugee status. The four children have applied for family reunion with this elder brother; but they do not qualify under the terms of the Dublin Convention, since he is not a parent. The fact that their father is dead and their mother sick in a refugee camp in Ethiopia does not alter the picture.

In another case, a 16 year old Turkish Kurd with a brother in the UK was sent back to a country he had passed through on his way to Britain. When this case came up in court the barrister representing the government justified the refusal to allow the boy to stay by arguing that since he had clearly been tortured by the Turkish regime he was not an ordinary 16 year old! Even within the limited scope permitted, family reunion is only for full refugees. The increasing queue of refugees awaiting a decision on their case and those granted only exceptional leave are thereby excluded from any family reunion rights.

The 1993 Asylum and Immigration Appeals Act

Those fleeing persecution face ever-increasing difficulties in seeking refuge in Britain. Recent figures reflect this. The number of asylum applications made in Britain has virtually halved in the last year. However, in an attempt to simplify procedures, streamline the exclusion process and fortify the country further against asylum seekers, the government passed a new Act of Parliament and new Immigration Rules on asylum. They include powers for immigration and police officers forcibly to fingerprint asylum-seekers, including children; they introduce a 'fast-track' procedure for asylum claims considered to be 'without foundation' by the government, with appeals heard within five days of being lodged and no further challenge possible, and they set severely curtailed time limits for lodging appeals, two days in the case of some asylum seekers refused on entry to Britain. Housing rights of asylum applicants are also severely curtailed.

Factors which the Home Office may take into consideration in dealing with an asylum claim include the destruction of documents, the failure to seek refuge in another part of the country from which the asylum-seeker is fleeing 'to which it would be reasonable to expect him to go', failure to apply for asylum 'forthwith' on arrival or to make a full disclosure of the facts, transit through a 'safe' third country, and membership of a group 'whose claims are clearly not related to the criteria for refugee status in the Convention'. Asylum claims may be refused on these grounds if no 'reasonable explanation' is offered for them.

The effect of these provisions on women asylum-seekers will be devastating. Often reluctant to trust an unknown official with their story, they will be penalised for not disclosing all details immediately on arrival. Given the widely acknowledged reticence in speaking about rape and other sexual assault cases, victims of gender-based persecution will be particularly disadvantaged. The shortage of female interviewers and interpreters, and the obligation therefore to present case histories through men will exacerbate the hurdles such women have to overcome. What is more the explicit exclusion of asylum claims not based on Geneva Convention grounds, discussed below, will increase the difficulties in presenting gender-based persecution claims. The Act does, for the first time, grant an oral right of appeal against refusal in all cases, but given the stringency of the time limits and the restrictiveness of the criteria this is unlikely to be an effective safeguard for the majority of asylum-seekers.

Decrease in percentage granted refugee status

As a result of these measures it is increasingly hard for refugees to get to Britain and other west European countries to present their asylum claims. But access is only one of the problems they confront; as the examples above illustrate, asylum-seekers who are clearly entitled to refugee status under the Convention are being denied this status, by the UK and other EC governments.[27] The reduction in the percentage of recognised refugees is matched by a corresponding increase in those granted the inferior status of exceptional leave to remain on humanitarian grounds.

This discredits the much propounded view that most asylum applicants are attempting to circumvent immigration control; if they were simply 'economic migrants' they would not get exceptional leave. Applicants who some years ago would have been granted full refugee status no longer do today. The extreme situations which push people to flee their own country have not altered. The Amnesty International Yearbook bears testimony to the widespread occurrence of torture and human rights violations but the political climate has changed and with it government policy.

Consequences of ELR instead of refugee status

The British government's grant of ELR instead of full refugee status has serious implications for refugees' rights. Full refugees get indefinite leave to remain (settlement) after four years; those on ELR have to wait for seven years. For many refugees the anxiety and distress of seven years of insecurity after the terror and chaos which precipitated their original flight are considerable.

Of even greater consequence to the majority of asylum-seekers is the effect on family reunion rights. Full Convention refugees have an immediate entitlement to family reunion with their spouse and minor children. What is more, there is a possibility of family reunion for other dependants, such as aged parents and siblings, if they were living in the same household as the refugee before the separation.[28] In practice this provision is applied increasingly restrictively by the government. Elderly parents, siblings and other relatives are only granted family reunion if they can prove exceptionally compassionate circumstances.

Mi Lan, a Vietnamese boat person, was separated from the rest of her family at the age of 13. After a period in a Hong Kong refugee camp she was accepted as a full refugee and came to the UK. She spent 10 years with no idea whether her parents and brother were alive. In 1989 she managed to establish her family's whereabouts, in a village in China. Her father is in poor health, elderly and unemployed and the family now live off the remittances from their daughter. In 1990 Mi Lan applied for family reunion; the Home Office took over two years to consider the application and finally refused it because the family's circumstances were not considered exceptionally compassionate.

Difficult though it is for full refugees to exercise family reunion rights, they do at least have a possibility of success. People on ELR have no such *rights*, even for the immediate family, but must instead depend on the exercise of *discretion* in their favour. What is more, extensive delays are built into the system. The Home Office has stated that an application for family reunion is only likely to succeed four years after the grant of ELR. Given that there is frequently a delay of two years or more between the application and grant of ELR, a person may be faced with a six year delay in effecting family reunion.

Ayse, a Turkish Kurd, arrived in the UK with her husband in 1989, leaving four children in Turkey, the eldest with cerebral palsy. The couple clearly qualified for full refugee status because of their experiences in Turkey; however, after considerable delay, they were eventually granted only ELR. An application to upgrade their status to full refugees was made so that they could qualify for family reunion straight away rather than after four years. This produced no result and as the eldest child's condition worsened, visa applications were made in Istanbul, in March 1990. Despite pressing pleas from the family no action was taken to deal with the case urgently. By the time the papers had found their way from Istanbul to the Asylum Division of the Home Office in London the child had died.[29]

The trauma of separation for the refugee applicant in the UK is often heightened by acute concerns over the dangers facing the relatives abroad. The Home Office is usually impervious to such concerns; even though its queueing procedure for dealing with family reunion applications allows for exceptional or particularly compassionate cases to be dealt with out of order, no published guidelines exist about how this system operates, and indeed given the arbitrariness of the decisions taken it remains a mystery. The story of Amina shows the failure to acknowledge compassionate circumstances.

Amina, a Somali refugee, fled with her husband Mohamed, their baby son and other relatives, to a refugee camp on the Somalia/Kenya border following the outbreak of war in Somalia. Mohamed eventually managed to raise the cost of one air fare and arrived in the UK in September 1990, leaving Amina and the baby behind in the refugee camp. Despite numerous attempts to have his case expedited Mohamed had to wait over two and a half years, until April 1992, for a decision on his case; refugee status refused but ELR granted. He applied for family reunion and informed the Home Office on numerous occasions that extremely worrying reports had reached him about safety and health conditions in the refugee camp. In early October 1992 he learned that his son had died of malnutrition and illness; less that one month later he was informed that Amina had been shot dead in the refugee camp as a result of inter-clan fighting. Four months later there was still no reply from the Home Office.[30]

One official justification for this policy of enforced separation is that some delay is advisable to establish conclusively whether circumstances may change in the country of origin, making it possible for people on ELR to return to their families. However available figures tend to discredit this argument: in both 1990 and 1991 only four applications for extensions of ELR were refused, while the numbers of initial grants in both those years were in four figures.[31]

Recent European policy decisions on asylum

The Dublin Convention, even though not fully ratified, has proved an effective tool for forcing refugees to make their asylum application in one EC state only, even if they have close ties with another country. However, this objective has now been superseded as EC states devise ways of keeping refugees out of the European fortress altogether. The means for achieving this more ambitious end were first publicised in December 1992, at the London EC Immigration Ministers meeting, when a series of resolutions, recommendations and conclusions concerning asylum-seekers were agreed.

The legal status of these measures is unclear, but nevertheless they are planned to be implemented by national governments by 1995. One proposal is for refugees to be sent back to 'safe' countries outside the EC and its surrounding buffer states, if they have transited through any such territory. Most refugee stopover points on the way to western Europe are third world countries. Under this proposal they will be stacking up thousands of refugees, with whom they are far less well-equipped to deal than the prosperous European states. Amnesty International has expressed concern that no measures have been taken to ensure protection against refoulement back to the country of origin by these 'host third countries'.[32]

According to another proposal, refugees would not be accepted from 'safe' third countries where there is 'generally no serious risk of persecution'. Such safe country lists represent a worrying development, since generalised, out of date or incomplete information is likely to override specific allegations made by individual asylum-seekers. A third proposal has already been anticipated by the provisions of the Asylum and Immigration Appeals Act; it sets out criteria for classifying an asylum application as 'without foundation' and provides for 'fast track procedures' for dealing with such applications. In such cases there is no guarantee of a fair hearing or adequate appeal rights.

The particular difficulties of women refugees

A majority of the adults who flee their country are women.[33] Men are more likely to have been killed in fighting, to have joined government or rebel military forces, to be the victims of imprisonment and torture. Yet most asylum applicants in western countries are men.[34] Women refugees face particular difficulties at all stages of the process of flight.

> Aycha is 19 and from the Horn of Africa. She arrived in her country of asylum after a two-week trek through the desert. Physically exhausted and suffering from blistering sores she was directed to a refugee settlement but her ordeal was not yet over. A policeman of the neighbouring town raped Aycha after having threatened to have her sent back to her country of origin if she did not comply. The act of rape was subsequently medically confirmed.[35]

Women often have to assume sole responsibility as head of the household for traumatised and disrupted families, performing traditionally-male tasks in addition to their own, in the absence of normal support systems. They may face increased physical dangers arising out of the absence of family members to protect them, or out of the frustrations of their male relatives with the stresses of the refugee situation. Many women refugees risk rape by soldiers, enforced prostitution as a means of survival for their families, domestic violence from male family members unable to adapt to their loss of status and role in society. Women also face particular legal difficulties.

The gender blindness of the refugee definition

The definition of refugee contained in the Geneva Convention is gender-neutral: it does not expressly recognise gender as a ground of persecution. It reflects the traditional preoccupation of human rights law with public (and therefore 'political') activities to the detriment of those conducted in 'private'.[36] A dual process can be identified. On the one hand, ill-treatment in the 'private' or domestic sphere has often been considered too prevalent and at the same time too trivial to warrant protection. On the other hand there has been a tendency to ignore the political nature of non-traditional forms of protest or political engagement, of seemingly private activities, and to redefine persecution against women as mere personal conflict.

This may not be a problem for many women refugees who flee 'traditional persecution', such as torture and imprisonment because of their race, religion, political opinion or other Convention ground, just as their male counterparts. It does however create difficulties for women whose fears of persecution arise out of forms of protest or ill-treatment not considered 'political'.

In order to qualify as a Convention refugee an asylum applicant must show that the ill-treatment feared amounts to *persecution*; he or she must then show that the reason for the persecution is *one of the recognised grounds* in the Convention definition. Since gender is not a Convention ground, women fearing gender-specific persecution have had to try and fit their claims into one of the recognised grounds. 'Particular social group' and 'political opinion' have been the most commonly used categories, the former obviously more appropriate for women who have not been associated with political activity.

Women persecuted through association with political opposition

Refugee law has evolved through the examination of male asylum applicants and their activities. Men have been considered the agents of political action and therefore the legitimate beneficiaries of protection from persecution resulting from it. Women who are related to or associated with male political activists may be at equal risk, either as a means of eliciting information or as an object of blackmail or revenge. The harassment of families of political opponents is often part of a terror campaign against the opposition and reflects a well-documented strategy affecting countless women.[37] Similarly women's contribution to political opposition may take a form not generally recognised as 'political activity' but none the less crucial or incontrovertibly partisan; cooking, washing clothes, tending the wounded, hiding wanted activists, passing information. Gender, rather than greater or less political commitment, defines the different form of activity.

However, the harm feared by female participants in 'rebel' movements or female relatives of activists has often been considered personal rather than political, thereby excluding them from protection as refugees. There are no reported British cases on this point but a widely discussed American case provides an extreme example. Sofia Campos-Guardado, a Salvadorean woman, was visiting her uncle and cousins, active in the agrarian land reform movement, when the family were attacked by government soldiers. Together with her female cousins she was first bound and forced to watch the uncle and male cousins being hacked with machetes and shot dead; the women were then raped and threatened with death unless they fled immediately. Sofia Campos-Guardado suffered a nervous breakdown and had to be hospitalised for fifteen days; one of the attackers continued to harass her and threatened to kill her if she revealed his identity. To escape further threats she fled to the United States and applied for asylum. Her application was rejected on the basis that the harm she feared was not political.[38]

In Britain anecdotal evidence suggests that Home Office practice in deciding on similar cases is inconsistent. Sometimes cases of asylum applicants from the same country, with very similar experiences, are decided differently depending on when the asylum application is made. People who apply at the start of a refugee exodus get full refugee status, cases presented later on, when alarm about numbers of possible applicants has altered official policy, do not. Often the decision about whether to grant full refugee status appears random, dictated more by political and foreign policy considerations than by a coherent legal interpretation of the relationship of these activities to the Geneva Convention definition of refugee. This is shown in the two following examples.

Mary, a Ugandan mother of five and opponent of the Museveni regime, fled her country when the body of her husband, a prominent activist, was deposited, cut up in pieces, on the family's doorstep. She left her children in the care of a younger sister and her mother. Some weeks after her escape she found out that her two eldest daughters and her sister had been captured by government soldiers; the sister was eventually killed, the daughters freed following the intervention of a well-connected family friend who managed to bribe the authorities. Mary applied to the Home Office for refugee status. Her application was rejected, but she was granted permission to stay exceptionally.

Zarah, an Eritrean woman, came from a family active in the Eritrean Liberation Front. She had joined the organisation at the age of 18. 'Mine was a supportive role. I used to collect membership fees for the supporters all over the village and about once a month I would go to town and buy groceries for the activists. I would buy things like soap, cigarettes, underwear.'[39] She married an ELF activist, who fled to Saudi Arabia after being seriously injured in the fighting. The Ethiopian army found out about her ELF activities, and came searching for her. She fled her village and went into hiding. Eventually she left Eritrea and walked, at night, together with a convoy of traders, into Sudan. After some years working in the Gulf, Zarah's husband managed to arrange for her join him. She worked in Saudi Arabia too for some time, and, shortly before the outbreak of the Gulf war, the couple flew to London using false Saudi travel documents. They entered as visitors but then applied for political asylum and were both granted full refugee status.

Lack of consistency characterises decision-making across Europe as much as within Britain. Opposite outcomes to very similar asylum applications demonstrate the arbitrariness of the adjudication process and the need for harmonisation. Thus an Eritrean woman, member of the EPLF, who had distributed leaflets and whose husband was an EPLF fighter, fled to the Netherlands and applied for asylum after she had been sexually abused and blackmailed by a member of the military. The Dutch court rejected her asylum application on the basis that her activities were not sufficient to have rendered her a political opponent of the regime.[40] By contrast a German court granted full refugee status to an Eritrean woman who had cooked, washed and cared for resistance fighters for three years.[41]

Women who transgress cultural norms

Feminists have long recognised the political nature of seemingly private acts which transgress customary norms. In many Islamic countries, for example, refusing to wear the veil[42] or wearing lipstick, refusing to marry the selected husband or committing adultery can be acts of political protest or subversion.[43] Frequently they are severely punished. In Iran offending against dress regulations was punished by 74 lashes initially, escalating with repetition.[44] An Iranian asylum-seeker in Germany reported having been detained by one of the Islamic Revolutionary Committees for two days because she had painted her finger nails.[45] An Iranian woman who sought asylum in Canada because she had been given 35 lashes and sacked from her job for not wearing a veil in her own home was refused in May 1990 and sent back to Iran. It was believed that she risked prosecution, not persecution, that her punishment had not left permanent injuries and she had not been deprived of her livelihood.[46]

Yet frequently these challenges to social norms — differing as they do from conventional forms of political contestation — have been considered 'personally motivated' and not categorised as political. Firdaus, for example, was born in the Yemen, but as her father was a diplomat, she spent much of her childhood abroad. When the family was posted to Britain, Firdaus studied design here but, in the middle of her studies, the family moved to Saudi Arabia and her father forced her to move there too as he considered she was becoming too independent. Her life there became intolerable as her father allowed her no freedom and physically assaulted her when she tried to assert her own views. She was unable to escape from the family as an unmarried woman cannot leave Saudi Arabia without her father's consent. When the family came to London in the summer of 1985, Firdaus gained the strength to tell her father she would not return. Her father threw her out of the house, retaining her passport and refusing to speak to her thereafter. With the help of friends made while a student in Britain she managed to find temporary work and continue her education. But the Home Office refused to allow her to stay as she did not fit into the immigration rules. The question of asylum was never seriously considered, on the grounds that her reasons to fear return were solely based on her family situation, not the society in which she had lived or the social group to which she belonged. Her appeal against refusal was lost, the adjudicator stressing that he dismissed it 'with very considerable reluctance' as he was 'wholly convinced that the circumstances of the case render it essential that [Firdaus] be permitted to remain in this country'. The Home Office eventually allowed her to stay exceptionally in early 1990, after five years of uncertainty.

Women persecuted for such transgressions have had difficulties bringing themselves within the Geneva Convention definition and therefore within the protection of refugee law. Two recorded British cases, concerning women from Islamic countries who rejected their society's strict behavioural requirements, illustrate this.

Mahshid worked as a finance manager with a company in Iran. She participated in a demonstration against the compulsory wearing of the veil and did not always wear it at work. She was summonsed before the Revolutionary Guards and warned that the next time she did not wear the veil she would be treated as a prostitute and taken to prison where she would be whipped and could face capital punishment. As a result of this warning, Mahshid suffered a nervous breakdown followed by a skin disorder. Her application for refugee status in Britain was rejected.[47] The Immigration Appeal Tribunal held that westernised, middle class women in Iran who refused to conform to Islamic dress codes did not constitute a social group within the meaning of the Geneva Convention, even though, in the words of the Tribunal, 'the evidence goes to show that in certain cases there were horrendous penalties administered...'. According to the Tribunal, such women could only claim persecution if they could prove they had been specifically singled out for treatment distinguishable from other similarly placed women in their society.

This was the situation in another case[48] where an Iranian woman managed to establish that she was a close associate of the Empress Farah, wife of the deposed Shah of Iran, and a member of 'the Shah's court'. Because of this the Tribunal accepted that the woman ran the risk of being persecuted. On this basis her claim for refugee status was successful, the rejection of strictly imposed social rules not having been deemed sufficient to bring her within the refugee definition.

In an attempt to keep refugee numbers down, governments increasingly demand evidence of *personal* as opposed to group fear, and construe 'membership of a particular social group' narrowly. Court challenge is therefore crucial to assert refugees' rights to asylum. Courts in other European countries have reacted differently to very similar cases, illustrating the scope for interpretation of the Geneva Convention obligations, and the reluctance of governments to explore these possibilities.

A German court upheld the refugee claim of an Iranian woman who had refused to wear the veil (and had been arrested and detained as a result) on the basis that she had a well-founded fear of persecution *on grounds of her political opinion*;[49] a French court granted full refugee status to an Armenian Christian woman who frequently did not wear the veil, *because of her membership of a particular social group*.[50] But a Dutch court refused refugee status to an Iranian woman who had been imprisoned twice for not wearing prescribed Islamic dress, and who had been dismissed from her job after joining a silent demonstration, on the basis that her activities were too slight.[51]

The situation of rebel, non-conformist feminists in several countries with strict Islamic codes of conduct has been widely publicised; as a result there is growing pressure internationally for recognition of their entitlement to refugee status. The Canadian authorities have begun to set important precedents on this issue. In 1990 a woman and her two daughters were granted refugee status because they were held to have a well-founded fear of persecution based on their membership of the particular social group 'consisting of women and girls who do not conform to Islamic fundamentalist norms.'[52] In 1993, following a highly publicised campaign involving women and human rights organisations, a Saudi feminist was granted permission to stay. In 1991 a young Saudi woman, identified only as 'Nada', applied for asylum in Canada and based her claim solely on gender persecution. She had been an active feminist in Saudi Arabia, espousing feminist beliefs openly and refusing to wear the veil. As a result she had been imprisoned. In her asylum application she detailed the position of Saudi women as second class citizens, prohibited from driving, choosing a husband, travelling without written permission of a male guardian and frequently targeted and searched by the mutawah or secret police. The Canadian authorities rejected the asylum application; however, as a result of the success of the campaign, the Minister eventually granted Nada permission to remain exceptionally.[53]

As feminist and human rights groups increasingly involve themselves in claims of this nature, it is hoped that pressure will successfully be put on governments to recognise these forms of protest as political, warranting the grant of refugee status to those persecuted as a result.

Women at the mercy of non-governmental persecutors

Just as certain forms of protest have been deemed non-political, so certain forms of ill-treatment have been considered personal or private matters, their victims thus rendered ineligible for refugee protection. This has affected women whose persecution arises out of the systematic failure of governments to protect them from non-governmental persecutors, be they battering husbands or relatives imposing female genital mutilation.

Rabia Janjua, a Pakistani woman, raped at 20, married her rapist to avoid the customary punishment for 'Zina' or sex outside marriage. Under the Hudood Ordinance introduced in Pakistan in 1979, a charge of Zina carries a possible sentence of 10 years imprisonment and public flogging of 30 lashes.[54] Rabia was brought to Britain by her husband, and subjected to years of harassment and violence, which resulted in her being hospitalised twice, once with a knife wound and the second time while pregnant with her second child. On this latter occasion, because she nearly lost the baby, she decided to tell the authorities what had happened and eventually obtained an injunction banning her husband from coming near her or the children. In revenge he reported her as an illegal entrant to the Home Office.

Entirely dependent on her husband, Rabia was unaware that she had violated British immigration law by following his instructions and entering the UK as a visitor despite intending to settle. The Home Office declared her an illegal entrant; in March 1990 she was arrested and detained at Harmondsworth Detention Centre separated from her two children, the youngest of whom she was still breastfeeding. Her case was taken up by the feminist organisation Southall Black Sisters, a campaign mounted, and she was eventually allowed to stay.[55] She was not, however, granted refugee status, despite facing punishment for Zina if returned to Pakistan.[56]

Until very recently there has been no public discussion about whether women fleeing domestic violence can claim refugee protection.[57] Even Rabia's feminist supporters did not entertain the possibility of opposing her deportation on the basis that she had a claim for refugee status; they simply campaigned for the exercise of discretion in her favour, accepting that the treatment she feared in Pakistan did not bring her within the Convention. This reflects the traditional failure of human rights law to include within international protection these human rights abuses. This failure is all the more serious as many governments condone gross acts of violence against women as customary and not warranting state intervention.[58]

However there are signs of change. The Canadian authorities have set several important precedents which can now be used to support an extension of refugee protection to women at the mercy of non-governmental persecutors. A Canadian Federal Court of Appeal in 1992 granted refugee status to a Trinidadian woman, whose husband had routinely beaten her, and threatened to kill her if she returned home. The court recognised that she belonged to the 'particular social group of Trinidadian women subject to wife abuse' and that there was virtually no protection from the local justice system for such women.[59] Following this decision, the Canadian Refugee Board awarded refugee status to a Zimbabwean woman forced, whilst still a minor, into marriage with a man who repeatedly physically and sexually assaulted her, and who over the course of a 17 year marriage was unable to obtain state protection against his violence.[60]

European courts have not so far accepted such claims. Customary practices, such as female genital mutilation or bride burning, have not been considered persecutory acts against women warranting refugee protection, and the claims of women fleeing domestic violence have not even been formulated in these terms. The tendency of governments to grant permission to such women exceptionally has often answered the immediate humanitarian needs. However, as discussed above, exceptional permission is an inferior status with fewer rights; the practice of refusing full refugee status is unjustified and should be challenged if progress in this area is to be achieved. This is precisely what is being done in a test case currently being conducted in France.

Aminata Diop, a Malian woman, applied for refugee status in France in 1991, having defied family, fiancé and heritage and fled her home the night before she was due to be subjected to the customary ritual of clitoridectomy. In many countries governments condone or tolerate this practice or one of the other forms of female genital mutilation, performed on approximately two million female children each year and estimated to affect some 100 million women worldwide. Diop applied for refugee status in France but was refused. She was granted permission to remain exceptionally but the refusal of refugee status is the subject of an appeal pending before the French Supreme Court.[61]

Women victims of rape

Perhaps the most extreme example of the gender-blindness of the Geneva Convention is the situation of refugee women who have been victims of organised rape by soldiers. They have faced difficulties bringing themselves within the definition because the authorities tend to view rape as an apolitical, 'personalised' act of random violence against individuals, rather than a component of a political strategy against persecuted groups.

> People tend to misunderstand the substantive function of rape; they see it as a sexual act, even think it's acceptable, a kind of morale booster or booty in war. They fail to see it as an act that's about power and about terror.[62]

Rape is still frequently viewed as a crime of honour rather than a crime of torture.[63] Yet in most refugee-generating countries there are reported cases of this or similar treatment against women, including sexual harassment, forced prostitution and the obligation to grant sexual favours in return for assistance.[64] In Sri Lanka, for example, women have been been sexually abused by the authorities while in jail in order to extract information about male relatives.[65] In India reports of rape in custody are widespread;[66] in Peru's civil war, both the military and the opposition Shining Path 'measure their tactical progress through the intimidation of women'[67] by the widespread practice of rape. What is more, raped women are often repudiated by their communities after the incident, so that many choose to remain silent and conceal their experiences; women courageous enough to break this taboo may be forced to resort to prostitution as a sole means of survival.

Yet governments frequently refuse refugee status to rape victims, whose governments are responsible for or collusive of the rape. Fadumo, a 27 year old Somali woman from the Issaq clan, was shopping in the market place in Hargeisa, a town in the north of the country, in May 1988, when a violent incident in the civil war broke out around her. After sheltering in a shop for a night, she was captured by government troops (hostile to her clan) and raped and beaten over a two day period before being able to flee. She managed to make her way to London. On arrival she applied for asylum but her application was rejected, despite the assaults and despite her having pointed out that her father had been killed by government troops and the rest of her family, in hiding in Nairobi, risked the same fate if returned to Somalia.[68] Fadumo was only granted exceptional leave to remain and so could not bring her family to join her in safety.

Given that rape is a grave human rights violation, a form of torture, it must amount to persecution where perpetrated or condoned by government; the asylum claims of women who fear or have been subjected to such rape should be clearly formulated in these terms to ensure that the issues are addressed in the determination process.[69] In Bosnia, according to press reports, as many as 20,000 Bosnian Muslim women have been systematically savaged by Serbian forces, sometimes in special 'rape camps' where they are detained to prevent abortion until they give birth.[70] Rape has clearly been part of the strategy of 'ethnic cleansing' in the Balkan war. Yet raped Bosnian women are being excluded from full protection under the Geneva Convention by the British and other EC governments. At their June 1993 bi-annual meeting, EC immigration ministers in Copenhagen decided on guidelines for the admission of 'particularly vulnerable' people from former Yugoslavia, short of recognising any as refugees. These included a recommendation that 'as far as possible, arrangements will be made for *contacts to be maintained* with close relatives [spouses and children who are minors]'.[71] 'Maintaining contacts' is not the same as allowing admission. The clear implication is that Bosnian atrocity victims, including raped women, are not to be treated as Convention refugees because they will not normally be allowed to bring even their immediate families to the host country.

Positive developments

It is clear that women refugees still face substantial difficulties in obtaining refugee status on the basis of gender-specific persecution. However the efforts in the last decade of both non-governmental organisations and international human rights bodies to highlight those difficulties and propose changes have begun to bear fruit.

Several intergovernmental bodies have formulated policies and guidelines concerning women refugees and their asylum applications. The European Parliament passed a resolution focusing on the special problems of refugee women in 1984. In 1985, the United Nations High Commission for Refugees (UNHCR) passed its first conclusion specifically on the problems of women refugees, and in 1991 it issued special *Guidelines on the Protection of Refugee Women*, describing the gender-based persecution claims which governments considering women's applications for refugee status may recognise.

At the governmental level, the Canadian authorities have set several important precedents. Not only have they recognised individual asylum applications from women persecuted for transgressing customary norms, or persecuted by non-governmental oppressors, as described above. But, in March 1993, the Canadian Immigration and Refugee Board published trend-setting *Guidelines for the treatment of women refugees fearing gender-related persecution*.[72] These guidelines provide the most detailed governmental analysis to date of the range of situations giving rise to women's claims for asylum. They set out wide-ranging recommendations and undoubtedly represent a most significant advance for refugee women. In a first test case of the new guidelines, a Chinese woman facing sterilisation after she was found to have violated China's 'one child policy', and her second child, were allowed to stay in Canada.[73] It is to be hoped that, despite the current widespread attack on refugee rights, this lead will be followed by other governments.

Conclusion

Mainstream politicians have exploited the spurious yet allegedly 'objective' distinction between 'economic' and 'political' refugees to justify inhumane exclusion policies. It is nearly as if, through the cynical pronouncements of ministers and the hate-ridden voicing of popular racism (directed against peoples of different cultures as well as different colour) the very word 'refugee' has become an accusation, a description of a deceitful method of gaining access to something to which the person is not entitled. (In fact, as shown above, a substantial proportion of asylum applicants are eventually allowed permission to stay on in the host country, a tacit endorsement of their reasons for fleeing.)

The prospects for any meaningful implementation of the post-war ideals of human rights protection for refugees in Europe seem bleak given the current European agenda: an agreed list of visa countries, a list of non-European 'safe' countries to which refugees can be sent back, carrier sanctions, an increasingly restrictive application of the definition of refugee to penalise those arriving without documents or so shell-shocked that they do not disclose all aspects of their case at the first opportunity. On the other hand, human rights abuses continue unchecked in many countries of origin, with western intervention limited largely to protecting economic self-interest. As the Balkan war illustrates, the need for effective refugee protection is as great now as it ever was.

The specific problems of women, both those challenging customary norms which discriminate against them, and those subjected to gender-specific persecution as opponents of their government, have yet to be fully addressed by governments and courts. Women refugees are often particularly vulnerable yet frequently excluded from the benefit of protection under the Geneva Convention on Refugees. Yet they are likely to find it ever harder to gain protection. Political hostility to extension of the Convention definition to encompass gender persecution, and streamlined decision-making based on statements made immediately on arrival, will militate against the consideration that many women refugees need for their asylum applications to be accepted.

The rising tide of racism and chauvinism sweeping across Europe and targeting settled immigrant communities as much as newly arrived refugees brings with it an ominous feel. Ministerial protestations of concern over starving orphans in Somalia or gassed Kurds in Iraq and sentimental gestures about individual Bosnian children are increasingly overshadowed by the shrill cries of European politicians anxiously guarding their gates and restricting entry to their fortress to those in need on behalf of the racists in their midst.

Conclusion

Women have long been discriminated against in British nationality and immigration legislation, though the ideology underpinning this discrimination has changed over time. The book has charted these changes as expressed in the law. It has also shown the complex interaction of race and sex discrimination in this field, with assumptions about women's dependence on men grafted onto government policies designed to exclude black and third world people from Britain.

The medieval perspective viewed a woman as her husband's property, so that she could pass on her British subject status to her children born abroad only if she had travelled with her husband's permission. In 1870 this perspective received further codification in the law when an Act was passed which made a woman's nationality dependent on that of her husband. That was the state of affairs until 1948 when, after prolonged campaigning, women were allowed to retain their own nationality on marriage. They were not, however, able to transmit this nationality to their children born abroad until 1983.

In immigration law there was no such linear progress. Throughout the history of immigration law prior to 1988, women settled in Britain were treated differently from men. Women's rights to be joined by their husbands have always been qualified, ranging from an almost complete ban in 1969, through the relatively liberal provisions of 1974, to the various setbacks and improvements of subsequent years. Men, by contrast, had clear legal rights to bring their wives to join them in Britain, though in practice black men often encountered difficulties and delays in exercising those rights. In the 1980s, immigration rules were passed which discriminated against women in spite of the modern ideology of sex equality. Assumptions about women being homemakers, rather than breadwinners, and therefore less of a threat to the British labour market, were cynically used to minimise the number of black men entering Britain. The rationale for this differential treatment was that, in Home Office terminology, men, unlike women, were the source of 'primary immigration'. The 1978 Select Committee on Race Relations and Immigration, for example, expressed the view that 'as male fiancés are prospective heads of families, they enter the UK not so much to join a family as to form a new family'; the same report referred to the 'traditional pattern of the bride joining the husband's family'.[1]

The argument used by the British government before the European Commission of Human Rights in May 1982, to justify the sex discrimination in its 1980 immigration rules on marriage, illustrated this point: 'Society still expects the man to go out to work and the woman to stay at home.'[2] (The Home Office legal team defending this position was predominantly female.) When it lost these cases, the Home Office responded negatively to the Court judgement that British immigration law was sex discriminatory, by first reducing, then abolishing men's unqualified entitlement to be joined by their wives. Since 1 August 1988, men and women — if they are settled in the UK or British citizens — are in the same legal position. They have no absolute entitlement to be joined by a partner, only a qualified right. As discussed in previous chapters, it is still generally easier for men to bring in partners.

At the time of writing the government had recently published a 'consultative document' which proposes the removal of most areas of remaining sex discrimination in the immigration rules. But substantial additional changes need to be made to present government policy and practice to achieve real sex equality. Much of the injustice now inflicted on women in the field of immigration is a consequence of indirect rather than direct discrimination. It results from the way in which discretion is exercised and from the disproportionate impact on women of rules which are formally non-discriminatory: the exclusion of Asian husbands through the primary purpose rule, the separation of mothers from children abroad by the sole responsibility rule, the restrictive application of the Geneva Convention definition of refugee to exclude gender persecution.

Removing discrimination from these areas of decision-making requires a reconsideration of the assumptions underlying policy. It requires acceptance of the fact that the base of a woman, whatever her ethnic origin, as much as that of a man, can determine the 'natural' home for a couple. It requires the government to recognise that women should not be penalised for having to leave their children behind when they emigrate to escape poverty and find work. It requires increased awareness of the gender-specific persecution of women and a reappraisal of what count as 'political' acts so that the asylum claims of many refugee women are indeed accepted within the terms of the Geneva Refugee Convention.

A just immigration policy would require a reappraisal of the rights of both men and women. It would necessitate a completely different approach to the question of family reunion, which should be viewed as a basic human right, an entitlement, rather than as a privilege reluctantly accorded. This presupposes a legal structure which relies on the fact of the family relationship per se, rather than on an analysis of underlying motives or surrounding behaviour. The family reunion provisions of EC law, evolved in the context of promoting freedom of movement for EC nationals within the Community, offer such a model. One of the purposes of Community law is to encourage a single market within the Community and therefore remove obstacles to the free movement of people travelling between countries, for work or other purposes, such as study. Family relationships are therefore defined generously and inclusively, to cover children up to the age of 21, grandchildren, and relatives in the ascending line such as parents, grandparents, even aunts and uncles, if they are dependent on the person they are joining. Primary purpose and sole responsibility are unknown concepts. The contrast between this definition of the family and the ever-more restrictive one operating in British immigration law for non-EC nationals is stark and unjust.

It also produces the anomalous situation that a British citizen who has never travelled outside the UK is in a worse position than one who has lived and worked in another EC country. The latter's family benefits from the liberal provisions of EC law whereas the former is covered by the much less generous British immigration laws. It is illogical for the government to maintain a provision such as the primary purpose rule when it is possible for couples and families to circumvent it by the expedient of living in another EC country for some months.

This difference is one manifestation of the racism characteristic of many British institutions today, from the Department of Social Security to the police. Because domestic immigration law has evolved to prevent the entry of black and third world immigrants, restricting numbers of possible entrants rather than ensuring the right to family life has been the dominant policy goal. For those who have managed to secure entry, internal controls have increased, both in number and in ferocity, to complement immigration controls at the borders.

The division between the rights of EC nationals exercising free movement and non EC nationals resident in Britain is indefensible; it divides the Community along race lines and institutionalises the hierarchised system of rights based on nationality, described earlier. The extension of free movement rights to nationals of the European Free Trade Association countries, but not to the countries of the Maghreb or Turkey for example, highlights the race divide. Many of the eight million non-EC nationals living within the European Community are not white. The assumption that being non-white means being subject to control is such that the onus is often put on ethnic minority EC nationals or their family members to prove that they are entitled to 'first class', EC rights. The book shows this racism and the difficulties such EC nationals or relatives of EC nationals have encountered. Citizenship should not divide residents within Britain or anywhere else within the EC; third country nationals living in the EC should benefit from the free movement rights within the Community that their EC national counterparts enjoy.

Of course extending EC law to non-EC European residents would do nothing for those excluded from the European fortress altogether. The book documents the restrictive measures increasingly directed against refugees. Here change is desperately needed if the human rights gains of the post Second World War period in Europe are not to be completely eroded. International obligations exist, declarations have been signed; what is needed is effective implementation through political will, backed up by a court or other international forum.

The particular difficulties of refugee women, the majority of the estimated 17.5 million refugees worldwide, must be resolved. Here an example has been set by the Canadian authorities. They have introduced

Guidelines on the Protection of Refugee Women which provide a model for other countries in recognising the hitherto excluded or ignored situations which give rise to persecution of women. The guidelines provide wide-ranging recommendations for the appropriate handling of women's refugee claims and the steps to be taken to ensure effective protection for them under the Geneva Convention. So far there has been minimal recognition in Britain of the distinctive problems of women refugees. Neither the government nor the courts have seriously discussed many of the arguments set out in the Canadian guidelines. This is partly a reflection of the fact that, until very recently, women's rights advocates themselves accepted leave granted exceptionally on compassionate grounds, rather than pressing for full refugee status for women persecuted for transgressing cultural norms, or persecuted by non-governmental oppressors. It is hoped that this book will contribute to an increased debate and public awareness of these issues so that change beneficial to women refugees can result.

Much policy and decision-making on immigration and refugee issues in Britain is now influenced if not directly governed by the EC process. The book charts the ever-expanding scope of EC political discussions: it demonstrates how intergovernmental meetings of senior EC civil servants and interior ministers play a central role in the formulation of European but also domestic immigration policy. This process, at the heart of the development of 'Fortress Europe', is frequently shrouded in secrecy, thereby removed from the arena of public debate and parliamentary scrutiny. Only some lobbying groups with a special interest, journalists, lawyers and academics, manage to keep track of evolving proposals and developments. By the time policy discussions become public knowledge they are already part of an agreed programme, not amenable to change by public campaigning.

For those opposed to these developments, the challenge for the coming period is to connect the legal and academic discussions with the organisations and groups involved in more broadly-based anti-racist campaigning; to share the ever more specialised expertise with individuals, interest groups and campaigning organisations whose intervention is crucial for effective opposition to government policy. If this book contributes to this process, it will have achieved its purpose.

Glossary

Ad Hoc Group Immigration A grouping of senior civil servants, from all EC countries, responsible for discussing immigration and refugee matters and formulating policies.

Alien Historically, any person not a subject of the British Crown. A citizen of any non-Commonwealth country, except Ireland; synonymous with **foreign**.

Asylum Another word for **refugee status**.

British citizen A term first used in the 1981 British Nationality Act, for people who were previously citizens of the UK and Colonies with the **right of abode.**

Carriers' Liability Act The legislation which allows the British government to fine airlines and shipping companies £2000 for each passenger they bring in without valid entry documents.

Dependant A term used in the **Immigration Rules** to refer to the wife and children of a person settled in Britain whose claim to come here depends on that relationship.

Deportation Sending a person out of Britain by order of the Home Secretary. This may happen when a person who entered legally overstayed his/her permission to remain or committed other crimes here or (rarely) to a woman, if she is married to a man being deported. See also **removal**.

Dublin Convention A Convention signed by all EC countries which lays down which country is responsible for deciding on an asylum application from a person who has entered the **EC**.

EC The European Communities, formerly the European Economic Community (EEC), which the UK joined on 1 January 1973. The other member states are Belgium, Denmark, France, Germany, Greece, Ireland, Italy, Luxembourg, the Netherlands, Portugal and Spain.

ECHR European Convention on Human Rights, an international instrument agreed by the Council of Europe, a wider grouping then the EC, to which Britain is a signatory. Individuals who believe that the British government has contravened their rights under this Convention can complain to the European Commission of Human Rights. If the Commission finds the case 'admissible' and the parties cannot arrive at a 'friendly settlement', the case is referred to the European Court of Human Rights for a final decision. Both the Commission and the Court are based at Strasbourg.

ECJ The European Court of Justice, the court established by the EC to rule on matters of European Community law. Its decisions are binding on domestic governments and courts. Cases only come before the Court if they are referred by domestic governments, domestic courts or the European Commission; individuals cannot petition directly. The Court is based in Luxembourg.

EEA European Economic Area, which comprises EC and EFTA countries. Nationals of all these countries (with the exception of Switzerland, which voted against this in a referendum, and Liechtenstein) have free movement rights within the EEA countries from 1 January 1994.

EFTA European Free Trade Association, comprising Austria, Finland, Iceland, Liechtenstein, Norway, Sweden and Switzerland.

Entry clearance Permission granted by the British authorities abroad to a person to come to the UK for a particular purpose. It may be called a visa (when it is compulsory for people of that nationality) or an entry certificate (for Commonwealth citizens who are not visa nationals).

EU European Union, a term to be used, under the Maastricht treaty, instead of EC when referring to justice, policing, immigration, defence and foreign policies decided in intergovernmental discussions.

Exceptional leave to remain/enter (ELR/ELE) The second-class status granted to the majority of asylum-seekers, when the Home Office is not satisfied that they qualify as **refugees** under the terms of the Geneva Convention relating to the Status of Refugees, but also does not believe that it is safe for them to return to their country of origin.

Foreign Any non-Commonwealth citizen. See also **alien**.

Illegal entrant A person who immigration officials believe has entered the UK in breach of the immigration laws, either by bypassing immigration control altogether, or by deception as to his or her identity or reasons for coming to the UK, or by entering in breach of a current deportation order.

Immigration appeals A system set up in 1969 to appeal against decisions of the Home Office or British posts abroad, separate from the courts system. An appeal goes first to a single adjudicator and it may be possible to appeal, on a point of law, to the three-person Immigration Appeal Tribunal, and (since 1993) to the Court of Appeal. Until 1987, adjudicators were appointed by the Home Office, but since then they and Tribunal members are appointed by the Lord Chancellor's department.

Immigration Rules The rules of practice, published by the Home Office, as to how immigration officials should carry out the law. They have the force of law and must be agreed, though not debated, by Parliament. At the time of writing, the main immigration rules were House of Commons papers 251 (March 1990) and 725 (July 1993), but new draft rules had been proposed in July 1993.

Migrant workers People coming to Britain specifically to work, usually for a limited period of time. Often those who have come on **work permits**.

New Commonwealth All Commonwealth countries except Australia, Canada and New Zealand. A government euphemism for black.

Old Commonwealth Australia, Canada and New Zealand.

Patrial Term used in the 1971 Immigration Act for people not subject to immigration control, mainly people who were UK citizens by their birth, naturalisation or registration in Britain, Commonwealth citizens with a parent born in Britain and Commonwealth women married to such men before 1983.

Public funds Public funds for immigration purposes are income support, family credit, housing benefit and housing provided under the homelessness provisions of the Housing Acts.

Refugee The Geneva Convention relating to the Status of Refugees defines a refugee as someone who 'owing to a well-founded fear of being persecuted for reasons of race, religion, nationality, membership of a particular social group or political opinion is outside the country of his nationality and is unable or, owing to such fear, is unwilling to avail himself of the protection of that country'. When the UK recognises people as refugees, it grants them **asylum**.

Removal Sending a person who has been refused entry at a port or airport, or is being treated as an illegal entrant, out of the country. A quicker and less cumbersome process than **deportation**.

Right of abode Being free of British immigration control and able to enter the UK freely at any time, however long the person has been away. Applies to British citizens and to those who were **patrial** Commonwealth citizens.

Schengen group A group of all EC countries except Britain, Denmark and Ireland, which is working towards a common immigration policy and common border controls.

Settled A person subject to immigration control, but with no limit on the length of time for which he or she may remain in Britain.

Sponsorship The act of supporting financially people who are applying to come to the UK. Sponsors may be asked to sign a formal undertaking, which gives the DSS Benefits Agency the power to reclaim from the sponsor any income support paid to the person sponsored.

Third country national Term used by EC governments to describe all non-EC citizens.

UK citizen Term used under the 1948 British Nationality Act, strictly 'citizen of the UK and Colonies', for a person who was a citizen of the UK or any of its colonies. The 1962 and 1968 Commonwealth Immigrants Acts removed the right of those from colonies or ex-colonies to come to the UK.

UK Passport Holder (UKPH) Government term for people who are British but who do not have an entitlement to enter and to live in Britain.

UNHCR The United Nations High Commission for Refugees, the UN agency with responsibility for resettlement and care of refugees. It attempts to influence government policies towards asylum-seekers but has no power to enforce its views.

Visas Compulsory **entry clearance**.

Work permit Permission given by the Department of Employment to an employer to employ a named worker in a particular job.

Notes

Introduction

1. If these proposals are implemented, the only areas where sex discrimination will remain in the regulations is in the power to deport a woman solely because her husband is being deported (a provision which has scarcely been used for a decade) and in the non-statutory special quota voucher scheme. See further discussion on these points on pages 117-9 and 113-7.
2. Melanie Phillips, *The Guardian,* 14 September 1990.
3. C. Pateman, *The sexual contract* (Polity Press, 1988).
4. For a general discussion of this point see Nira Yuval-Davis, 'The citizenship debate: women, ethnic processes and the state', *Feminist Review*, no. 39.
5. See, for example, *Hansard* reports of debate on 1968 Commonwealth Immigrants Act.
6. *Campaign for citizenship rights*, Campaign against Racism and Fascism, No 15, July/August 1993, p. 5, col. 1.
7. During the 1979 general election campaign, Margaret Thatcher, then leader of the Conservative Party, declared that she stood by her statement on the television programme *World in Action* of 31 January 1978: 'People are really rather afraid that this country might be swamped by people with a different culture'.
8. *The Independent*, 20 May 1993, page 3, col. 7.
9. *New York Times*, 12 June 1993, Section 1, page 2, col 1.
10. *R v Secretary of State for the Home Department, ex parte Ejaz, The Times,* 23 July 1993.
11. Bridget Anderson, *Britain's secret slaves: an investigation into the plight of overseas domestic workers* (Anti-Slavery International and Kalayaan, London, 1993).
12. See Francesca Klug, 'Oh to be in England': the British case study' in *Woman — nation — state,* ed. Nira Yuval-Davis and Floya Anthias (Macmillan, 1989).
13. United Nations, Vienna Declaration and Programme of Action, 25 June 1993, para 18.

Chapter 1
'As a woman I have no country': women and nationality

1. See Clive Parry, *Nationality and Citizenship Laws of the Commonwealth and Ireland* (Stevens & Sons, 1957), Mervyn Jones, *British Nationality Law and Practice* (Clarendon Press, 1947) and Ann Dummett and Andrew Nicol, *Subjects, citizens, aliens and others: nationality and immigration law* (Weidenfeld and Nicolson, 1990).
2. De Natis Ultra Mare, an Act of 1351.
3. M. Jones, *British Nationality Law and Practice*, p.66; see also Parry, *Nationality and Citizenship Laws*, pp.33-4.
4. Collingwood v. Pace, 1664.
5. For example see Parry, *Nationality and Citizenship Laws*, p. 71.
6. HC 115 (HMSO, 1923).
7. The quotations from the proceedings of the British Nationality and Status of Aliens Bill 1914 are taken from *Hansard*, 13 May 1914 and 29 July 1914.
8. Laura Aberconway writing in *Jus Suffragii, The International Woman Suffrage News*, vol. 8, no. II, 1 July 1914.
9. For a discussion of the difference between citizenship and nationality see Ann Dummett, *Citizenship and Nationality* (Runnymede Trust, 1976).
10. Related by C. Scott Dickenson MP, during the course of the British Nationality and Status of Aliens Bill 1914.
11. For more details, see Elizabeth Sarah, 'Female Performers on a Male Stage', in Scarlet Friedman and Elizabeth Sarah, eds, *On the Problems of Men* (Women's Press, 1982).
12. Vol. 4, no. 97, 16 April 1915.
13. Aberconway, *Jus Suffragii.*
14. Section 10, as amended by the British Nationality and Status of Aliens Act 1918.
15. Section 7a.
16. British Nationality (Married Women) Bill 1922.
17. Select Committee Report, *The Nationality of Married Women*, HC 115 (HMSO, 1923).
18. Quoted in the British Nationality and Status of Aliens Bill, *Hansard*, 9 November 1933.
19. *Jus Suffragii*, vol. 27, no. 7, April 1933.
20. British Nationality and Status of Aliens Bill.
21. The quotations from the proceedings of the British Nationality Bill 1948 are taken from *Hansard*, 7 July 1948 and 13 July 1948.
22. *Ibid.*
23. United Nations Treaty Series, vol. 309, United Nations 1958, p. 65.
24. *Hansard*, 7 February 1979.

Chapter 2
Travelling third class: women and immigration

1. Quoted in Peter Fryer, *Staying Power: The History of Black People in Britain* (Pluto, 1984).
2. Andrew Nicol, *Illegal Entrants* (Runnymede Trust, 1981).
3. *Aliens: Instructions to Immigration Officers,* Cmnd. 4296 (HMSO, 1970).
4. Paul Foot, *Immigration and Race in British Politics* (Penguin, 1965).
5. See *ibid* for a fuller account of British immigration policy in this period.
6. Ceri Peach, *West Indian Migration to Britain: A Social Geography* (Oxford University Press/Institute of Race Relations, 1968).
7. CO 926/38, 1952/54, quoted in John Solomos and Stephen Woodhams, *The politics of Cypriot migration to Britain*, Birkbeck research papers no 4, 1993.
8. CO 926/359, 1954/66, quoted *ibid.*
9. For a full and unique analysis of this process, see A. Sivanandan, *A Different Hunger: Writings on Black Resistance* (Pluto, 1983).
10. The quotations from the proceedings of the 1962 Commonwealth Immigrants Bill are taken from *Hansard*, 6 and 7 February 1962.
11. *Commonwealth Immigrants Act 1962: Instructions to Immigration Officers,* Cmnd. 3064 (HMSO, 1966).
12. *Ibid.*
13. David Smith, *The Facts of Racial Disadvantage* (PEP, 1976), Colin Brown, *Black and White in Britain* (Policy Studies Institute/ Heinemann, 1984) and OPCS *Labour Force Survey*, 1990-1991.
14. For a fuller explanation of this development, see, for example, David Steel, *No Entry: The Background and Implications of the Commonwealth Immigrants Act 1968* (C. Hurst & Co., 1969), and Anthony Lester, *Citizens without Status* (Runnymede Trust, 1972).
15. The quotations from the proceedings of the 1968 Commonwealth Immigrants Bill are taken from *Hansard*, 28 February 1968.
16. Cmnd. 4298 (HMSO, 1970).
17. For example, see the current Rules, *Statement of Changes in Immigration Rules*, HC 251 (HMSO, 1990).
18. The quotations from the proceedings of the 1971 Immigration Bill are taken from *Hansard*, 30 March 1971, 1 April 1971, 25 May 1971 and 16 June 1971.
19. See, for example, the debate on the Commonwealth Immigrants Bill 1962, summarised above, and the debate on the Commonwealth Immigrants Bill 1968, *Hansard*, 28 February 1968, cols 1426-8.
20. *British Nationality Law: Discussion of Possible Changes*, Cmnd. 6795 (HMSO, 1977).
21. Joint Council for the Welfare of Immigrants, *On the Eve of the Nationality Act* (1982).
22. The quotations from the proceedings of the British Nationality Bill 1981 are taken from *Hansard*, 28 January 1981, 17 February 1981, and 4 June 1981.

Chapter 3
Till laws us do part: the ban on husbands

1. David Ennals, *Hansard*, 24 July 1968.
2. *Hansard*, 7 November 1968.
3. *Hansard*, 30 January 1969.
4. *Ibid.*
5. David Renton, *Hansard*, 6 February 1962.
6. *Aliens: Instructions to Immigration Officers*, Cmnd. 4296 (HMSO, 1970).
7. *Ibid.*
8. All these cases are quoted in National Association of Asian Youth, *Which Half Decides? A Contribution to the Debate on Sex Discrimination, British Nationality and Immigration Laws* (1979).
9. Quoted in Dilip Hiro, *Black British, White British* (Eyre & Spottiswoode, 1971), p.163.
10. *Immigration Rulés for Control on Entry: Commonwealth Citizens*, HC 79 (HMSO, 1973).
11. *Immigration Rules for Control on Entry: EEC and Other Non-Commonwealth Nationals*, HC 81 (HMSO, 1973).
12. Cmnd. 4298 (HMSO, 1970).
13. House of Lords *Hansard*, 28 March 1974.
14. Spouses of UK Citizens (Equal Treatment) Bill 1974.
15. *Hansard*, 21 June 1974.
16. *Hansard*. 27 June 1974.
17. Cmnds. 5715-18 (HMSO, August 1974).
18. *Hansard*, 3 December 1974.
19. *Hansard*, 24 May 1976.
20. *Ibid.*
21. *Hansard*, 5 July 1976.
22. *Ibid.*
23. *Ibid.*
24. HC 238-41 (HMSO, March 1977).
25. Shirley Summerskill, Home Office minister, *Hansard*, 10 January 1978.
26. *Hansard*, 24 May 1977.
27. Joint Council for the Welfare of Immigrants, *Checks on Immigrant Marriages* (1977).
28. *First Report from the Select Committee on Race Relations and Immigration*, HC 303 (HMSO, 1978).
29. Speech, Leicester, 7 April 1978.
30. *Hansard*, 4 December 1979.
31. Equal Opportunities Commission, *Briefing on Removing the 'Concession' Allowing British Women to Marry Foreign Men and Live in Britain*, 13 August 1979.
32. Hazel Carby, 'White Woman Listen: Black Feminism and the Boundaries of Sisterhood', in *The Empire Strikes Back: Race and Racism in 70s Britain* (Centre for Contemporary Cultural Studies/Hutchinson University Library, 1982). See also

Jenny Bourne, 'Towards an Anti-Racist Feminism', *Race and Class*, vol. 25, summer 1983.
33. *Guardian*, 19 November 1979.
34. *Times*, 5 December 1979.
35. The quotations from the debate on the 1979 White Paper are taken from *Hansard*, 14 November 1979 and 4 and 5 December 1979.
36. HC 394 (HMSO, February 1980).
37. *Ibid.*
38. House of Lords *Hansard*, 7 November 1979.
39. Parita Trivedy, 'Asian Women in History', in *Many Voices One Chant: Black Feminist Perspectives, Feminist Review*, no. 17, autumn 1984.
40. Office of Population, Censuses and Surveys, *Labour Force Surveys*, for 1981 and 1990-1991 (HMSO, 1982 and 1991).
41. European Commission of Human Rights, Document E56.486.06.2.
42. The quotations from the debate on the 1983 Rules are taken from *Hansard*, 15 December 1982 and 15 February 1983.
43. *Guardian*, 15 February 1983.
44. Case of Abdulaziz, Cabales and Balkandali, European Court of Human Rights, (15/1983/71/107-109), [1985] 7 EHRR 471.
45. *Ibid.*
46. *Hansard*, 6 June 1985, col. 431.
47. *Statement of changes in immigration rules*, HC 169, HMSO, 1983.
48. *Hansard*, 15 February 1983.
49. *Hansard*, 16 December 1983.
50. *The Guardian*, 21 March 1984.
51. See for example *Ravinder Singh* (3352) and *Lahmber Singh* (3353).
52. *Vinod Bhatia* (3456).
53. Calculated from Home Office, *Control of immigration: statistics*, UK, 1991, Home Office Statistical Bulletin 14/93 and *Hansard*, 16 July 1993, col. 696.
54. *Hansard*, 16 July 1993, cols. 674-678.
55. *R v Immigration Appeal Tribunal ex parte Arun Kumar*, [1986] Imm AR 446.
56. *Immigration Appeal Tribunal v Amirul Hoque and Matwinder Singh*, [1988] Imm AR 216.
57. *Iqbal*, [1993] Imm AR 270.
58. *Majid*, (9317).
59. *Surinder Singh*, Case C-370/90, 7 July 1992.
60. *Berrehab*, [1988] 11 EHRR 322.
61. Women, Immigration and Nationality Group, *Immigration Widows Kit* (1983).
62. *Wirdestedt*, [1990] Imm AR 20.
63. *Webb*, (5387).
64. In a telephone conversation with one of the authors, 1992.
65. See, for example, Sanjiv Sachdeva, *The primary purpose rule in British immigration law* (Trentham, 1993) and David Pannick, ed., *The primary purpose rule: a rule with no purpose* (Young JUSTICE, 1993).

Chapter 4
Divide and rule: wives under immigration law

1. See Jean Gardiner, 'Women, Recession and the Tories', and Lynn Segal, 'The Heat in the Kitchen', in Stuart Hall and Martin Jacques, eds, *The Politics of Thatcherism* (Lawrence & Wishart, 1983) for a discussion of the Conservatives' attitudes to women (ignoring the position of black women).
2. For a readable description of how the system worked, see Robert Moore and Tina Wallace, *Slamming the Door: The Administration of Immigration Control* (Martin Robertson, 1975) and *Immigration control procedures: report of a formal investigation* (Commission for Racial Equality, 1985).
3. *Report of the Committee on Immigration Appeals*, under the Chairmanship of Sir Roy Wilson QC, Cmnd. 3387 (HMSO, August 1967).
4. See Moore and Wallace, *Slamming the Door*, p.70.
5. Mary Dines, 'Entry Certificates: Report on a Visit to India and Pakistan', *The Immigrant*, no. 4 (Joint Council for the Welfare of Immigrants, September 1969).
6. 'Commonwealth Immigration: Advice for Dependants Overseas', Sir Derek Hilton MBE, 15 September 1969.
7. *Hansard*, 8 November 1966.
8. *Immigration control procedures: report of a formal investigation* (Commission for Racial Equality, London, 1985).
9. 'Immigration from the subcontinent: Report from Mr Lyon to the Home Secretary', January 1975.
10. 'Report of a Visit to Posts in the Subcontinent made by Mr D. F. Hawley', January 1976, Foreign Office, unpublished.
11. 1978 White Paper on Immigration from the Indian subcontinent (quoted in CRE report).
12. CRE report, p.52.
13. CRE report, pp. 85-86.
14. 'Internal Document to British High Commission, Dacca', October 1976.
15. *Ibid.*
16. From the files of the Joint Council for the Welfare of Immigrants. For further examples, see Mohammed Akram and Sarah Leigh, *Where Do You Keep Your String Beds? A Study of the Entry Clearance Procedure in Pakistan* (Runnymede Trust, 1974), Mohammed Akram and Jan Elliott, *Appeal Dismissed: The Final Report of the Investigation into Immigration Control in the Indian Subcontinent* (Runnymede Trust, 1977).
16. Ranjit Sondhi, *Divided families* (Runnymede Trust, 1987), and Sushma Lal and Amrit Wilson, *But my cows aren't going to England* (Manchester Law Centre, 1986).
17. From the files of the Joint Council for the Welfare of Immigrants.
18. Ian Martin, *Entry Certificate Delays in Dacca* (JCWI, 1975).
19. *Divided Families Campaign Briefing* (1984) available from Bangladesh Cultural Centre, Main Road, Oldham, Lancs.
20. *Hansard*, 21 February 1992, col. 293.
21. Amrit Wilson, 'Atrocity at Heathrow', *Spare Rib*, no. 55, February 1976, pp.20-1.

22. *Regina v Secretary of State for the Home Department, ex parte Phansopkar* [1975] 3 AllER 437.
23. Central Policy Review Staff, *Review of Overseas Representation* (HMSO, 1977).
24. This was a recommendation of the 1978 Select Committee on Race Relations and Immigration, *First Report*, HC 303, (HMSO 1978).
25. 'They're Killing us in Here', *Spare Rib,* no. 84, July 1979, p.33.
26. Sir Henry Yellowlees, *The medical examination of immigrants: Report by the Chief Medical Officer* (DHSS, 1980).
27. CRE report, op. cit., 1985.
28. CRE report, page 128.
29. *Regina v Entry Clearance Officer, Bombay, ex parte Amin (Times Law Report*, 8 July 1983).
30. Home Office, *Control of immigration: statistics*, (HMSO), 1983, 1991 and Home Office statistical bulletin, 14/93.
31. For examples, see Paul Gordon, *Deportations and Removals* (Runnymede Trust, 1984).
32. Personal communication from the Afia Begum Campaign.
33. *Ibid.*
34. 'No More Deportations', *Outwrite*, no. 26, June 1984.
35. *You and yours*, 15.5.91.
36. The issue is discussed in detail in their evidence to the Parliamentary Home Affairs Committee investigation into domestic violence, 1992.
37. See British Nationality Act 1981, Schedule 1 Para.1(3) for a small exception to this.
38. See S. Whitfield, *When is a Wife not a Wife?* (Birmingham CDP, 1975) for a detailed discussion of this problem.
39. *Hussain v Hussain*, *Times Law Report*, CA 24 June 1982.
40. *Today*, 22 March 1986.
41. Quoted in *The Independent*, 2 April 1991.

Chapter 5
Childless mothers: children kept out

1. See Friends of Anwar Ditta, *Bring Anwar's Children Home* (Manchester Law Centre, not dated).
2. CRE report, page 37.
3. From an entry clearance officer's statement in a case dealt with by the Joint Council for the Welfare of Immigrants.
4. Sir Henry Yellowlees, *The Medical Examination of Immigrants: Report by the Chief Medical Officer* (DHSS, 1980).
5. Lord Trefgarne, written answer to a parliamentary question from Lord Avebury, *Hansard,* 28 January 1982.
6. Edward White, 'The Use of X-rays for Age Determination in Immigration Control' (unpublished, 1981).
7. William Whitelaw, written answer to a parliamentary question from John Wheeler, Hansard, 22 February 1982.

8. CRE report, page 41.
9. *DNA profiling in immigration casework: report of a pilot trial by the Home Office and Foreign and Commonwealth Office*, July 1988.
10. Families appealing against an entry clearance refusal may qualify for assistance under the green form legal aid scheme, which will pay for the tests.
11. *Hansard,* 14 June 1989, cols. 463-5.
12. *Hansard,* 3 July 1992, cols. 742-3.
13. *R v Immigration Appeal Tribunal ex parte Manshoora Begum*, [1986] Imm AR 385.
14. International Social Service, *Immigrants at London Airport and their Settlement in the Community* (London Airport Project Report, June 1967).
15. Select Committee on Race Relations and Immigration, *The West Indian Community,* session 1976-77, vol. 3: *Evidence and Appendices* (HMSO, 180-111, 1977) p. 573.
16. G. W. Farmer and E. J. T. Housden, 'Report on a Tour of the Caribbean Area', 20 January to 14 February 1974 (unpublished).
17. Roy Jenkins, written answer to a parliamentary question from Helene Hayman, *Hansard*, 28 July 1975.
18. Select Committee, *The West Indian Community.*
19. *The West Indian Community: Observations on the Report of the Select Committee on Race Relations and Immigration*, Cmnd.7186 (HMSO, April 1978).
20. For more information on this issue, see John Plummer, *Divide and Deprive* (JCWI, 1978).
21. CRE report, op. cit., page 72.
22. *The Guardian*, 3 August 1992.
23. *The Independent*, 1 June 1993.
24. *The Independent on Sunday*, 8 August 1993, *The Guardian*, 3 August 1993.
25. *The Guardian*, 3 August 1993, *The Independent,* 5 August 1993, CARF September/October 1993.
26. Christine Harvey, *The children of deportees,* unpublished M.Ed dissertation, University of Nottingham.
27. *The Independent*, 1 September 1993.
28. *First Report from the Select Committee on Race Relations and Immigration,* HC 303 (HMSO, 1978).
29. CRE report, *passim.*

Chapter 6
Hard labour: migrant women workers

1. *Hansard*, 25 February 1993, col. 713.
2. For more information about migrant women workers, see, for example, Annie Phizacklea, ed., *One way ticket: migration and female labour* (Routledge & Kegan Paul, 1983), Swasti Mitter, *Common fate, common bond: women in the global economy* (Pluto, 1986).
3. *Hansard*, 5 February 1993, col. 353.
4. J. S. and L. D. MacDonald, *The Invisible Immigrants* (Runnymede Industrial Unit, 1972).
5. Leila Maw, *Immigrants and Employment in the Clothing Industry: The Rochdale Case* (Runnymede Trust, 1974).
6. *Ibid.*
7. *Observer*, 24 December 1972.
8. *Hansard*, 11 November 1971.
9. *Hansard*, 1 November 1973.
10. *Hansard*, 13 August 1977.
11. *Employment Gazette* (Department of Employment, March 1982).
12. Mentioned in passing in MacDonald, *The Invisible Immigrants,* for example.
13. *Zamir v. Secretary of State for the Home Department* [1980] A 11 ER 768, gives the widest definition of illegal entry. The concept and its expansion is discussed in Andrew Nicol, *Illegal Entrants* (Runnymede Trust, 1981).
14. *Claveria v. Immigration officer, London (Heathrow) Airport* [1978] Imm AR 176.
15. Migrants Action Group, *Migrant Women under Threat* (1980).
16. Migrants Action Group, *On the Road to Repatriation* (1981).
17. *Khawaja v. Secretary of State for the Home Department* [1983] 1 765 HL.
18. Home Office press release, 23 February 1993.
19. This was provided in the Statement of changes in immigration rules, HC 725, which were mainly about asylum-seekers.
20. Letter, David Waddington MP to Lord Avebury, 26 July 1983.
21. See, for example, Paddington Migrants/Immigrants Employment Rights Unit, *Annual Report, 1982/3*, and letter to *The Times*, 30 July 1983.
22. Bridget Anderson, *Britain's secret slaves: an investigation into the plight of overseas domestic workers* (Anti-Slavery International and Kalayaan, London, 1993).
23. *The Independent,* 10 February 1992 and 2 February 1993.
24. *Hansard,* 6 May 1993, col. 178.
25. Peter Brown, 'Immigration Control and the Overseas Nurse Learner' (unpublished, 1977).
26. *Birmingham Mail*, 27 October 1976.
27. Quoted in *No Pass Laws Here! Bulletin*, July 1983.
28. For minor variations in the rules for children of different categories of EC nationals, see page 282, note 26.
29. *Unger v Bestuur der Bedrijfsvereniging voor Detailhandel en Ambachten*, (Case 75/63, CMLR 319).

30. See Paul Gordon, *Passport raids and checks* (Runnymede Trust, 1982), Manchester Law Centre, *The thin end of the white wedge* (1981), Michael Nunoo, *The challenge of internal immigration controls* (Hackney Anti-Deportation Campaign, 1989) and Campaign against Racism and Fascism journal, *passim.*
31. *Police and immigration activity in the London area*, JCWI briefing paper, 1990.
32. Mark Ashford, *Detained without trial: a survey of Immigration Act detention* (JCWI, 1993).
33. *Migration News Sheet,* June 1993, reported that France has had a similar situation but a law enacted in May 1993 provided for 'generalised identity checks...in places and for a period which these legal authorities determine' thus giving the police an ever freer hand.
34. *The Independent,* 23 August 1993.
35. Letter, DHSS to JCWI, 22 July 1981.
36. Letter, Timothy Raison MP to Hugh Rossi MP, 15 June 1981.
37. See, for example, Michael Nunoo, *The challenge of internal immigration controls* (Hackney Anti-Deportation Campaign, 1989).
38. *R v Secretary of State for the Environment ex parte Tower Hamlets London Borough Council,* Court of Appeal, 7 April 1993.
39. Home Office press release, *Home Office announces study of inter-agency co-operation on illegal immigration*, 212/93, 13 October 1993.
40. Quoted in *Sunday Telegraph*, 10 January 1993.
41. Nony Ardill and Nigel Cross, *Undocumented lives: Britain's unauthorised migrant workers* (Runnymede Trust, 1988).
42. *Hansard*, 3 March 1986.
43. *Hansard,* 5 February 1987.
44. *Black Bag,* 27 August 1993.
45. *The Guardian, Daily Mail,* 19 May 1992.
46. *Daily Telegraph, Daily Mail,* 22 July 1993.
47. *Migration News Sheet*, February and March 1993.
48. *Migration News Sheet,* September 1993.

Chapter 7
Sex equality and race division: migration and Fortress Europe

1. For a list of EC countries see Glossary.
2. Select Committee on Race Relations and Immigration, session 1977- 78, Minutes of evidence, 19 April 1978, Home Office, HMSO 410-1.
3. The original EEC consisted of six countries: France, Belgium, the Netherlands, Luxembourg, Italy and the Federal Republic of Germany. Ireland and Denmark joined at the same time as Britain; Greece joined in 1979, Portugal and Spain in 1985.
4. The European Economic Community (EEC), together with the European Coal and Steel Community and Euratom, are called the European Community or EC for economic policy, but from 1994 the European Union (EU) for immigration and foreign policy.
5. A very small group, consisting mainly of people with a connection with British India who did not gain Indian nationality on independence and who had lived in the UK for at least five years. British subjects without the right of abode, mostly of Indian ethnic origin, are not Community nationals.
6. By Article 135 of the Treaty of Rome, the inhabitants of such territories which have 'special relations' with Member States may be granted freedom of movement within the EC by agreements 'concluded subsequently with the unanimous approval of Member States'. No such agreements have ever been made.
7. Article 8a of the Treaty of Rome as amended by the Single European Act 1986.
8. *De Falco v Crawley Borough Council* [1980] 1 All ER 98.
9. Equal Treatment Directive 76/207/EEC.
10. For a detailed survey of international and European instruments aimed at eliminating racial discrimination see J. Niessen, *International Instruments to Combat Racial Discrimination in Europe,* Churches Committee for Migrants in Europe Briefing Paper no. 8. For a summary of the activities of European institutions aimed at combating racial discrimination see page 214.
11. *Levin v Staatssecretaris van Justitie* (Case 53/81) [1982] ECR 1035.
12. *Unger v Bestuur Der Bedrijfsvereniging Voor Detailhandel en Ambachten* (Case 75/63) CMLR [1964] 319.
13. By virtue of the so-called 'June Directives', Council Directives Nos.90/364/EEC, 90/365/EEC, and 90/366/EEC of 28 June 1990.
14. This simply means economically self-sufficient and not requiring recourse to public funds to support oneself; it is not the test of substantial wealth which operates within UK immigration law.
15. Because of their fears of uncontrolled immigration, these member states have indicated that checks will continue until the External Borders Convention, which provides for effective controls at the outer borders of the Community, is in force (see pages 217-20 for more details).
16. *State v Royer* (Case 48/75) [1976] 2 CMLR 619.
17. *Roux v The State* (Belgium) (Case C-363/89) [1993] 1 CMLR 3.
18. *Adoui and Cornouaille*, Cases 115 and 116/81, [1982] ECR 1665.

19. R. Plender, *The Implementation of European Principles*, Paper delivered to the Immigration Law Practitioners' Association conference on Immigration and Asylum Law in the European Context, 2 October 1992, p. 3.
20. However, the 1993 draft immigration rules give women students this right.
21. This was established by the European Court of Justice in the case of *Diatta v Land Berlin,* Case 267/83 [1986] 2 CMLR 164, ECJ. But if the EC national leaves the host member state then the protection of Community law no longer extends to the remaining spouse, see *R v Secretary of State for the Home Department, ex p Sandhu* [1983] 3 CMLR 131, CA.
22. For a description of the shortcomings of the British immigration rules in this respect see *JCWI Bulletin,* vol. 5 no. 3, p. 5 col 1.
23. Home Office Internal Instructions *Marriage and Children* DP/2/93 para 10.
24. ed. Kees Waalduk and A. Clapham, *Homosexuality: a European Community issue* (Martinus Nijhoff Publishers, 1993), p. 100-101.
25. See *Netherlands v Reed,* Case 59/85 [1987] 2 CMLR 448, ECJ.
26. For EC nationals exercising Treaty rights to study, or as retired or self-supporting persons, by virtue of the so-called June Directives, family reunion for children is limited to dependent children, of whatever age. Non-dependent children under 21 do not therefore qualify under these provisions.
27. The wording of the EC Regulation and Directive is not entirely clear on this point, and so far no caselaw exists. However the European Commission has indicated that this interpretation is acceptable, and in practice the British authorities allow it.
28. Letter from I. Phelps, 17 August 1992, quoted in C. Vincenzi, *The Consequences of Non-Implementation of Community Free Movement Rights in the United Kingdom,* paper given at a seminar at the Institute of Advanced Legal Studies, summer 1993.
29. See case of *Morson and Jhanjan v Netherlands* [1983] 2 CMLR 221, ECJ.
30. For a detailed description of this case see page 86.
31. *R v Secretary of State for the Home Department ex p Ayub* [1983] Imm AR 20.
32. For a careful analysis of how TCNs could be given free movement rights within the EC see W.R. Bohning and J. Werquin, *The Future Status of Third Country Nationals within the European Community*, Churches Committee for Migrants in Europe, Briefing Paper No. 2.
33. For example 800,000 Algerians in France, and an estimated 700,000 Commonwealth nationals in the UK. See International Labour Organisation, Informal Consultation Meeting on Migrants from Non-EEC Countries in the Single European Market After 1992, Geneva (April 1989), Informal Summary Record, Appendix 6, p.31. No. 34.
35. Arguably the Commission has breached its obligations by handing over decisions on TCNs and asylum to intergovernmental structures. See A. Cruz, *Community Competence over Third Country Nationals residing in an EC Member State,* Churches Committee for Migrants in Europe Briefing Paper No. 5.
36. *Re the Immigration of Non-Community Workers: Germany and others v EC Commission* (Cases 281/85, 283-285/85 and 287/85), [1988] CMLR11.
37. For a clear summary of the various bodies dealing with immigration and asylum issues in Europe see A. Cruz, *Schengen, ad hoc Immigration Group and other*

European Intergovernmental bodies, Churches Committee for Migrants in Europe Briefing Paper No. 12.

38. Convention Between the Kingdom of Belgium, the Grand-Duchy of Luxembourg, and the Kingdom of the Netherlands on the Transfer of control of persons to the external frontiers of the Benelux territory, 11 April 1960. Cited in D. O'Keefe, *The Schengen Convention: A Suitable Model for European Integration?*, Yearbook of European Law 1993, p. 187.
39. See for example *Europe: Harmonisation of Asylum Policy—Amnesty International's concerns* (Amnesty International, November 1990).
40. *Migration News Sheet,* September 1993, p. 1, col 1. There are now nine member states within Schengen, all the EC states except Britain, Denmark and Ireland.
41. A new EC structure is due to replace the proliferation of ad hoc groups. Known as the K4 Committee, its membership will consist of the 'Rhodes Group' Coordinators and it will include three steering groups, one on immigration and asylum policy. See *Statewatch*, July/August 1993, p 7, col 1.
42. Its full name is the draft Convention of the Member States of the European Communities on the Crossing of their External Borders.
43. For details of the lists of visa and non-visa countries see A. Cruz, *Schengen, ad hoc Immigration Group and other European Intergovernmental bodies,* Churches Committee for Migrants in Europe, Briefing Paper No. 12, May 1993, Annex A, p. 30.
44. *Migration News Sheet* July 1993 p 7 col 1.
45. Michael Hanley and Ronan Toal, *Report of Visit to Kenya*, January 1993, p. 10, unpublished.
46. Africa Watch Women's Rights Project, *Seeking refuge, finding terror: the widespread rape of Somali women refugees in north eastern Kenya,* 4 October 1993, p.2.
47. *ibid.*, p. 14.
48. One criterion is the 'reasonable belief that the person is planning to commit a serious offence'; another is the commission of 'serious' immigration offences.
49. Its full name is the Convention Determining the State Responsible for Examining Applications for Asylum Lodged in One of the Member States of the European Communities.
50. *Independent,* 13 August 1992, p. 3.
51. *Guardian,* 13 August 1992, p. 2 and *Independent,* 13 September 1992, p. 16.
52. *Migration News Sheet,* May 1993, p. 7, col. 2.
53. *Press Release: Meeting of Ministers with Responsibility for Immigration* (Copenhagen, 1 and 2 June 1993) p. 2.
54. Commissioner Flynn quoted in *Migration News Sheet* , August 1993, p. 2, col. 2.
55. For more details of this process see *Statewatch*, March-April 1993, p. 4.
56. *Press Release: Meeting of Ministers with Responsibility for immigration* (Copenhagen, 1 and 2 June 1993), Draft recommendation concerning checks on and expulsion of third country nationals residing or working without authorization, p. 4, para 2.
57. See *Moustaquim v Belgium* (31/1989/191/291), *Beldjoudi v France* (55/1990/246/317), *Lamguindaz v United Kingdom*, (ECHR Application No. 16152/90).

58. However, unlike the European Convention on Human Rights which applies irrespective of nationality, the rights guaranteed under the European Social Charter only apply to nationals of the contracting states.
59. See for example United Nations Convention on the Rights of the Child Article 1; Children Act 1989 section 1(1); International Labour Organisation Convention No. 143, Article 13; European Convention on the Legal Status of Migrant Workers, Article 12.
60. See for example W.R. Bohning and J. Werquin, *The Future Status of Third-Country Nationals in the European Community,* CCME Briefing Paper No.2. See also D. O'Keefe, *The Free Movement of Persons and the Single Market,* European Law Review 1992, vol 17, no. 1, p. 17.
61. EFTA countries include Norway, Sweden, Finland, Iceland, Liechtenstein, Austria and Switzerland.
62. Agreements have been entered into with Turkey, Poland, Hungary, Romania, Bulgaria, the Czech Republic, Slovakia, Morocco, Algeria and Tunisia.
63. Immigration officers and police arrested, among others, 55 Czechs and 21 Poles in a fruit farm in Kent, reporting that 'these clandestine workers were living in tents under appalling conditions'. *Migration News Sheet* August 1993, p. 12, col. 2.
64. See for example *The Times Magazine* 28 August 1993, p. 12-14. The traffic in women and enslavement into enforced prostitution is a growing European industry. 17 young Filipino women were freed from forced prostitution following a raid on an Antwerp hotel in August 1993. *Migration News Sheet,* September 1993, p. 3, col. 2.

Chapter 8
A well-founded fear of exclusion: the legal problems of women refugees

1. Inter Press Service, *Human Rights Coordinator*, 4 November 1991; *The Activities and Programmes of the United Nations High Commissioner for Refugees on Behalf of Refugee Women*, UN Doc. A/Conf.116/11, 30 April 1985, p. 5.
2. The numbers seeking asylum within the EC rose from about 150,000 in the mid 1980s, to 420,150 in 1991, to 556,947 in 1992. United Nations High Commission for Refugees (UNHCR) quoted in *The Guardian*, 1 June 1993, p. 6, col. 1.
3. 437,996 refugees applied for asylum in Germany in 1992. Germany received 61% of all EC asylum applications in 1991, and 79% in 1992. *World Refugee Survey*, 1993, p 121.
4. In 1985, 4389 refugees applied for asylum in the UK; by 1991 this figure was 44,845. Refugee Council, *UK Asylum Statistics 1982-1992*, Table 1, p. 10.
5. The Refugee Council, *UK Asylum Statistics 1982-1992*, p. 2.
6. *Independent on Sunday,* 15 August 1993, p. 1, col. 7.
7. *Migration News Sheet*, September 1993, p. 2, col. 1.
8. *Independent on Sunday*, ibid.
9. Inter Press Service, *Human Rights Coordinator*, 4 November 1991.
10. See Louise London, *British Immigration Control Procedures and Jewish Refugees 1933-1939*, in ed. Werner Mosse, *Second Chance: two centuries of German-speaking Jews in the United Kingdom*, ed. J.C.B. Mohr (Paul Siebeck), Tubingen, p. 485.
11. In 1992 there were 24,610 asylum applications in Britain, less than half the number for the preceding year. *Hansard*, 18 May, col 98. The figures for the first half of 1993 (11,440) suggest an even lower rate. *Exile* July/August 1993, p. 4.
12. There are approximately 70 extreme right-wing, racist parties in Germany with 40,000 members. 6,336 anti-foreigner offences were recorded in 1992, of which over 2,000 were directed against asylum-seekers, resulting in 17 deaths and 600 injuries. *The Economist*, 5 June 1993, p. 47; Lawyers Committee for Human Rights, *Asylum in Decline*, July 1993, p. 24-30.
13. *New York Times*, 8 September 1993, p. A7, col. 1.
14. See C. Tomuschat, 'A Right to Asylum in Europe', *Human Rights Law Review*, Vol.13 No.7-8, p. 257-265.
15. Article 2, *Convention governing the specific aspects of refugee problems in Africa*, 10 September 1969.
16. M. Ashford, *Detained without trial: a survey of Immigration Act detention* (JCWI, 1993), p. 65.
17. *Independent,* 1 September 1987, quoted in M. Ashford, *op.cit.*, p. 67.
18. 'Prisoners of Asylum', *CARF*, April/May 1993, p. 8-10.
19. Between 1985 and 1991 only 67 Sri Lankans (available figures do not specify the numbers who were Tamils) received full refugee status, compared with 6282 grants of ELR. Refugee Council, *UK Asylum Statistics 1982-1992*, p. 14-15.
20. For a description see M. Ashford, *op.cit.*, p. 49 and 71 and *JCWI Bulletin*, vol. 5 no. 3, Summer 1993.

21. Home Office *Press release*, 21 July 1993.
22. Only when refugee status is granted is the fine usually waived.
23. *Migration News Sheet*, July 1993, p.7, col.1.
24. With the exception of Denmark where it was adopted in June 1991.
25. See discussion of this Convention at pages 220-221.
26. At the time of writing, it had only been ratified by the following six states: Denmark, Greece, Italy, Luxembourg, Portugal and the UK, A. Cruz, *Schengen, ad hoc Immigration Group and other European Intergovernmental bodies*, Churches Committee for Migrants in Europe, Briefing Paper No. 12, p. 16, 1993.
27. The Refugee Council, *UK Asylum Statistics 1982-1992*, p. 6, Figure 6, shows that 59% of asylum-seekers in the UK were granted refugee status in 1982 and only 2.6% in 1992. 11.8% were granted exceptional leave in 1982 and 33.8% in 1992. The picture in other European countries is similar, reflecting a converging recognition rate; in the 1970s about 80% of applicants were granted refugee status, in the 1980s this had dropped to below 30%; by 1990, in Germany for example, only 4.4% of applications were approved. *The Economist*, 17 August 1991, p. 41.
28. Paragraph 185, *UNHCR Handbook on procedures and criteria for determining refugee status*, Geneva, September 1979.
29. Home Affairs Committee, *Delays in the Immigration and Nationality Department*, Second Report, evidence submitted by the Immigration Law Practitioners' Association, 15 February 1993, p. 46.
30. Evidence to Home Affairs Committee, *op. cit.*, p. 44.
31. *Hansard* 12 November 1992, col. 875, quoted in E. Guild, *The Family Unit: consequences of a definition*, unpublished paper presented at European Seminar on Family Reunification for Refugees in Europe, 15-17 May 1993.
32. Amnesty International, *Europe: Harmonisation of Asylum Policy*, November 1992, p. 9.
33. Amnesty International, *Women in the Front Line*, March 1991, p 48.
34. In Britain government figures on asylum applications are not categorized according to gender; however in countries where they are, male applications invariably outnumber female ones. See Dutch Refugee Council, *Report on Female Refugees*, forthcoming, for figures on the Netherlands and France.
35. S. Forbes Martin, *Refugee Women* (Zed Books, 1991), p. 19.
36. See Joanna Kerr, ed., *Ours by right: women's rights as human rights* (Zed Books, 1993), for further discussion of this point.
37. For a description of this strategy world-wide, see Amnesty International, *Women in the Front Line*, p.11; see also, as a specific example Amnesty International, *Tunisia, Female Victims of harassment, torture and imprisonment*, June 1993.
38. *Campos-Guardado v INS*, 809 F.2d 285 (5th Circuit, 1987).
39. Statement by client in support of her asylum application.
40. Dutch Refugee Council, *Refugee Women*, Case 3.12, p. 31.
41. Dutch Refugee Council, *op. cit.*, Case No. 4.15, p. 54.
42. For an interesting discussion on the significance and 'rhetoric' of the veil by an Arab feminist see L. A. Odeh, 'Post-colonial feminism and the veil: thinking the difference', *Feminist Review*, vol. 43, p. 26.

43. See M. Poya, 'Double Exile: Iranian Women and Islamic Fundamentalism' in ed. G. Sahgal and N. Yuval-Davis, *Refusing Holy Orders: Women and Fundamentalism in Britain* (Virago, 1992), p. 141.
44. Dutch Refugee Council, *op. cit.*, p. 52.
45. *Ibid.*, p. 53.
46. Quoted in Joanna Kerr, *op. cit*, p. 5.
47. Unreported decision of the Immigration Appeal Tribunal, 25 February 1987, (5216).
48. *Dina Djahanara Tadayon v Secretary of State for the Home Department*, (5379).
49. *Oberverwaltungsgericht Niedersachsen und Schleswig-Holstein*, 18 March 1988, Dutch Refugee Council, *op. cit.* Case no. 4.9, p. 50-51.
50. *Commission des Recours,* 19 December 1989, 60025, Dutch Refugee Council, *op. cit.,* Case No. 5.10, p 66.
51. *Department of Justice 17 February 1989*, Dutch Refugee Council, *op. cit.*, Case No. 3.7, p. 28.
52. T. O'Connor, *Gender and the Convention Refugee Definition*, unpublished ILPA (Immigration Law Practitioners' Association) Paper, p. 7.
53. Inter Press Service, *Human Rights Coordinator*, 24 February 1993.
54. Amnesty International, *Women in the Front Line*, March 1993, p. 34.
55. This case summary is drawn from a leaflet produced by Southall Black Sisters.
56. This law has been described by Amnesty International in its March 1990 newsletter as cruel and degrading treatment, contrary to Article 3 of the European Convention of Human Rights. Someone with a well-founded fear of such treatment should clearly qualify as a refugee.
57. For a full discussion of this topic as applied to the United States see P. Goldberg, 'Anyplace but Home: Asylum in the United States for Women fleeing Intimate Violence', *Cornell International Law Journal*, 38, (1993).
58. See Women's Rights Project of Human Rights Watch and Americas Watch, *Criminal Injustice: Violence Against Women in Brazil*, 1991. Women's Rights Project of Human Rights Watch and Middle East Watch, *Punishing the Victim: Rape and Mistreatment of Asian Maids in Kuwait*, 1992.
59. *M.E.I. and Mayers, Marcel,* F.C.A. No. A-544-92, 5 November 1992.
60. Canadian Refugee Board Decision U92-06668, E. R. Smith, Daya, February 19, 1993.
61. A. L. Bardach, 'Tearing off the Veil', *Vanity Fair* (US Edition), August 1993.
62. Dorothy Thomas, Director of the Women's Rights Project at Human Rights Watch, quoted in Mary Walsh Williams, 'Female Asylum Seekers Raise New Questions About Refugees', *Los Angeles Times*, 23 February 1993, from Human Rights Coordinator, 5 March 1993.
63. At the 1993 Vienna UN World Human Rights Conference, a Tribunal organised by feminist human rights activists sought to highlight this distinction.
64. UNHCR, *Guidelines on the Protection of Refugee Women*, Geneva 1991, p. 9. See also Amnesty International, *op. cit.*, ch. 3.
65. See for example *The Sri Lankan Monitor*, April 1992, p. 3, col. 3; op. cit., May 1992, p. 2, col. 3. Amnesty International, *An Assessment of the Human Rights Situation*, p. 12, col. 2, February 1993.

66. Amnesty International, *Women in the Front Line,* p. 19.
67. J. Phillips, 'Crossfire's Targets: Women in Peru Fight Violence from both Sides', *Village Voice*, 13 July 1993, p. 28.
68. *Independent,* 30 September 1992.
69. see J. Castel, 'Rape, Sexual Assault and the Meaning of Persecution', *International Journal of Refugee Law*, vol. 4, No. 1, p. 37.
70. See Amnesty International, *Bosnia-Herzegovina: Rape and Sexual Abuse by Armed Forces*, January 1993.
71. 'Ministers Agree moves to reinforce Fortress Europe', *Guardian,* 2 June 1993, p. 20, col. 3.
72. Immigration and Refugee Board, *Guidelines Issued By the Chairperson Pursuant to Section 65(3) of the Immigration Act: Women Refugee Claimants Fearing Gender-Related Persecution* (Ottawa, Canada, 9 March 1993).
73. *Ting Ting Cheung and Karen Lee v Minister of Employment and Immigration,* Federal Court of Appeals, No. A-785-91.

Conclusion

1. *First report from the Select Committee on Race Relations and Immigration,* HC 303, HMSO, 1978.
2. European Commission of Human Rights, Document E56.486.06.2.

Selected bibliography

Amos, Valerie, 'Black women in Britain: a bibliographical essay', *Sage Race Relations Abstracts,* vol. 7, no. 1, February 1982

Anderson, Bridget, *Britain's secret slaves: an investigation into the plight of overseas domestic workers*, Anti-Slavery International and Kalayaan, London, 1993

Ardill, Nony and Cross, Nigel, *Undocumented lives: British unauthorised migrant workers,* London, Runnymede Trust, 1988

Ashford, Mark, *Detained without trial: a survey of Immigration Act detention,* London, JCWI, 1993

Berger, John and Jean Mohr, *A seventh man,* Harmondsworth, Penguin, 1975

Bourne, Jenny, 'Towards an anti-racist feminism', *Race and Class,* vol. 25, no 1, summer 1983

Commission for Racial Equality, *Immigration control procedures: report of a formal investigation*, 1985

Cronin, Kathryn, *Children, nationality and immigration,* London, Children's Legal Centre, 1985

Davis, Angela, *Women, race and class*, London: Women's Press, 1982

Divided Families Campaign, *Give us a happy ending: how families are kept apart by British immigration law,* c/o South Islington Law Centre, 131/2 Upper Street, London N1 2UN, 1990

Dummett, Ann, *A portrait of English racism*, Harmondsworth, Penguin, 1973 (reissued CARAF, 1984)

Dummett, Ann, *Europe and 1992: focus on racial issues*, Catholic Association for Racial Justice, 1990

Dummett, Ann and Nicol, Andrew, *Subjects, citizens, aliens and others*, Weidenfeld & Nicolson, 1990

Dutch Refugee Council, *Report on legal problems of women refugees*, 1993

Feminist Review, *Many voices, one chant: black feminist perspectives*, no 17, autumn 1984

Gillespie, Jim, *Report on immigration and asylum procedure and appeal rights in the 12 members states of the European Community*, Immigration Law Practitioners' Association, 1993

Gordon, Paul, *Fortress Europe? the meaning of 1992*, London, Runnymede Trust, 1989

Gordon, Paul and Klug, Francesca, *British immigration control: a brief guide,* Runnymede Trust, 1985

Immigration Widows Campaign, *Trial by separation*, c/o South Islington Law Centre, 131/2 Upper Street, London N1 2UN, 1983

Joint Council for the Welfare of Immigrants, *Immigration and nationality law handbook,* 1992

Joly, Danièle and Nettleton, C, *Refugees in Europe,* London, Minority Rights Group, 1990

Kerr, Joanna, ed., *Ours by right: women's rights as human rights*, Zed Books, 1993

Lal, Sushma and Wilson, Amrit, '*But my cows aren't going to England*': *a study in how families are divided*, Manchester Law Centre, 1986

Macdonald, Ian and Blake, Nicholas, *Macdonald's immigration law and practice,* Butterworths, 1991

Manchester Law Centre, *Immigration controls: how they affect black people, how they affect women*, 1980

Martin, Susan Forbes, *Refugee women,* Zed Press, 1991

Mole, Nuala, *Immigration: family entry and settlement*, Bristol, Jordan & Sons, 1987

Moreno, Clara et al, 'Resident domestics campaign', in Ann Curno et al, eds, *Women in collective action*, Association of Community Workers, London, 1982

National Association of Asian Youth, *Which half decides? a contribution to the debate on sex discrimination, British nationality and immigration laws*, London, 1979

Pannick, David, chair, *The primary purpose rule: a rule with no purpose,* Young JUSTICE, 1993

Phizacklea, Annie, ed., *One way ticket: migration and female labour,* London, Routledge and Kegan Paul, 1983

Powell, Phil, *Notes for immigration lawyers on custom and practice in the Indian subcontinent,* 1990 et seq

Sachdeva, Sanjiv, *The primary purpose rule in British immigration law*, Trentham Books, 1993

Sondhi, Ranjit, *Divided families: British immigration control in the Indian subcontinent*, London, Runnymede Trust, 1987

Vincenzi, Christopher and Marrington, David, *Immigration law: the rules explained,* London, Sweet & Maxwell, 1992

Ward, Anna, Jeanne Gregory and Nira Yuval-Davis, eds. for the European Forum of Socialist Feminists, *Women and citizenship in Europe: borders, rights and duties: women's differing identities in a Europe of contested boundaries*, Trentham, 1992

Wilson, Amrit, *Finding a voice: Asian women in Britain*, London, Virago, 1978

Yuval-Davis, Nira and Floya Anthias, eds., *Woman —nation —state*, Macmillan, 1989

Many articles in such journals as *Immigration & Nationality Law & Practice, JCWI Bulletin, Migration News Sheet, Race & Class, Statewatch.* Selected decisions of the courts and Immigration Appeal Tribunal are printed in quarterly Immigration Appeals Reports (known as the green books).

Index

'ABC cases', 8, 72-3, 76-7, 88, 113
Abdulaziz, Nargis *see* ABC cases
Aberconway, Laura, 22
Ad Hoc Group Immigration, 216-7, 220, 221, 265
Adoption/adopted children *see* Children
Adoui and Cornouaille, 206, 281
Africa, 7, 9, 12, 33, 36
Afro-Caribbean
  see Caribbean
Aitken, Jonathan, 61
Ajani, Abeke, 157
Akhtar, Nasreen, 103-4
Ali, Merle, 185
Aliens, 12, 30-1, 94-5, 206, 220, 265
  marriage to, effect on nationality, 8, 15-28, 50-1
  undesirable alien, 30, 215, 220
Aliens Act 1905, 12, 20, 30, 33
Aliens Order 1920, 167
Aliens Order 1953, 31
Aliens Restriction Act 1914, 31
Aliens Restriction (Amendment) Act 1919, 31
Amnesty International, 241, 244
Amoako, Dora, 193
Anti-racist movement
  see Racism, fight against
Anti-Slavery International, 182
Argentina, 23, 50
Asia/Asians, 9, 33, 37, 63, 66, 70, 74, 85, 98, 111-2, 142, 201
  see also Bangladesh, India, Indian subcontinent, Pakistan, Sri Lanka
Asian husbands, 56-7, 62, 70, 79, 211, 260
Asian women, 2, 6, 7, 12, 38, 51, 66, 70, 88, 94, 102-6, 111
Association and Co-operation Agreements, 225-6
Asylum *see* Refugees
Asylum and Immigration Appeals Act 1993, 9, 139, 155, 158, 194, 236, 240-1, 244
Asylum-seekers, 14, 192, 194, 197, 220, 221, 229, 230, 231, 233
Au pairs, 13, 180
Aung San Suu Kyi, 10
Australia, 35, 42, 52, 60, 164, 218, 267
AWAZ, 112

Balkandali, Sohair *see* ABC cases
Balkans *see* Yugoslavia, former
Bangladesh/Bangladeshis, 1, 37, 96, 99, 105, 106, 110, 120-1, 125, 133, 136-7, 140-1, 145, 154, 155
  see also Asia, Indian subcontinent
Begum, Afia, 120-1
Begum, Manshoora, 138-9
Belgium, 23, 197, 205, 214, 266
Belstead, Lord, 68

Benelux Economic Union, 214
Bennett, Frederick, MP, 46
Berrehab, 86
Bhatia, Vinod, 81
Black women *see* Feminist movement
Bogus marriage *see* Marriage
Bongay, Leove, 123
Bosnia/Bosnians *see* Yugoslavia, former
British Brothers League, 30
British citizenship *see* Citizenship
British Embassy, 97, 139, 209
  see also British High Commission
British High Commission, 51, 96-7, 99, 114, 133-5, 139, 144, 145- 6, 147, 209
British Imperial Conferences, 20
British Nationality Act 1730, 17
British Nationality Act 1948, 4, 8, 12, 26, 28, 206, 259, 268
British Nationality Act 1981, xi, 4, 8, 12, 28, 48-53, 72, 91, 124, 150-2, 225, 259, 265
British Nationality and Status of Aliens Act 1914, 4, 18, 19, 20, 22-3, 31, 73
British Nationality and Status of Aliens Act 1933, 24
Brittan, Leon, MP, 120
Brockway, Lord Fenner, 59
Budgen, Nick, MP, 78
Butcher, John, MP, 23, 24
Butler, R.A., MP, 35

Cabales, Arcely *see* ABC cases
Callaghan, James, MP, 56, 95
Campos-Guardado, Sofia, 246
Canada, 1, 10, 35, 42, 52, 58, 154, 164, 221, 236, 248, 250, 252, 255, 262-3, 267
Carby, Hazel, 65-6
Caribbean, 37, 95, 141-4, 146-7, 227
Caribbean women, 7, 13, 38, 41, 70, 130, 154, 164-6, 184
Carr, Robert, MP, 175
Carriers' Liability Act, 218, 237-8, 256, 265
Chaffee, Najat, 71, 121-2
Chavrimootoo, Prakash, 123
Child tax allowances, 148
Children, 44-6, 99, 101, 118, 126, 127, 130-152, 160-1, 191-2, 208, 219-20, 223
  adopted, 52, 130-1, 149-50, 209, 223
  'bogus', 99, 113, 133
  born abroad, 40, 47-8, 52-3, 260
  'illegitimate', 45-6, 143-4, 187
  'over-age', 130, 131, 137-9
  under 1981 British Nationality Act, 51-3, 126, 150-2
  under 12, 144-5
Chile, 23
Chopra, Mamta, 123
Churchill, Winston, MP, 5-6
Citizenship
  British citizenship, 3, 4, 49, 67, 123, 126, 193, 200, 211, 224, 262, 265
  British Dependent Territories citizens, 5, 49-50, 200, 202
  British Overseas citizens, 49, 50, 51, 53, 113-7, 193
    see also UK passport holders
  British subjects, 14-8, 19, 23, 26, 34, 49, 200, 259
  UK and Colonies citizenship, 26, 39, 42, 49, 269
Clarke, Kenneth, MP, 180
Claveria, Florida, 177-8
Clothing trade, 7, 173-4, 195-6
Cohabitation/cohabitees *see* Wives, common-law
Colville, Viscount, 59
Commission for Racial Equality, 96, 98, 112-3, 133, 135, 155, 161
Commission of the European Communities *see* European Commission
'Common-law wives' *see* Wives
Common Market *see* European Community
Commonwealth citizens, 26, 33, 36, 42, 49, 56, 89, 97, 163, 199, 201, 235, 267
Commonwealth Immigrants Act 1962, 34, 35-7, 57, 130, 166, 269
Commonwealth Immigrants Act 1968, 39-41, 50, 142, 269
Council of Europe, 72, 77, 266
Council of Ministers, 213, 214

'Courier wives' *see* Wives
Crossman, Richard, MP, 40
Cyprus/Cypriots, 12, 33-4, 38, 117-8
Czechoslovakia, 155

Denmark, 52, 90, 206, 208, 266
Denning, Lord, 203
Department of Social Security *see* Social Security, Department of
Dependants, 12, 55, 95, 138-9, 160, 210, 222, 223, 265
  women treated as, 70-71, 100, 113-4
Deportation, xii, 45, 61, 85, 103, 116-9, 120, 121-3, 157, 158-60, 187, 195, 206, 265, 268
  freedom from, 36
  under Prevention of Terrorism Act, 49
Detention, 85, 109-10, 121, 123, 159-6, 183, 197, 206, 235, 236
Diamond, John, MP, 36
Diop, Aminata, 253
Discrimination *see* Racism, Sex discrimination
Distressed Relatives Scheme, 33
Ditta, Anwar, 71, 132-3
Divided Families Campaigns, 88, 108
Divorcées, 18, 41, 42, 114, 152
DNA testing, 101, 107, 132, 135-7, 161, 210
Domestic servants/slavery, 7, 13, 164, 168, 174, 175, 181-4
  see also Resident domestic workers
Domestic violence, 91, 100, 103, 119, 120, 121-3, 144, 157, 191, 222, 245, 251-3
Dublin Convention, 220-1, 238-40, 243, 266

East African Asians, 39-41, 42, 50, 51, 113-7, 201
Eastern Europe *see* Europe
Ede, John Chuter, MP, 27, 35
Egypt, 47-8, 52
Ejaz, Naheed, 6, 123-4
Elizabeth I, 29
Employment vouchers, 35, 37-8, 39, 166
Ennals, Lord David, MP, 41
Entry certificates, 57, 95-6, 141
Entry clearance, 55, 61, 94-9, 100, 104-7, 109-11, 113, 120, 125, 130, 133-4, 142, 183, 204, 266
Entry clearance officers, 84, 99, 101-3, 105-6, 132, 145, 156
Equal Opportunities Commission, 47, 65, 115
Ethnocentrism, 8, 65, 81, 102-7, 126, 129, 141-2, 143
Europe/Europeans, 4, 43-4, 53
  Eastern, 9, 32, 180, 197, 222, 226, 230,
  Southern, 7, 168
  Western, 180
European Commission, 204, 213, 215, 224
European Commission of Human Rights, 72-3, 160, 222, 260, 266
European Community, 1, 9, 13, 43-4, 92, 129, 153, 199-227, 229, 236, 261, 263, 266
  EC nationals, xii, 1, 4, 11, 49, 75, 85-6, 161, 187-8, 198, 199, 202, 262
European Convention on Human Rights, 2, 72, 73, 76-7, 86, 91, 211, 222, 223, 233
European Court of Human Rights, 2, 8, 9, 72, 76-8, 86-7, 88, 113, 213, 222, 266
European Court of Justice, 9, 85-6, 204, 205, 211, 213, 220, 221, 225, 266
European Economic Area, 225, 226, 266
European Free Trade Association, 225, 262, 266
European Information System, 220
European Parliament, 88, 121, 204, 214, 255
European Social Charter, 222-3, 284
European Voluntary Workers Scheme, 32-3, 163
Exceptional leave to remain, 10, 11, 235-7, 240, 241-3, 267
'Exclusion undesirable', 130, 142, 146-8
Extended families *see* Families
External Borders Convention, 217-20

Falkland Islands/Malvinas, 4, 50
Families, 102, 129, 140-1, 157, 187

divided, 96-7, 107-8, 131-2, 137-8
extended, 11, 129, 152-3, 210, 239
reunion, 1, 2, 6, 99-100, 130-1, 207-10, 211, 220, 222, 237, 239, 241, 242-3, 261
unity of, 93-4, 99, 127-8, 239
'Fast track' procedure, 240, 244
Female genital mutilation, 219, 251-3
Feminist movement, xi, 2, 3, 7-8, 12, 22, 27, 34, 60, 62
black, 65-6, 68, 71-2, 112, 120
Fiancées, 80, 100, 111-3, 125, 126
Fiancés, 61, 62-4, 80, 100
Fingerprinting, 240
'Fortress Europe', xii, 14, 215, 217, 219, 222, 236, 243, 262, 263
Fox, Marcus, MP, 78
France, 6, 26, 52, 200, 202, 214, 215, 218, 220, 225, 238-9, 250, 253, 266
Franchise Act 1918, 19
Freedom of movement, 86, 187-8, 199, 201-10, 262

Galiara, Zahira, 109-10
Gardner, Joy, v, xii, 158-9, 161
Gay men, 11, 89-90, 208
Geneva Convention on Refugees, 10, 14, 232-4, 240, 245, 249, 257, 261, 263, 267, 268
Germany, 5, 52, 211, 214, 221, 222, 229, 230, 231, 239, 248, 250, 266
Ghana/Ghanaians, 76, 98, 144-5, 154, 155, 183, 196
Gibraltar, 5, 49-50, 200
Glyn-Jones, W. S., MP, 20
'Guestworkers', 167

Hadzimuratovic, Irma, 230
Hague Convention, 24
Hailsham, Lord, 96
Hale, Lord, 16
Hampson, Keith, MP, 71
Harcourt, Lewis, MP, 19
Harmonisation, European, 199, 212, 214, 221-3, 226, 243, 248
Hart, Dame Judith, MP, 35, 37
Harvey, Edward, MP, 18
Hawley Report, 61, 97
'Head of household', 4, 13, 41, 113-7, 119, 244
Hong Kong, 38, 49, 82, 200, 242
Hoque, Amirul, 83-4
Hotel and catering industry, 7, 168, 174-5, 178-9, 195
Housing, 105, 139-41, 142, 145, 173, 193-5, 240
Howard, Michael, MP, 195
Huen, Lisa, 123
Husbands, 1, 37, 44-5, 50-1, 55-92, 79, 117, 192, 260
Commonwealth, 58-9
of 'career wives', 37
foreign, 8, 32, 59
Hussain v Hussain, 125-6

Idrish, Muhammad, 118
Ifekaozor, Francisca, 183
Illegal entrants, 177-9, 191, 222, 251-2, 268
Immigration Act 1971, 41-6, 99, 118, 130, 166, 184, 200, 268
Immigration Act 1988, 89, 126, 131
Immigration Appeal Tribunal, 57-8, 81, 86, 90, 104, 107, 117-8, 140, 249, 267
Immigration appeals, 82, 95, 96, 106-8, 126, 155-6, 158-60, 267
Immigration Appeals Act 1969, 95
Immigration (Carriers' Liability) Act 1987 *see* Carriers' Liability Act
Immigration officers, 32, 43, 94, 121, 158, 197
Immigration Rules, 43, 53, 73, 87, 89, 97, 99, 108, 122, 125, 130, 140, 142, 146, 149, 152, 153, 155, 156, 160, 167, 181, 193, 195, 198, 267
1973 rules, 43-5, 58, 130-1
1974 rules, 59-61, 69, 259
1977 rules, 62-3, 69, 122
1980 rules, 53, 65, 66-8, 69, 72, 73, 91, 131, 138, 147, 180, 260
1983 rules, 69, 71, 73-5, 78, 79, 91
1985 rules, 69, 78, 89, 91, 122, 192
1988 rules, 69, 89, 122, 260
1989 rules, 7, 100, 167-8
1990 rules, 100, 186, 267
1993 rules, 180, 240, 267

1993 consultative document, 3, 100, 119, 131, 150, 153, 186, 260, 267
Immigration Widows Campaign, 8, 87-8, 108-9
Imperialism, 17-8, 19, 165
Independent means, 204
India/Indians, 50, 58, 62, 76, 110, 114-6, 155, 164, 183, 218
Anglo-Indians, 46
Indian subcontinent, 3, 6, 12, 62, 70-1, 79, 82, 97-8, 101, 106, 111, 113, 132, 136, 139
Instructions to immigration officers, 31, 36, 41, 43, 57, 59, 75, 80-1, 87, 91, 94, 152, 208
Internal immigration controls, xii, 5, 13, 164, 188, 193-5, 198, 222, 262
International Council of Women, 20
International Social Service, 141-2
International Woman Suffrage Alliance, 20, 22, 23, 28
Iqbal, Iram and Tanveer, 84
Iran/Iranians, 189, 234, 237, 248, 249, 250
Iraq/Iraqis, 218, 230, 256
Ireland/Irish, 12, 49, 209, 223, 266
Islam, 125-6, 249-51
Italy/Italians, 168, 187, 266

Jamaica/Jamaicans, 34, 124, 149, 152-3, 158, 165, 206, 222
James, Winifred, 24
Janjua, Rabia, x, 251-2
Japan/Japanese, 164, 218
Jeffreys, Alec, 135
Jeger, Lena, MP, 40-1, 59-60
Jenkins, Roy, MP, 60, 61, 62
Jews, 12, 20, 25, 29, 30, 32, 231
Joint Council for the Welfare of Immigrants, ix, x, 51, 72, 80, 178

Kalayaan, 183
Kaur, Baljit, 82
Kaur, Dalvinder, 159-60
Kaur, Manjit, 191-2
Kenya/Kenyans, 39, 51, 114-6, 219-220
Khan, Parveen, 191-2
Knight, Jill, MP, 45, 47
Kumar, Arun, 83
Kumari, Santosh, 83
Kumari, Vijay, 81
Kurds, 12, 230, 236-7, 239, 242, 256
see also Turks, Iraqis
Kus, 225-6
Kusah, Sarah, 100

Labour Party Women's Conference, 59
Lane, David, MP, 61
Latin America/Latin Americans, 12, 149, 176
League of Nations, 10
Lesbians, 11, 89-90, 208
Levin, 203, 207
Liberty *see* National Council for Civil Liberties
Luczak, Lilli, 91
Lyon, Alex, MP, 63

Maastricht, 200, 216, 217, 224, 267
MacDonald, Ramsay, MP, 24
Malawi, 39
Malaysia/Malaysians, 38, 42, 50, 76, 157, 186
Marriage
arranged, 64, 65, 67-70, 74, 77-8, 84-5
assumptions about, 64, 102-4, 111-2, 118
'bogus', 26, 62-3, 67, 208
breakdown, 103, 118-9, 123, 128, 208
common-law, 35, 91, 152, 208,
effects on nationality, 6, 12, 16-22, 24, 28, 50-1, 60, 76, 124-6
importance for immigration, 99, 101, 113-7, 176-9, 207-8, 259
polygamous, 11, 124-6
Maugham, Viscount, 27
McCarran-Walter Act, 165
Medical examinations, 112, 134, 135
Migrant workers, 12, 31, 163-4, 167-8, 267
see also Women workers
Migrants Action Group, 178-9
Mokolo, Florence, 183
Morocco/Moroccans, 75, 98, 121, 176, 207, 218, 220
Morson and Jhanjan, 211, 282

Mothers, 45-6, 129-61
  lone, 131, 140-8
Mothers' Union, 20
Mozambique, 218
Mudd, David, MP, 78

National Council for Civil Liberties, 65, 72
National Federation of Women's Institutes, 23
National Health Service, 7, 33, 34, 166, 175, 185-6, 189-90, 208
  see also Nurses
National Union of Women Workers, 20
Nationalism, 11, 20
The Nationality of Married Women, 17
Naturalisation Act 1844, 17
Naturalisation Act 1870, 17, 19
Naturalisation, 27, 42, 48, 49, 51, 76
Netherlands, 86, 90, 203, 208, 214, 215, 266
Nigeria/Nigerians, 98, 119, 155, 159, 183, 196
Non-marital relationships *see* Same-sex couples *and* Wives, common-law
Nurses, 13, 165, 166, 184-6, 208
Nwokedi, Dorothy, 159

Onwualu, Elizabeth, 183
Organisation of African Unity, 234
Organisation of Women of African and Asian Descent, 66
Overstayers, 116-7, 190, 191, 193

Pagkakaisa ng Samahang Pilipino, 178
Pakistan/Pakistanis, 37, 58, 95-6, 98, 102, 103, 125, 155-6, 226, 251-2
  'concern' over Pakistani boys, 130, 141-2, 145-6
Pankhurst, Christabel, 22
Parents, 11, 61, 130-1, 152-3, 210, 223, 241-2
Pasqua, Charles, 6
Passports , 151-2, 188-9, 190, 204
  see also Internal immigration controls
Patrials/patriality, 41-3, 45-6, 50, 61, 110-1, 124, 268
Patriarchy, 14, 15, 46, 59
Persecution, 10
  gender, 10, 14, 240-1, 245-55, 261
Phansopkar, 110
Philippines/Filipinos, 3, 12, 13, 76, 108-9, 147-8, 153, 173-4, 176-9, 183, 197, 208
  Filipino Chaplaincy, 178
Police, 122, 135, 158-9, 188-9, 195-6, 206, 215
  registration with, 24
Portugal/Portuguese, 168, 176, 201, 210, 218, 221, 266
Powell, Enoch, MP, 39, 44, 52, 58, 61, 97
Prevention of Terrorism Act, 12, 49
'Primary purpose', 1, 2, 68, 75, 78-85, 86, 89, 92, 101, 108-9, 211, 223, 260, 261
Proctor, Harvey, MP, 74
Prostitutes, 30, 101, 197, 206, 226, 245, 249, 253, 253
'Public funds', 31, 36, 104-5, 187-8, 191-3, 268
Purewal, Rashpal, 86, 211

Queues, entry clearance, 95-7, 105-6, 113, 148
Quota vouchers *see* Special quota vouchers

Racism, 1-2, 29, 34, 57, 175, 201, 231
  fight against, xi, 5, 7, 11, 201, 212, 214, 223-4, 263
  in immigration, nationality and refugee law, xii, 11, 12, 39-42, 77, 80, 82, 88, 175, 205-6, 225, 256
  of feminist movement, xii, 65-6
Rai, Mahesh Kumari, 183
Raison, Sir Timothy, MP, 52, 70
Rape, 10, 46, 146, 219, 231, 240, 244, 245, 251, 253-5
'Recourse to public funds', 89, 99, 103, 118-9, 131
Rees, Merlyn, MP, 47, 48
Refugees, xii, 9-10, 14, 30, 32, 123, 151, 159, 215, 229-57, 265, 268
  refugee women, 14, 189, 219-20, 221, 240, 244-55, 263
Register of dependants, 97

Registration, 27, 28, 47-8, 49, 50, 58, 76, 124-6, 151
Removal of Aliens Act 1848, 29
Renton, David, MP, 36, 37
Repatriation, 176
Residence permits, 205, 207
Resident domestic workers, 7, 176-9, 180
Resident Domestics Campaign, 8, 71, 178-9
Retired persons, 204, 223
Rhodes Group, 217
Richardson, Jo, MP, 53
Right of abode, 42, 50, 110-1, 126, 265, 268
Romania, 9, 150
Roux, Danielle, 205
Royer, 205

Saint Helena, 49
Same-sex couples, 13, 89-90, 208
Sandys, Duncan, MP, 39
Sari Squad, 120-1
Schengen, 214-8, 220, 268
Secret instructions *see* Instructions to immigration officers
Select Committee on Race Relations and Immigration, 63-4, 142, 144, 160, 199, 260
Self-employed, 204, 205
Sex discrimination
  fight against, xi, 7-8, 11, 47-8, 71-3
  in immigration and nationality law, xii, 1, 2-3, 8, 11, 35-6, 40-7, 62, 70, 73, 77, 82, 119, 126, 131, 168, 200, 202, 203, 227, 259, 260
  lack of attention to, xi-xii, 263
Sex Discrimination Act 1975, 47, 60, 76, 115
Sex Disqualification (Removal) Act 1919, 19
Sexism *see* Sex discrimination
Sharples, Richard, MP, 44, 45
Simpson, Myrna, 158-9
Singh, Matwinder, 83-4
Singh, Surinder, 86, 211
Slavery *see* Domestic slavery
Social Security, Department of, 125, 187-8, 190-3, 197
'Sole responsibility', 41, 130, 141-6, 179, 208-9, 211, 261
Somalia/Somalis, 218, 230, 233, 239, 243, 254, 256
Southall Black Sisters, x, 123, 252
Southall Indian Workers' Association, 58
Southern Europe *see* Europe
Soviet Union, 23
Spain/Spanish, 168, 266
Special quota vouchers, 41, 50, 113-7
Sponsors, 30, 156, 193, 268
Sri Lanka/Sri Lankans, 155, 183, 230, 234-9, 253
Stanbrook, Ivor, MP, 52, 62
Statelessness, 11, 21, 45, 151
Steel, Sir David, MP, 44, 64
Students, 3, 8, 45, 61, 100, 127, 151, 184-6, 190, 204
Suffragettes, 22
  see also Feminist movement
Swami, Laxmi, 182-3

Tamils *see* Sri Lanka
Thailand/Thais, 3, 108-9
Thatcher, Margaret, MP, 5, 48, 63, 64, 66, 74, 91
'Third-country cases', 238, 240, 244, 256
'Third-country nationals', 204, 212-4, 218, 224-6, 262, 268
Thomas, Josey, 156-7
Torture, 9, 233, 236-7, 239, 244, 245, 254
Tower Hamlets council, 140-1, 194
Townsend, Cyril, MP, 67
Treaty of Rome, 187, 200, 206,
Treaty on European Union *see* Maastricht
Trevi group, 216
Trinidad, 146, 165, 185, 222, 252
Turkey/Turks, 5, 12, 52, 117, 120, 155, 176, 195, 225-6, 230, 236-7, 239, 242, 262

Uddin, Shorif, 137-8
Uganda, 39, 155, 201, 237, 247
Unauthorised workers, 164, 181, 195-7, 226
Undertakings, 193, 268
Unger, 188, 204, 281 note 12
UK passport holders, 39-41, 201, 269

see also Citizenship
United Nations Convention on the Nationality of Married Women, 28
United Nations Convention relating to the Status of Refugees *see* Geneva Convention on Refugees
United Nations High Commission for Refugees, 219, 220, 255, 269
United Nations World Conference on Human Rights, 14
United States, 23, 52, 53, 164, 218, 236, 246
Universal Declaration of Human Rights, 232

Violence *see* Domestic violence
'Virginity test', 111-3, 127, 134
Visas, 95, 139, 150, 154-6, 186, 204, 215, 217, 218, 234-7, 242, 256, 266, 269
Visitors, 8, 115-7, 139, 145, 153-6, 181, 186, 197

Waddington, (Lord) David, MP, 77, 80, 81, 82, 120, 181
Wainwright, Edwin, MP, 36
White, Eirene, MP, 35
Whitelaw, Lord, MP, 48, 53, 61, 62, 64, 68, 70, 78
Widows, 3, 18, 41, 42, 114, 120, 152-3
Widowed daughters, 130
Wilkins, W.H., 30
Williams, Aneurin, MP, 18
WING *see* Women, Immigration and Nationality Group
Wirdestedt, Lars, 90
Wives, 3, 32, 93-128
as appendages, 7, 45, 100, 117-121
'career wives', 37
'common-law wives', 11, 13, 35, 90-1, 152, 208
Commonwealth wives, 44-5
'courier wives', 145-6
foreign wives, 8, 32
married women and nationality, 8, 15-28, 50-1
Women against Racism and Fascism, 65
Women, Immigration and Nationality Group, xi, 71-2, 73, 87
Women workers, 7, 12, 30-1, 37-9, 73, 147, 163-98
see also Migrant workers
Women's Campaign against Deportations, 156-7
Women's Institute, 65
Women's International League for Peace and Freedom, 23
Women's movement, 21, 60, 65-7
see also Feminist movement
Women's Social and Political Union, 22
Work permits/work permit holders, 7, 31, 38, 61, 89, 92, 100, 163-4, 167-72, 184-6, 225-6, 267, 269
Worlds Apart, ix, x, xi, xii, 3, 11, 12

X-rays, 134-5

Yellowlees, Sir Henry, 112
Yugoslavia, former, 155, 218, 220, 230, 233, 254, 256